# NORTH AND NORTH EASTERN FRONTIER TRIBES OF INDIA

# NORTH AND NORTH EASTERN FRONTIER TRIBES OF INDIA

**Compiled in the**

**INTELLIGENCE BRANCH**
**DIVISION OF THE CHIEF OF THE STAFF**
**ARMY HEAD-QUARTERS INDIA**

GYAN

*Published by*

Gyan Publishing House
5, Ansari Road
Daryaganj, New Delhi-110002
Phone: 011-47034999, 9811692060
E-mail: books@gyanbooks.com

*Distribution Network*
gyanbooks.com
India, USA, Canada, UK, Australia, France



ISBN : 978-81-212-1972-3 (PB)
First Published, 1907

2nd Impression 2021

*Printed at:* Gyan Press, Delhi.



**North and North Eastern Frontier Tribes of India**
Compiled in the Army HQ.

# CONTENTS.

## PART I.

## NEPAL.

### CHAPTER I.

*THE COUNTRY AND PEOPLE.*



### CHAPTER II.

*MILITARY OPERATIONS.*



## PART II.

## SIKKIM.

### CHAPTER III.

*THE COUNTRY AND PEOPLE.*



### CHAPTER IV.

*MILITARY OPERATIONS.*

# PART III.

## TIBET.

### CHAPTER V.

*THE COUNTRY AND PEOPLE.*



### CHAPTER VI.

*MILITARY OPERATIONS.*



# PART IV.

## BHUTAN.

### CHAPTER VII.

*THE COUNTRY AND PEOPLE.*

## CHAPTER VIII.

### MILITARY OPERATIONS.



# PART V.

## ASSAM.

## CHAPTER IX.

### ASSAM PROPER.



## CHAPTER X.

### THE NORTHERN HILL TRIBES.



## CHAPTER XI.

### THE NORTH-EASTERN HILL TRIBES.



## CHAPTER XII.

### THE SOUTHERN HILL TRIBES.



## CHAPTER XIII.

### THE NAGA HILLS.

## CHAPTER XIV.

### *MANIPUR.*



# PART VI.

## THE LUSHAIS.

## CHAPTER XV.

### *THE COUNTRY AND PEOPLE.*



## CHAPTER XVI.

### *MILITARY OPERATIONS.*



## LIST OF MAPS.

# NEPAL.

## CHAPTER I.

### *THE COUNTRY AND PEOPLE.*

THE modern kingdom of Nepal is a narrow tract of country extending for 520 miles along the southern slopes of the Himalayas, with a varying breadth of from 90 to 140 miles. It is bounded on the north by Tibet; on the east by Sikkim and the river Mechi; on the south by Bengal, Oudh, and Rohilkhand; and on the west by Kumaun. Nepal is thus surrounded on three sides by British territory. Of the fourth, or Tibetan, frontier, formed by the main range of the Himalayas, little is known. Previous to 1815 the kingdom included the country up to the river Sutlej, and also the Sikkim territory west of the Tista river.

The country consists of four distinct zones running east and west: namely, the Terai, the Dhuns, the Hill Country, and the Alpine Region.

The Terai.

The Terai is a belt of country, thirty miles wide, skirting the British frontier, and divided into the open Terai and the Bhaver. Of these the open Terai is marshy land slightly lower than the adjoining plains, and is now almost entirely cultivated. The climate is exceedingly unhealthy in the hot weather and rains. The Bhaver, or primæval *sàl* forest, has a climate even more malarious than that of the Terai. There are small patches of cultivation in the heart of the forest, and the Terai edge of the forest is gradually retiring, as fresh land is brought under cultivation. This jungle is almost uninhabited, and is only valuable for its timber and elephants.

At two points the Nepal Terai is broken, *viz.*, between the Oria and the river Gandak, and at the Dundwa hills. Here British territory advances to the Sandstone range.

Dhuns or Marris.

Separating the *sàl* forest from the second zone is the Sandstone range; a more or less pronounced ridge running along the whole frontier, rising to about 3,000 feet above the sea, or to 600 or 800 feet above the surrounding country; it is covered with dense jungle, and is impassable, except at the passes, in none of which is there a good road. The Dhuns are valleys lying behind the sandstone range, generally 2,500 feet above the sea. Their soil is alluvial and is capable of very high cultivation. From motives of isolation policy the Nepalese allow these valleys to remain covered with jungle.

Hill country and Alpine region.

North of the Dhuns lie the Himalayas, hill succeeding hill, until they culminate in a vast snowy range. This region may be divided into two zones:—The first, up a height of 10,000 feet, includes numerous well watered, populous, and highly cultivated valleys, at an average elevation of 4,000 feet. The second is the Alpine region, in which cultivation is carried up to a height of 13,000 feet. This country is divided, by four massive offshoots from the main Himalayan range, into three mountain basins. These, with Nepal Proper, or the valley of the Baghmati river, and the Terai, form five natural provinces, namely—

1. The Terai.
2. Eastern Nepal, or the Kosi basin.
3. Nepal valley.
4. Central Nepal, or the Gandak basin.
5. Western Nepal or the Karnal basin.

The whole of the communications throughout Nepal may be classed as bad. The Nepalese have always set their faces against any improvement in this respect, trusting to the natural inaccessibility of the country as the best means of preventing invasion. Only one route is open to Europeans—that from Segowlie *viâ* Etaunda to Khatmandu. All authentic information ceases as soon as the Sandstone range is passed. Most of the routes are only practicable for hill ponies or mules, and some of those into Tibet only for sheep and yaks. The numerous hill rivers are only to be crossed by country rope bridges.

People.

The original inhabitants of Nepal would appear to have been of Mongolian origin. With them there is now an admixture of Hindu stock. Thakur and Khas are descendants of Brahman invaders and form the highest social class. Next to them come Magars and Gurungs, aboriginal tribes who have been admitted by the Hindus to the privileges of the Kshatriya caste. The Limbus, Rais, and

Sunwars are also aboriginals. All the above are termed Gurkhas. The term Gurkha is not limited to any class or clan, but is applied to all those whose ancestors inhabited the country of Gurkha, fifty-five miles west of Khatmandu, and from which they extended their conquests. Other aboriginals are the Newars, an intelligent people living in the Nepal valley; Lepchas and Bhatias, hill tribes; Dhotials, the inhabitants of Western Nepal; and the Tharus, low caste Hindus who dwell in the Terai and are immune to malaria. We enlist the first four classes named above, and also a few Newars. Limbus, Rais, and Sunwars have also served us well in Burma. There are at present (1906) about 22,000 Gurkhas serving in the British Army, to keep up which strength Nepal furnishes annually 1,667 recruits.

As compared with other orientals Gurkhas are bold, enduring, faithful, frank, very independent, and self-reliant; in their own country they are jealous of foreigners and self-asserting.

The population of Nepal was estimated by us (1883) at 2,000,000; by the Nepalese in 1901 at 5,000,000; and by Colonel Vansittart (1906) at 4,000,000.

The standing army has been estimated—

| | | |
|---|---|---|
| in 1814 | at | 5,600 |
| 1817 | ,, | 8,333 |
| 1870 | ,, | 19,100 |
| 1876 | ,, | 35,365 |
| 1889 | ,, | 50,205 |
| 1892 | ,, | 44,217 |
| 1905 | ,, | 35,333 |

In addition there is an army reserve by which it is thought that these numbers could be very quickly doubled. In 1839 it was estimated that the fighting tribes would produce 109,000 able-bodied fighting men.

Arms.

The real national weapon is the *kukri*, a short, curved, broad-bladed and heavy knife. No exact statement can be made of their other arms. In 1814 they were in possession of a considerable number of matchlocks. In 1892 it was thought that the whole army could be provided with Snider rifles. In 1894 the Government of India, to stop smuggling, provided the Nepalese with 8,000 Martini-Henry rifles. In 1905 the Resident reported that there were 107 serviceable guns. There is a factory at Soondrijal, where maxims, mountain guns, rifles, and ammunition have been manufactured. As to its work Colonel R. Pears reports in 1902 that the rifles, a modification of the Martini-Henry, seem to him "serviceable."

Outline of History.

In 1749 Prithwi Narayan, King of the Gurkhas, began to extend his territory and absorb the small states about the Nepal valley. The last of the independent Newar Rajas appealed to the British for help, and an expedition under Major Kinloch was despatched. It did not, however, penetrate beyond the Terai, and Prithwi Narayan captured Khatmandu. By the year 1790 the Gurkhas had obtained possession of all the country from Bhutan to Kashmir, and from Tibet to the British provinces.

About this time the Nepal regency, tempted by the great riches of the monasteries in Tibet, determined to make an attempt upon them. The pretext of the war was that the Tibetans insisted on circulating base coin. A Gurkha Army, 18,000 strong, covered the 398 miles to Shigatse with great rapidity, and plundered the palace. The Tibetans meantime entreated help from Pekin, and, upon the Nepalese defying the Chinese demands, a Chinese Army of 70,000 men, provided with leathern guns, advanced. They defeated the Gurkhas at Tengri Maidan, and then finally crushed them at Naiakot near Khatmandu. Peace was made on terms humiliating to Nepal. She was to restore the plunder; to pay an annual tribute to the Emperor; and to send an embassy to Pekin once in five years.

Mission, 1792.

Unable to withstand the Chinese, the Gurkhas had appealed to the British Government; and a Mission under Colonel Kirkpatrick reached Naiakot in March 1793. By that time, however, peace had been concluded. A commercial treaty [1] between the British and Nepalese Governments was signed, but the Nepalese appeared determined to avoid closer acquaintance, and Kirkpatrick quitted Nepal in 1793. The policy of the British at this time seems to have alienated both the Gurkhas and Chinese. [2]

[1] Aitchison's *Treaties, Engagements, and Sanads*, Vol. II, No. LII.
[2] *Vide* page 77.

In 1801 another treaty[1] was signed, and Captain W. D. Knox was appointed Resident at the court of Nepal. Being dissatisfied with the political conduct of the Nepalese, he withdrew in March 1803, and in January 1804 Lord Wellesley formally dissolved the alliance. From this time the Nepalese carried on a system of outrage and encroachment on the frontier which led to the declaration of war by the British in 1814. After a series of operations[2] Sir David Ochterlony penetrated to Mokwanpur, and the treaty of Segowlie[3] was signed in December 1815, by the terms of which the kingdom of Nepal was limited to its present eastern and western boundaries; a large part of the Terai was ceded to the British; and a British Resident was appointed.

Expedition, 1814.

In 1839, upon the overthrow of the veteran prime minister Bhim Sen Tappa, hostility towards the British Government assumed an open form. The British success, however, in Afghanistan, and the presence of a British corps of observation on the frontier, had their effect, and the Nepal Durbar promised good behaviour.

In 1848 an offer to assist the Indian Army against the Sikhs was made, but declined. This was the first sign of attachment to the British Government. In 1850 Jung Bahadur visited England, and was ever after an enthusiastic ally of the British.

In 1854 the Gurkhas entered into a war with Tibet which terminated favourably for Nepal.

In 1857 the Nepalese again offered help to the British Government, but it was not until the 26th June, after Delhi had been taken and Lucknow relieved, that the offer was accepted. In all 10,000 men were sent down, and took part in the campaigns of 1857 and 1858 against the rebels. In return for this service the portion of the Terai ceded in 1816 was restored to Nepal.

In 1884 a dispute arose with Tibet, which was settled by the payment of an indemnity by the Tibetan Government.

In 1885 the Nepal Durbar offered 15,000 men for service in Afghanistan, and also a contingent to take part in the Delhi camp-of-exercise. This offer being conditionally accepted, the massing of picked men was made the occasion of internal revolution, and Bir Shumshere seized the office of prime minister.

[1] Aitchison No. LIII. [2] See Chapter 2.
[3] Aitchison No. LIV.

In 1892 Lord Roberts, Commander-in-Chief in India, was present at a review of the Nepal Army at Khatmandu, and Bir Shumshere visited the manœuvres at Muridki and Rawalpindi.

Nepal pays no tribute to the British Government. A Mission used to be sent every five years to Pekin with presents, but this was discontinued in 1852, and after that date no Mission was sent until 1866. In 1885, on the occasion of Bir Shumshere's seizing the chief power, a special Mission was despatched to Pekin to pray that he should be recognized.

# CHAPTER II.

## *MILITARY OPERATIONS.*

### Expedition under Major Kinloch, 1767.

THE first British expedition into Nepal was undertaken as long ago as 1767, when a force under Major Kinloch advanced on Hariharpur. The circumstances which led to this body of troops being despatched were briefly these. In the middle of the eighteenth century, Prithwi Narayan, the King of the Gurkhas, began to overrun the territories of the neighbouring rajas, and, commencing operations against the Newar Rajas of Nepal proper, gradually subjugated Mokwanpur and the valley of Nepal. Before he had finally conquered the country, the Newars appealed to the British Government for aid against him. An expedition was undertaken at the recommendation of Mr. Golding, the Commercial Agent at Bettiah, who feared that the success of the Gurkhas would ruin the trade he had before carried on with Nepal, and which had been interrupted for three or four years in consequence of the subjugation of Mokwanpur. Major Kinloch commanded the party destined for the relief of the Nepal Raja. He was a good officer, but advanced into the hills at least a month too early (in October 1767), and had not strength enough to establish a chain of depôts to secure his communications with the plains; consequently, having penetrated to Hariharpur, he was detained there by a *nala* not then fordable, and the bridge and raft he constructed were carried away after a fall of rain which swelled the torrent unnaturally. The delay thus experienced exhausted his supplies and produced sickness, and he was finally obliged to return early in December, the time when he should really have set out.

### Nepal War, 1814-15.

After the expedition of Major Kinloch no further invasion of Nepal took place until a series of outrages and insults on the part of the Nepalese brought about the war of 1814-15. The causes which led to this war were briefly as follows :—

Owing to a claim by the Gurkhas to the districts of Butwal and Seoraj, which had been in dispute for several years, and to their aggressions in the Bettiah district in 1811,[1] Major Paris Bradshaw, First Assistant to the Resident at Lucknow, was nominated by Lord Minto to settle these frontier questions, and with this object met the Gurkha Commissioners during the winter of 1812-13 in the Gorakhpur Terai. The investigation proved that the Gurkhas had no shadow of right on their side; the Nepalese Commissioners, however, declared themselves not satisfied, and begged to refer to Khatmandu. Lord Minto being perfectly satisfied with Major Bradshaw's proceedings, demanded the immediate evacuation of Butwal and Seoraj, but an answer received in December 1813 declared that the investigation had clearly established the rights of the Gurkhas to both districts.

Lord Hastings, who had in the interval assumed charge of the Government, now addressed a peremptory requisition to the Raja of Nepal for the evacuation of the districts, and authorized the Magistrate of Gorakhpur to advance and occupy the contested lands with troops, if the Raja's order for their evacuation did not arrive within twenty-five days. The Gurkha Government were further informed of the Magistrate's orders. The Gurkhas, on receipt of this letter, after much deliberation, determined on war in April 1814, and no orders were issued for the evacuation of the provinces of Butwal and Seoraj. In the meantime the Magistrate of Gorakhpur, Sir Roger Martin, on the expiration of the period of twenty-five days, marched three companies into the districts and occupied them. The Gurkhas retired without opposition, and for nearly a month attempted nothing, but allowed the Magistrate to establish three police *thanas* in Butwal, at Chitwa, Bisourea, and Sourah, and one with two subordinate outposts in Seoraj.

Outbreak of hostilities.

The above arrangement was made with a view to the ordinary administration of the district, and wholly without anticipation of attack or hostility by the Gurkhas. Early in the morning of the 29th May 1814, before

[1] Consisting in the occupation of twenty-two villages round about the ruins of Simraon on the Champaran frontier.

the regular troops had reached Gorakhpur on their return, the three *thanas* were simultaneously surrounded and attacked, and a number of men killed; the *daroga*, or chief officer, of the *thana* of Chitwa was murdered in cold blood after he had surrendered, in the presence of Munraj, the late Gurkha Governor of Butwal and the leader of the enterprise. As the season was too late for our troops to take the field, the *thanas* were ordered to concentrate and retire on Bansi, thus relinquishing for the present all that had been occupied.

Whilst hostilities had thus broken out at Gorakhpur, the disputes on the Champaran frontier were fast coming to the same issue, and Lord Hastings had ordered the annexation of the twenty-two villages. The tract was consequently occupied by a few companies. For several reasons the declaration of war was postponed until after the rains, but was at length issued from Lucknow on 1st November 1814. The frontier which was to be the scene of the war stretched from the Sutlej to the Kosi, a distance of about 600 miles: and the enemy had command of all the passes of the forests as well as the hills. Lord Hastings resolved to take the offensive against the enemy along the whole line, and the following was the allotment ultimately made of this space to the several divisions that were brought into the field:—

Disposition for the campaign.

Major-General Ochterlony, from Ludhiana, was to operate in the hilly country lying near the Sutlej, south of Simla; this force which was composed exclusively of native infantry and artillery amounted to 6,000 men, and included a train of two 18-pounders, ten 6-pounders, and four mortars and howitzers.[1]

Major-General Gillespie, from Meerut, was to proceed first against Dehra Dun, and after taking it, which operation was not expected to be attended with any difficulty, the force was to divide, and, while a detachment attacked Srinagar, in the Garhwal district, the main body was to proceed to Nahan to aid General Ochterlony's operations against Umar Singh. General Gillespie's force consisted of about 1,000 Europeans (made up of His Majesty's 53rd Foot, some artillery, and a few dismounted dragoons), and 2,500 native

[1] The district in which General Ochterlony was to act was commanded by the Gurkha Chief, Umar Singh, a man of great influence and military talent.

infantry. This division and that of General Ochterlony were ordered into the field towards the end of October. Kumaun and Almora (its capital) were to be attacked from Rohilkhand, but according to the original plan this was to follow the occupation of Garhwal.

Major-General John Sullivan Wood was given command of a force from Benares and Gorakhpur, with instructions to penetrate by Butwal into Palpa. This division consisted of His Majesty's 17th Foot, 950 strong, and about 3,000 native infantry; it had a train of seven 6 and 3-pounders and four mortars and howitzers, and was ordered to leave Gorakhpur on the 15th November.

Major-General Marley was given a force, collected from Patna and Murshidabad, amounting to nearly 8,000 men and including His Majesty's 24th Foot, 907 strong. This division was to make the main attack direct on Khatmandu by the passes between the Gandak and the Baghmati. It had a train of four 18-pounders, eight 6-pounders, and fourteen mortars and howitzers. The Ganges was to be crossed by the troops from Patna on the 15th November, and a further brigade was formed from troops at more distant stations to follow this force and secure its depôts and rear as it advanced into the hills.

In addition to these four columns, Major Latter was furnished with 2,000 men beyond the Kosi for the defence of the Purniah frontier. He was instructed to open communication with the Sikkim Raja and, short of an actual advance of his troops for the purpose, was to give him every assistance and encouragement to expel the Gurkhas from the eastern hills.

Such were the dispositions for the campaign. Major-General Gillespie was the first to penetrate the enemy's frontier. On the 22nd October 1814 he seized the Timri pass over the Siwaliks into the Dhun, and occupied Dehra without opposition. The whole hill country to the west was under Umar Singh, who had detached a force of 600 men under Bulbhudur Singh for the defence of the Dhun. About five miles from Dehra is a hill 500 to 600 feet high which was surmounted by a fort of no great size or strength, called Nalapani. Here Bulbhudur made his stand and strengthened the works, which were still unfinished when General Gillespie arrived in the neighbourhood. General Gillespie resolved to carry the fort by assault, and, throwing up a hasty battery at 600 yards distance, formed his division

*Operations of General Gillespie's Division.*

in four parties during the night for the assault next day; these parties were to move simultaneously from four different points, and, surrounding the fort, were to escalade the walls with ladders. The advance was to be by signal guns not before 10 A.M.; but the General, having fired for some time at the walls without effect, got impatient and gave the signal an hour before the time. Only two of the parties answered to it, one 611 strong, the other 930 all told. The result of this assault, which was repulsed, was most disastrous, General Gillespie being killed whilst leading the attack, and the total loss, besides the General, being 4 officers and 29 men killed and 15 officers and 213 men wounded. Colonel Mawbey of the 53rd now succeeded to the command, and withdrawing to Dehra, waited there until reinforced by some heavy guns from Delhi on the 24th November. On the 25th operations were renewed; a battery of 18-pounders was erected at 300 yards, and a breach was made by the 27th. An assault was made on the 28th as the breach was deemed practicable. The result was more disastrous than in the first assault; 4 officers, 15 privates, and 18 sepoys were killed, and 7 officers, 215 privates and 221 sepoys wounded. Thus, including the casualties in the first attack, this fort had already cost a greater loss than the entire number of its garrison. It was now determined to bombard the place, and efforts were directed to cutting off the defenders' water; the result of this was that the fort was evacuated after three days. If this simple measure had been adopted at first, the long list of casualties, the loss of two months of the favourable season, and the disgrace of two disastrous failures, would have been averted. Bulbhudur escaped with 70 survivors, all that remained of his garrison of 600, and the fort was razed to the ground by the British.

Disasters at Nalapani.

General Martindell, who had been appointed to the command of the division, leaving a detachment in the Dhun, now moved into the valley below Nahan *viâ* the Kolapari pass on the 19th December. Nahan was found to have been evacuated and was occupied on the 24th December. Colonel Runjoor Singh,[1] who had held this place with 2,300 of the *élite* of the Gurkha army, had retired to the fort and position of Jythuk, 3,600 feet above the sea, in accordance with

[1] Umar Singh's son.

Umar Singh's orders. General Martindell endeavoured to occupy two ridges on the flanks of the main position with two detachments of 738[1] and 1,000[2] men, respectively; but one detachment was routed by the enemy and lost 31 Europeans and 120 natives killed and wounded, including 1 officer killed and 3 wounded. The other detachment made good their object, but their reserve ammunition went astray, and owing to the failure of the first column they were ordered to retire; this they were only able to do with many losses. Had they been supported by reinforcements and ammunition they could have maintained their position easily, as their casualties up to the time of retiring had been very trifling. Their loss was 3 officers killed, 5 wounded, and 78 men killed and 220 wounded.

General Martindell now believed that his force was inadequate to the task assigned to it, and remained long inactive at Nahan. In the interim several reinforcements reached him, and the Commander-in-Chief continually urged the recommencement of active operations. Towards the beginning of February, a ridge within range of the enemy was occupied without opposition, and by the greatest exertions some 18-pounders were dragged to its summit without any attempt by the enemy to prevent the movement. Runjoor Singh was also joined by reinforcements, one body of which, numbering about 200 fighting men, defeated a force of 2,000 irregulars under Lieutenant Young, who had been sent to intercept it. General Martindell now became vacillating in the extreme, and, although he had a force of 5,000 native regulars and a European regiment, he would not bring on an action, in spite of the fact that the enemy never had more than 2,500 men. This caution and vacillation were due to the early disasters, and were strongly animadverted on by the Commander-in-Chief.

Having relinquished his idea of obtaining a useful end with heavy artillery, Martindell at last resolved to surround Runjoor and starve him out. Though the end of March was late to commence such an operation, there can be no doubt it would have been effective had not the fall of Jvthuk been now brought about

[1] Major Richard's Force: Light Company, His Majesty's 53rd; 3½ Light Companies, Native Infantry; 2 Companies, 13th Native Infantry, and some Pioneers.

[2] Major Ludlow's Force: 1 Company, His Majesty's 53rd; 3½ Light Companies, Native Infantry; 9 Companies, 6th Native Infantry and some Pioneers.

by the successes of General Ochterlony and the surrender of Umar Singh, the Gurkha commander.

Operations of General Ochterlony's Division.

General Ochterlony, who took the field in middle of October, was opposed by Umar Singh in person and formed from the first a just estimate of the character of his enemy and of the difficulties he would have to encounter. He resolved therefore to proceed with the utmost caution. On the 31st October he reached Plasi, situated in a valley within the hills. Umar Singh was then at Erki, some distance further in the hills, which here run in broken ridges, north-north-west, each ridge affording a series of positions. The outermost ridge was surmounted by the fort of Nalagarh, which, with an outpost at Taragarh, commanded the principal route into the hills. On the next range stood Ramgarh, Jorjoru, Chamba, and a second Taragarh ; above this again towered the heights of Malaun, behind which lay Erki on one side, and on the other the capital of Umar Singh's ally, the Raja of Bilaspur. Between these two places was a comparatively large valley, from which Umar Singh could draw his supplies in case of his occupying any of the above ridges.

General Ochterlony, resolving to leave nothing to hazard, made a road with great labour and breached Nalagarh with his heavy guns, when it capitulated, together with Taragarh, on the 5th November. Umar Singh now occupied the Ramgarh ridge, leaving garrisons at Erki and Subathu. General Ochterlony then advanced from Nalagarh and tried to turn the left of Umar Singh's position, of which Ramgarh formed the right, standing nearly in the middle of the ridge. He endeavoured to batter a stockade on the left wing, but after making roads and getting a battery of 6-pounders in position, the range was found too great. This led to a reconnaissance, in which the party were partially cut off, one officer being killed and ninty-five sepoys killed and wounded.

About this time news of the disaster at Nalapani arrived and General Ochterlony had serious doubts of an ultimate success in the struggle. He feared that our native army with all its discipline was ill-adapted to warfare in a country too rugged to admit of its superior tactics being brought into play. These apprehensions were, however, expressed to none but the Commander-in-Chief.

He now won over the Plasi Raja and, with a view to carrying some points in Umar Singh's rear, made him aid in making a road from Mukran to Nehur (Nori), three miles north-north-east of Ramgarh, where he fixed his head-quarters. On the 29th December, one battalion of native infantry and an additional train of light guns joined the force. Colonel Thomson was thereupon detached with fourteen strong companies, two guns, and two howitzers to attack two stockades opposed to our right, which were situated on a kind of spur from the Ramgarh ridge, projecting north-east in Umar Singh's rear. Colonel Thomson gained the ridge, and the Gurkhas evacuated one stockade in the night. The same night, however, they made determined attempts to dislodge the British, but without success. General Ochterlony reinforced the party with a battalion, and the post was stockaded and otherwise secured. It was a most important position, as it was in rear of Umar Singh's centre, entirely intercepted his supplies from Erki, and threatened the communication with Bilaspur. The Gurkha General now threw back his left, still keeping his right at Ramgarh. As, owing to the rugged nature of the intervening ground, the stockades of the main position could not be approached from Colonel Thomson's position, a new plan of operation was devised, and on the 16th January, General Ochterlony, seeking to straiten the enemy's supplies, which were now drawn wholly from Bilaspur, crossed the river Gambhar from Nehur and marched along the Erki road till he turned Malaun ridge, whence he advanced on Bilaspur. By the 18th January the heights commanding Bilaspur and the valley of the Sutlej were occupied, and Colonel Thomson was at Jynuggur. Colonel Arnold was left in Colonel Thomson's former position to watch the Gurkhas. Umar Singh now retired to the stronger Malaun position, fearing the British would occupy it, and Colonel Arnold marched along the Ramgarh ridge and into Bilaspur, subsequently reducing the fort of Ratimgarh, which was detached from the Malaun ridge, but directly between it and Bilaspur. Small Gurkha garrisons had been left in the stone redoubts of Ramgarh, Taragarh, Chamba, and Jorjoru, the reduction of which took some time. Up to this time nothing decisive had been done by either side. The British force now amounted to nearly 7,000 men, while Umar Singh never had more than 2,800 to 3,000; this fact was the best possible proof of his capabilities as a soldier, and his skill in availing himself of the advantage of ground. The forts of Ramgarh and Jorjoru capitulated to Colonel

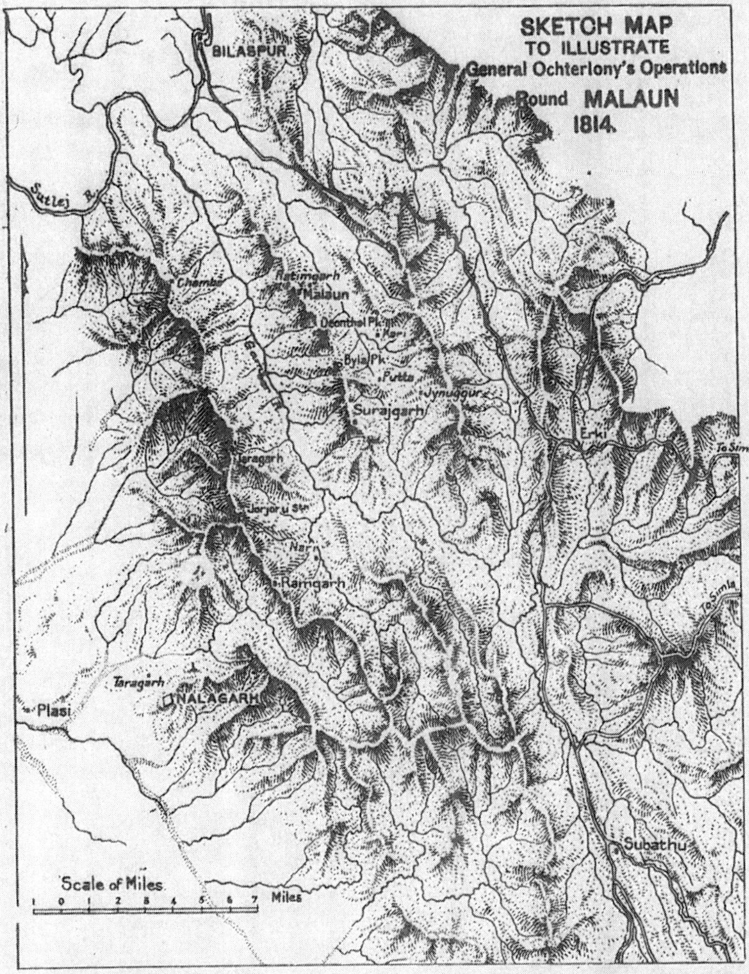


I. B. Topo. Dy No 6.686
Exd. C. J. A.. October 1907.

No. 4,185-I., 1907.

Cooper on the 16th February, having been regularly besieged. On the 10th March, Colonel Cooper brought a battery to bear on Taragarh, breached it next day, and it was evacuated by the enemy in the night. Chamba was next attacked and surrendered on the 16th March after a day's battering. Colonel Cooper's force now followed the main army to take part in the last operation against Malaun, and on the 14th April all was prepared for the combined movement which the General had been maturing for some time.

Operations against Malaun.

Umar Singh's position, stretching between the stone forts of Malaun and Surajgarh, presented a series of connected peaks, more or less abrupt, each crowned with a stockade, except two, called the Byla peak and Deonthal. The former was conveniently situated for operations against Surajgarh, which it would cut off from Malaun; the latter was in the very heart of the Gurkha position, and not 1,000 yards from Malaun itself. It was to be expected that the whole force of the Gurkhas would oppose the occupation of Deonthal, which was the main objective of the attack. General Ochterlony reckoned that even if he failed there, the possession of Byla would still be a great advantage, and that the movement on both points at once would contribute to distract the enemy. Five columns were told off to occupy those two points on the 15th. The first, from Putta, under Lieutenant Fleming, was to make a secret night movement on Byla and show a light as a signal to the other columns; the second column, under Captain Hamilton, was then to follow from Jynuggur, while the third column, under Major Jones, was also to march on Byla from General Ochterlony's head-quarters. The fourth column, under Major Lawrie, consisting of one native battalion, was destined for the attack of Deonthal from their position on the right at Halee (Kari), supported by the fifth column under Lieutenant-Colonel Thomson, consisting of one native battalion and two field pieces, from General Ochterlony's head-quarters. Two smaller detachments under Captains Bowyer and Showers were to demonstrate against the main Gurkha cantonment at Malaun.

The three columns established themselves on Byla without opposition. The columns for the attack of Deonthal, after hard fighting, obtained a footing on the peak, and desultory fighting continued all day, while in the evening and during the night every effort was made to throw up defences round the hill, under the conviction that the real struggle for the post had yet to come. The detachments directed on the cantonments completely succeeded in their object and drew off the Gurkhas from the main point.

The absolute necessity of dislodging the British from Deonthal was but too apparent to Umar Singh and his council. Two whole battalions with two field pieces were now in position there, with hastily improvised works. For the attack 2,000 Gurkhas were collected under Bhagtia Thapa next morning, the 16th April. The attack took place from all sides on the morning of the 16th and was carried out with furious intrepidity, but the enemy were repulsed with the loss of about 500, and Bhagtia Thapa, who led the final charge, was killed. The total loss of the British on the 15th and 16th was 2 officers and 59 natives killed and 5 officers and 288 men wounded.

The dispositions for the operations exhibited great skill, and the precision with which the movement of the different detachments was calculated reflects the greatest credit on those who collected the intelligence and furnished the materials on which the plan was designed.

General Ochterlony now commenced a road for heavy artillery up to Deonthal, and closed his position round Malaun. The Gurkhas concentrated round the latter place, abandoning Surajgarh and all other points. News of the fall of Almora [1] now reached them and Umar Singh's *sirdars* urged him to accept terms for himself and his son Runjoor at Jythuk. He, however, refused, thinking that the rains would force the British to withdraw. The chiefs then began to desert him, and he, retiring into Malaun with about 200 men, held out until the batteries were ready to open on the fort; he then capitulated, signing an agreement that the Gurkha nation should retire to the east of the river Kali, and resigning to the British all the provinces from Kumaun westwards. Runjoor Singh, opposed to General Martindell at Jythuk, was of course included in these terms. Many of the Gurkhas took service with the British, and three battalions were at once formed. Kumaun was made a

Umar Singh capitulates.

[1] See page 22.

British province, but the remaining hill country was restored to the Rajas from whom it had been conquered by Umar Singh.

Operations of Major-General John Sullivan Wood's Division.

The division assembled at Gorakhpur under General John Sullivan Wood should have taken the field on 15th November; but owing to want of transport and supplies it was late in December before that officer entered the Terai. Having ascertained that the Gurkhas, under Colonel Wazeer Singh, had taken post at the mouth of the pass within which Butwal is situated, and had built a stockade there called Jitgarh, General Wood resolved to reconnoitre the works and carry them. On 3rd January he marched from Simra in the Terai with twenty-one companies of infantry. The route led along the banks of the Tenavi, and for the last seven miles through *sál* forest. General Wood had been told to expect an open space in front of the stockade, but while with the advanced guard, still in the thick of the forest, he suddenly found himself in front of the stockade and not more than fifty yards from it. A destructive fire was opened on the advanced guard, but the General waited for the main body to come up before attacking. The stockade was merely a hollow one, and a position was gained on the enemy's left flank completely commanding it. The capture of the work was assured, and the enemy were already retreating from it, when General Wood, thinking it not possible to capture the hill behind the work, ordered a retreat, to the great disappointment of the troops, who were flushed with the prospect of a certain and easy victory. The British loss was 24 killed and 5 officers and 104 wounded. The enemy lost a *sirdar* and many more men than the British, but our retreat gave to them the triumph of a decided victory. The result of the action, and the bravery of the enemy, left on the General's mind an impression of the inadequacy of his force for the object assigned which influenced all his future measures; and instead of endeavouring to penetrate the hills he now confined his operations to the defensive.

Parties of irregular horse were added to the force, and the 8th Native Cavalry was sent to assist in scouring the country. Report magnified the Gurkha army to 12,000 men, whereas their regular troops scarcely reached as many hundred. The General, however, believed the reports, threw up works to defend the road to Gorakhpur, left a garrison in them, and moved with his main force to repel an incursion into Nichlaul. These measures made the enemy bold, and they raided daily in our territory, burning and plundering villages. This state of things continued throughout January, February, and March. Though reinforced by another native battalion and further artillery, General Wood still considered himself too weak to act offensively. What had been going on simultaneously on the Champaran frontier tended unfortunately to confirm this impression, and he could also not divest himself of the idea that Wazeer Singh commanded an army numerically stronger than his own. Being strongly urged to ascertain this point by coming into actual contact with the enemy, General Wood was induced in April to appear again before Butwal, and, drawing up his army before it on the 17th, he opened a desultory and futile fire on the walls for a few hours, after which he again retired. This operation the General described as "a reconnaissance calculated to create a diversion by alarming the enemy on this frontier, at the same time that it enabled him to ascertain that he had not miscalculated the strength of the army opposed to him." Immediately after this, having laid waste the Gurkha portion of the Terai, General Wood retired to cantonments at Gorakhpur.

Operations of Major-General Marley's Division.

Major Bradshaw, the negotiator for the frontier disputes, remained during the rains of 1814 in charge of the disputed lands near Simraon, and established posts which remained unmolested. In November the Gurkhas sent an envoy with a letter and presents for the Governor General, quite ignoring the fact that war had been proclaimed on the 1st November. Major Bradshaw refused to allow him to pass, and this decision was confirmed by Lord Hastings, who further ordered the envoy to be desired to return to Khatmandu or remain on the frontier at his peril. Notwithstanding this, the envoy, Chundur Seekur, remained in the Terai. Major Bradshaw having now heard that General Marley had crossed the Ganges, resolved to defer active operations no longer, and attacked the Gurkha post of Barharwa, situated on the right bank of the Baghmati, close to the frontier, preparatory to occupying the whole Terai. He took the post on the 25th November, and seized Chundur Seekur, the envoy, and his papers, which proved that the whole object of his mission was to gain time. The Terai was immediately evacuated by the Gurkhas and was temporarily annexed to the British Government. Major Bradshaw then established the undermentioned posts for its defence till General Marley should arrive: Captain Hay, with the head-quarters of the Champaran Light Infantry, at Baragarhi; Captain Blackney, with a wing of the 2-22nd Native Infantry, at Samanpur; and Captain Sibley, with about 500 men, at Persa, on the high road to Etaunda, some distance to the left of Baragarhi.

General Marley arrived on the frontier with the main army on the 12th December. An outpost of Captain Hay's had been driven back on the 7th, and the Gurkhas, though keeping within the *sál* forest, showed an actively hostile spirit. Some attempts at poisoning the wells and pools were discovered, and their spies were busy, several having been detected in our camps. General Marley formed his army in three divisions, intending himself to attempt the Bichia Koh and Etaunda pass with 2,200 men, while Colonel Dick, with about 1,500 men, was to take the route of Hariharpur to the eastward, and Major Roughsedge with 1,280 men was to move by Jurjuri and the Suktikhola pass, between the other two columns and in advance of Baragarhi. The remainder of the army was to be prepared to support either division that might need it, and to keep open the communications through the forest until the arrival of the brigade allotted for this purpose, which had not yet assembled.

The month of December was spent in maturing this plan and in collecting information. In the meantime the main army was encamped behind Baragarhi. The posts remained as before, that of Captain Sibley being twenty miles to the left of the main army, at Persa; Captain Blackney at Samanpur was nearly as far to the right. Both were without support, and notwithstanding the time that they had occupied the same ground no substantial works had been thrown up by either officer. This state of things induced the Gurkhas to plan an attack on both posts simultaneously. The main army of the Nepalese was at Mokwanpur under Colonel Rundher Singh, but the forest was occupied by parties who were always on the alert. Rundher ordered the posts to be attacked on the morning of the 1st January. Captain Blackney was completely surprised

Gurkha attack on Persa and Samanpur.

at Samanpur: he himself and Lieutenant Duncan, his 2nd-in-command, were at once killed, and in ten minutes the sepoys broke and fled in every direction; Lieutenant Strettell, the only surviving officer, retreated to Gora Sohun with the remnant of the detachment. Captain Sibley at Persa was more on his guard. He had expected an attack and had asked for reinforcements; a party under Major Greenstreet was consequently sent to his assistance on 31st December, but unfortunately did not reach Persa till too late. The small garrison made a good fight for it, but was surrounded and overpowered; the fugitives met the reinforcing detachment three miles off. Our loss out of 500 men was 123 killed and 187 wounded, besides 73 missing. The proximity of Major Greenstreet's detachment alone saved the wounded and stragglers, as the enemy were eager to secure their booty.

The activity and enterprise shown in these attacks was so unexpected by General Marley that he began to fear for his train of heavy artillery coming up from Bettiah in rear. He therefore strengthened Baragarhi with Major Roughsedge's detachment from Janikpur, and himself moved westward to cover his train. Moreover, considering his force to be insufficient, he abandoned all idea of penetrating the hills according to his first plan. His brigadiers agreed with him in this, and perhaps they were not far wrong.

The Marquis of Hastings was much disappointed at all these untoward occurrences and strained every nerve to strengthen all the divisions in the field.

General Marley, notwithstanding the daily approach of fresh troops, continued inactive during the whole of January. He made some marches in the open Terai, but never ventured into the forest. Repeated orders were sent from head-quarters for offensive measures, but the General was unable to come to any resolution. In the meantime the enemy burnt several villages not far from his camp and even threatened to attack Baragarhi, which had a garrison of over 1,000 men. A stockade was erected close to the post, and the Gurkha commander was ordered to attack, but wisely refrained. The Gurkha post was unmolested by us, but was removed on 7th February.

On the 10th February, General Marley, unable longer to endure the irksomeness of his situation, and feeling unable to carry out

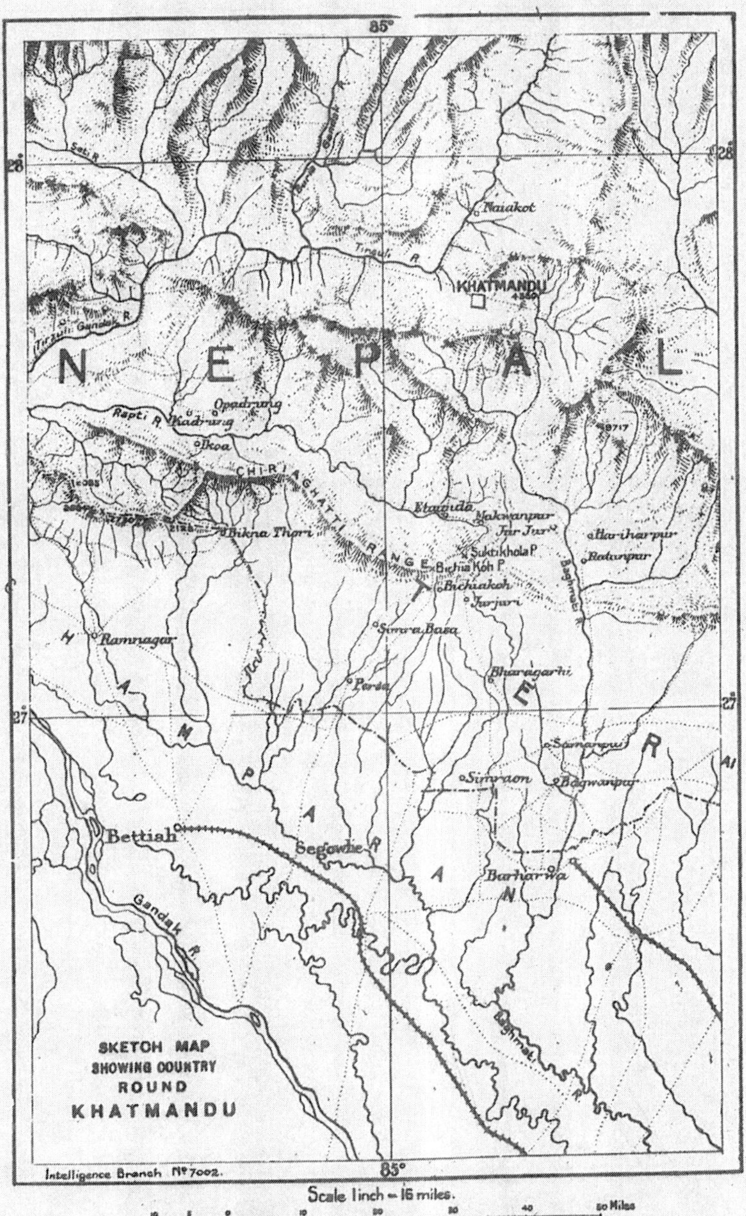
85°
28°
27°
NEPAL
Naiakot
Tirsuli R.
KHATMANDU
Sati R.
Gandak R.
Opadrung
Rapti R.
Kadrung
Ikoa
CHIRIAGHATTI RANGE
Bikna Thori
Etaunda
Makwanpur
Jur Jur
Suktikhola P.
Bichia Koh P.
Bichiakoh
Jurjuri
Hariharpur
Ratanpur
Baghmati R.
Simra Basa
Ramnagar
Parsa
Bharagarhi
Samanpur
Simraon
Bagwanpur
Bettiah
Segowlie
Barharwa
Gandak R.
Baghmati
TERAI
CHAMPARAN
SKETCH MAP
SHOWING COUNTRY
ROUND
KHATMANDU
Intelligence Branch No 7002.
Scale 1 inch = 16 miles.
10 5 0 10 20 30 40 50 Miles

the expectation of the Commander-in-Chief, took the sudden and extraordinary course of leaving his camp, then at Bunjari Kokhra, without intimating his intention to any one or providing for the ordinary routine of command. Lord Hastings had already intended to supersede General Marley, and Major-General George Wood, who had been ordered up to take his place, joined on the 20th February. The very day before his arrival an event occurred that struck terror into the enemy and raised the courage of the army to the highest pitch. Lieutenant Pickersgill, an active officer of the Intelligence Department, discovered, while reconnoitring, a party of about 500 Gurkhas at no great distance from the camp. He at once sent to inform Colonel Dick, who was in command; Colonel Dick immediately despatched a party of irregular horse under Colonel Hearsey to strengthen Pickersgill, who had remained watching the enemy, and followed himself with all the picquets. The Gurkhas, meanwhile, thinking Pickersgill unsupported, attacked him, but just then the cavalry came up, and, charging the enemy, cut the whole detachment to pieces. The Gurkhas were so intimidated by this that they hastily evacuated all their posts in the forest and Terai, and when General Wood arrived next day not a Gurkha was to be found below the hills. A month was still left in which to make an offensive effort, and the army were eager to be led on, but the General adopted an opinion that the fever season had commenced, and that it would be risking his fine army, now amounting to 13,400 men, to penetrate the forest. He accordingly contented himself with sweeping its skirt and marching to Janikpur and back; thus the season closed without his seeing an enemy.

Operations in Kumaun.

Whilst Lord Hastings was on his tour through Rohilkhand in December 1814, he ascertained that the province of Kumaun was quite destitute of troops, as they had all been despatched westwards to Malaun and Jythuk. He consequently thought that a diversion in this quarter might lead to important results and even to the conquest of the province. The Kumaunese also were known to be disaffected to the Gurkhas, and this point was reckoned on as a strong factor of the probable success. There were no regular troops to be spared, but the Rohillas of Rohilkhand, of Pathan origin, were a race trained to arms from infancy. Lord Hastings therefore selected two officers accustomed to irregular troops, Lieutenant-Colonel Gardner and Major Hearsey, to raise Rohilla levies. Lieutenant-Colonel Gardner was to penetrate from Kashipur in the Moradabad district, and Major Hearsey from Pilibhit, by the passes near Champawat and Khyrigarh, where the river Kali, or Sarda, enters the plains. Both officers received their instructions late in December and commenced to raise levies.

Lieutenant-Colonel Gardner, with the Honourable E. Gardner as Political Agent, commenced his march from Kashipur on the 11th February 1815. The Rohillas behaved in the most creditable manner, and by the 22nd March he had penetrated to near Almora after a few skirmishes, and by the 20th had established himself on the ridge immediately facing that place.

Major Hearsey advanced about the same time from Pilibhit and penetrated to Champawat without opposition. Finding the inhabitants inclined to declare in his favour, he formed posts along the Kali, and began to think of co-operating with Lieutenant-Colonel Gardner by moving on Almora. On the 31st March, however, he was defeated in an engagement; his raw levies deserted him, and he himself was wounded and made prisoner.

Towards the end of March Lord Hastings, perceiving the favourable condition of affairs, determined to support Lieutenant-Colonel Gardner before Almora, and despatched Colonel Jasper Nicolls[1] with a force of 2,500 native infantry and ten pieces of artillery to his assistance.

Colonel Nicolls marched on the 5th April, and advanced to join Lieutenant-Colonel Gardner, hearing on his way of Major Hearsey's defeat. After joining Lieutenant-Colonel Gardner there was a good deal of fighting round Almora, but by the 25th of April more guns had been brought up, and a position taken only seventy yards from the fort. Seeing his position desperate, Bam Sah, the governor of the province, proposed an armistice for the purpose of negotiating surrender. On the 27th April a formal convention was signed. In this the surrender of the province of Kumaun was stipulated, with all its fortified places; also the retirement, within ten days, of all Gurkha troops east of the Kali; and Major Hearsey's unconditional release. It was agreed that the Gurkhas should be allowed to take all their military stores and

[1] Afterwards Sir Jasper Nicolls, Commander-in-Chief in India.

private property away with them, the British supplying the necessary transport. These articles were faithfully executed, and the defensive line of the Kali taken up to protect our possessions.

General remarks on campaign of 1814-15.

It will be noticed that of the four divisions with which the campaign was originally commenced, the operations of three were total failures. Not only did they effect nothing, but the commanders succeeded in lowering our name throughout India to such an extent that the native princes of India began to think that it was time to take advantage of circumstances, and intrigues were set on foot through every independent state. The Marquis of Hastings, however, looked forward with confidence to his ultimate success. Every check to our arms was clearly traceable to a want of due precaution in the commanders, and to the fact that the soldiers and sepoys were unaccustomed to fighting in forests and mountains. The Gurkhas, on the other hand, never followed up their successes, and were quite satisfied with repelling an attack or cutting off an outpost, and their tactics were purely defensive. To the officers of the Bengal Army the lessons of the war were in the highest degree salutary; precipitancy and want of caution were qualities bred in them by an uninterrupted course of easy victory. From the days of Clive to those of Lord Lake, they had only to show themselves and march straight against the enemy to insure his precipitate flight. They carried to the hills the same contempt for the foe, and by painful experience found out their mistake. More than one of the officers in high command were examples of how easily the mind passes from one extreme to the other, their conduct changing from suicidal rashness to excessive caution and despair. General Ochterlony's well-directed and cautious operations stood out in brilliant contrast to those of Generals Gillespie, Martindell, J. S. Wood, Marley, and George Wood, whose conduct had scarcely a redeeming feature. The timely strategical movement on Kumaun, however, was the real means of bringing the war to a termination, for the fall of Almora influenced the surrender of Umar Singh.

Peace negotiations.

Upon the conquest of Kumaun the Nepal Government showed a decided desire to re-establish friendly relations, a desire which was reciprocated by us. Most of the Nepal Chiefs appeared to have become convinced that their confidence of security in the ruggedness of their mountains was a vain illusion; but there was still a faction inclined to continue the war. In May 1815, Guru Gujraj Misser was sent down, with full powers under the red seal, to negotiate with Major Bradshaw, the British Political Agent, for an entire adjustment of existing difficulties. The terms demanded by Lord Hastings were as follows :—

> *1st.*—The perpetual cession of all the hill country taken in the campaign, *viz.*, from the river Kali westwards.
>
> *2nd.*—A like cession of the entire Terai from the foot of the outer hills along the whole line of the remaining territory of the Gurkhas.
>
> *3rd.*—The relinquishment by the Gurkhas of the footing they had gained in the territory of the Sikkim Raja, and the surrender to him of the stockaded forts of Nagri and Nagarkot.
>
> *4th.*—The reception of a Resident with the usual escort and establishment at Khatmandu, and the customary stipulation not to receive or give service to Europeans without special sanction of Government.

As the Guru stated he had no authority to treat for the cession of the Terai, he returned to Khatmandu. In the meantime the army, which had been collected on the Simraon frontier, was cantoned to the north of the Ganges or at Dinapur and kept ready equipped to again take the field immediately the favourable season should return.

## Nepal War, 1816.

The Marquis of Hastings, thinking a second campaign inevitable, determined to take such measures as should crush this ambitious and aspiring nation for ever. Preparation was made for penetrating with a brigade from Kumaun, where Lieutenant-Colonel Adams had succeeded Colonel Nicolls. Colonel Nicolls, with the army of Major-General J. S. Wood, considerably reinforced, was to act against the Butwal and Palpa frontier. Major-General Ochterlony was at the same time to be summoned from the north-west to take command of the Simraon troops, which were destined to penetrate into the valley of Nepal.

Causes which led to the campaign.

Whilst making provision for war the efforts of Government to procure peace were in no way relaxed. Negotiations were again opened in August, and as the chief objection to the cession of the Terai was their high estimate of its pecuniary value, and the fact that most of the principal officers of the Nepal Court held *jagirs* there, Lord Hastings made concessions and offered to pay the estimated value of the stipend, amounting to from two to three lakhs of rupees. The reception of the Resident was greatly objected to by the Nepalese, but this was insisted on as a *sine qua non*. A treaty was finally drafted,[1] in which the cession of the Terai from the river Kali to the Gandak was all that was insisted on, and two lakhs of rupees were offered in compensation for the retained lands. The Nepalese envoys declared that they could not venture to accede to these terms without submitting the draft to their Court, but they engaged to give a definite answer in fifteen days, and forwarded a copy to Khatmandu. The negotiators then took their leave on the 29th October, promising to return in twelve days with the treaty signed. Owing to the extreme reluctance of the Nepalese to come to terms, the British Indian Government was even preparing to make further concessions, either in lieu of the stipends or in addition to them, when Guru Gujraj Misser returned from Khatmandu and signed the treaty according to the original draft. This was done at Segowlie on the 28th November 1815, and was ratified by Government with the usual salute, on the 9th December. The Government now determined to make the further concessions determined on, gratuitously, and never doubted the sincerity of the enemy. Under the impression that peace was restored, the preparations for the second campaign were suspended, and the commissariat officers, in their zeal for economy, went beyond the bounds of due discretion, discharging a great part of the transport establishment and selling much of the grain collected in the frontier depôts. Of this precipitancy there was soon reason to repent. It was a stipulation of the treaty that the ratification under the red seal (the royal assent) should be delivered to Lieutenant-Colonel Bradshaw in fifteen days. This period expired without the ratification, and it was ascertained, during December, that after animated discussion at Khatmandu the war faction had prevailed over that which favoured the proposed treaty. A renewal of hostilities appeared now inevitable, though it was expected that the Gurkhas would endeavour to waste as much as possible of the favourable season still remaining, in offers of negotiation.

[1] Aitchison LIV.

Sir David Ochterlony was at once ordered into the field, and every exertion made to furnish the stores and establishments necessary to render the army efficient. Notice of the approach of the army was sent to the Raja of Nepal, but he was told that the consequences of his want of faith might still be averted, if the treaty, duly ratified, were sent to meet the General in the Terai. The war party at Khatmandu, however, prevailed; the Gurkhas determined on hostilities; and with this view every precaution was taken to fortify and render impregnable the passes through the first range of hills (the sandstone range).

Outbreak of hostilities.

The principal route into the valley of Nepal is by the Bichia Koh over the Chiriaghatti range. On this the Gurkhas erected three successive lines of fortifications, the last of which was considered absolutely impregnable; all the other known routes were similarly defended. Behind these defences the Gurkhas awaited the arrival of Sir David Ochterlony, leaving him the passage of the forest altogether free.

The British force was already moving to the Terai when, in the beginning of February, it was met by Gujraj Misser with a formal intimation that the Nepalese were about to recommence war.

Sir David Ochterlony had a force of nearly 15,000 effective men, including three European regiments, Her Majesty's 24th, 66th, and 87th.[1] He divided this force into four brigades under Colonel Kelly of the 24th, Lieutenant-Colonel Nicoll of the 66th, Lieutenant-Colonel Miller of the 87th, and Colonel Dick, 9th Native Infantry. Colonel Kelly, with the 1st Brigade, was detached to the right by Bagwanpur with orders to penetrate, if possible, by Hariharpur. Lieutenant-Colonel Nicoll, Commanding the 2nd Brigade, was detached to Ramnagar on the left with orders to penetrate to the valley of the Rapti and thence move up the valley towards the main body. The 3rd and 4th Brigades,[2] under the command of Sir David Ochterlony, were to penetrate by the Bichia Koh, and to operate against the forts and valley of Mokwanpur.

General Ochterlony joined the main body at camp Bullwee on the 24th January, and by the 8th of February all troops had joined

[1] For detail of force see Appendix.

[2] The 4th Brigade was commanded by Lieutenant-Colonel Burnet, 8th Native Infantry, as Colonel Dick never joined the force.

his command, and precautions for the safety of his communications had been taken. Bettiah had been made into a fortified depôt and formed his immediate base; Persa was formed into a depôt and fortified, as also was Simrabasa about six miles beyond, this post being protected by a stockade. On the 9th February General Ochterlony advanced from Simrabasa through the forest with the 3rd Brigade and arrived at Bichia Koh, twelve miles, without opposition, the march occupying from 7 A.M. to 3-30 P.M. He there took up a position in the channel of the *nala* and was joined by the 4th Brigade next day. By this date also the brigades under Colonels Nicolls and Kelly were ready to advance from Ramnagar and Bagwanpur, respectively, and their movements commenced the next day.[1]

Bichia Koh, which was situated at no great distance from the first Nepalese stockade, was quickly converted into a fortified depôt. The enemy's works were reconnoitred and found unassailable, and information was earnestly sought as to the possibility of turning the pass by some route unknown to the enemy. Four days were spent by Captain Pickersgill, of the Quartermaster General's Department, in reconnoitring all the watercourses, and he at length found a practicable route along the Balu Khola to the foot of the hills; here some smugglers were induced by a high reward to show him a pass over the hills by which they were in the habit of smuggling goods into Nepal, a route which they averred was unknown to any servant of the Nepal State. This pass proved practicable, though difficult. On the 14th February at 9 P.M. General Ochterlony, with the 3rd Brigade, marched from Bichia Koh, leaving all tents standing. The route led by very intricate paths, through the deep and narrow ravine of Balu Khola, bringing the detachment out to a watercourse leading up a very steep acclivity by which the range was passed. It was 8 A.M. before the advance guard reached the point from which the ascent to the summit led. The difficulty of the ascent far exceeded anticipation, and the whole of the troops had not reached the crest until after sunset. On reaching the summit the brigade had to advance five miles beyond to obtain water, and the rear did not come in until 9 P.M., having been twenty-four hours on the march. The pass by which the brigade marched

[1] The record of the movements of these brigades is very incomplete.

was totally impracticable for any cattle, even elephants; and the 16th, 17th, and 18th were spent in making the road practicable for the latter animals. In the meantime the troops were almost wholly without provisions, and suffered great privations, being two days without food. They, however, cheerfully submitted, under the full conviction that the object of the movement was gained and the line of the Chiriaghatti successfully turned.

On the 15th instant Colonel Burnet, with the 4th Brigade, marched from Bichia Koh at daylight and took up a position at Semelbasa.[1] On a reconnaissance being made the first stockade was found to be evacuated, and the second was deserted by the enemy on approach of the reconnoitring party, which was thus enabled to proceed almost to the summit of the pass. Here it was received with a heavy fire from the heights, and had to fall back with some loss.

On the morning of the 17th it was ascertained that the enemy had retired owing to the successful movement of the 3rd Brigade, and the pass was occupied without opposition. On the 19th General Ochterlony joined the 4th Brigade at Etaunda, on the Rapti, where works were thrown up for the protection of the depôt established there. Having provided for the defence of Etaunda the 3rd Brigade moved on the 27th towards Mokwanpur, taking up a position on open level ground about two miles distant from the hills covering the fortified heights and detached defences; the following morning General Ochterlony was joined by the 4th Brigade with the battering train.

On the afternoon of the 28th the Gurkhas attacked a detached post called Sekha Khuttri, situated on a hill to the left of the camp. The enemy attacked with about 2,000 men and several guns, but the post in the village was obstinately and gallantly defended by the small detachment there. General Ochterlony successively detached one European and three native battalions in support, and the enemy were at length beaten off. The British casualties were 2 officers and 222 men, but the loss of the enemy, by their own subsequent account, had exceeded 800.

In the meantime the 2nd Brigade, under Colonel Nicoll, had crossed the range by the Bikna Thori pass and moved forward,

[1] Two miles north of Bichia Koh.

without experiencing any opposition, by the valley of the Rapti to Etaunda. Colonel Nicoll reached Ikoa on the 25th February and left there two native battalions and a proportion of field guns, in order to check any attempt by the enemy on the valley of the Rapti from their fortified posts of Kadrung and Opadrung, to which they had retired on his advance. The remainder of the brigade marched up the valley of the Rapti and joined head-quarters on the 29th, the day after the action at Mokwanpur.

At the same time Colonel Kelly, with the 1st Brigade, marching by one of the Baghmati routes, reached Ratanpur on the 27th February, having been obliged to make short marches owing to the nature of the road, which he described as "a bed of large stones." He experienced no opposition *en route.* On the evening of his arrival at Ratanpur he made a reconnaissance with a view to obtaining information and making a dash at Hariharpur, if it should promise a successful issue. The enemy showed in considerable force in a very strong stockade when half the ascent of the hill on which Hariharpur stands had been made, and Colonel Kelly ascertained that there were 1,000 men with two guns in the fort. On the 29th February he moved to Jur Jur, four miles to the west of Ratanpur, the road having to be made for the guns. On reaching Jur Jur it appeared from another reconnaissance that a strong point, 800 yards from one of the Gurkha stockades, had not been occupied. As the occupation of this neglected point appeared to be of great moment, Colonel Kelly considered it advisable to take it by surprise. A force of European and Native infantry, with two 3-pounder guns carried by bearers, started at 3 A.M on the 1st March, under Lieutenant-Colonel O'Halloran, and seized the position by 6 A.M., dislodging a Gurkha picquet. The enemy in very considerable numbers made a most desperate and obstinate attempt to recover this point, and a reinforcement was despatched by Colonel Kelly to cover the rear of the post, which was threatened. It was impossible, from the nature of the ground, to close or use the bayonet, and the musketry continued without intermission until 11-30, when the arrival of two 6-pounders and two 5½-inch howitzers on elephants decided the affair in a few minutes, and left the British in possession of an almost natural redoubt, very advantageously situated for further operations. This success, however, was

Action near Hariharpur.

not gained without some loss, five officers and fifty-four men being killed and wounded. After this repulse the Gurkhas apparently became disheartened, and on the 4th March, during a storm of rain. evacuated the fort and hill. From the date of the General's arrival at Etaunda a desire for peace had evidently pervaded the minds of the Nepalese chiefs, and an unsuccessful attempt had been made on the 25th February to obtain a suspension of hostilities.

Peace negotiations.

The intelligence of their reverses at Sekha Khuttri and Hariharpur, however, spread consternation at Khatmandu, and the Durbar immediately resolved to make a tender of unqualified submission as the only means of averting the most disastrous consequences.

The red seal having been hurriedly affixed to the Treaty of Segowlie it was despatched to the Gurkha Commander, Kazi Baktawar Singh, one of the chief *sirdars*, who on 3rd March informed the General of the fact, and said he would forward it to Chundur Seekur, the Nepal envoy. In reply he was informed that the Gurkha Government must not now expect the same terms as before the war, but if he had power to treat, Sir David Ochterlony would receive him. In the meantime approaches were pushed to within 500 yards of the defences of Mokwanpur, and a battery thrown up to open on the fort. Chundur Seekur soon appeared with the ratified treaty and pressed its acceptance in a submissive and abject manner. Sir David Ochterlony was instructed to ascertain that the spirit of hostility was completely annihilated, and that the foe was sufficiently humbled, before accepting this treaty. In order to put their humility to the test it was explained to Chundur Seekur that the letter of the treaty would now give to the British all the territory in their occupation and would include the valley of the Rapti as well as Etaunda and Hariharpur. At the same time he was assured that he must expect no concession beyond that stated in the treaty, and was made to give a specific note in writing to this effect, and further to engage that the Raja should confirm the declaration in a letter to the Governor General. To all this the envoy readily assented, and even presented the ratified treaty on his knees at the General's Durbar, before all the *vakils* in camp. The General then accepted the treaty and despatched Lieutenant Boileau of his staff to act as Resident at Khatmandu until one should be nominated by the Governor General.

The contest with the Nepalese was thus terminated in the beginning of March, and the requisite orders for the retrograde movement of the troops was at once issued to the leaders of the different columns engaged in the campaign. Lord Hastings was much pleased with the result to which Sir David Ochterlony had brought the campaign in so short a space of time, more particularly so because the late period at which the operations had unavoidably been commenced, after the interruption to the preparations which occurred in November and December, had made him apprehensive of the arrival of the unhealthy season before there would be time to effectually humble the enemy. Sir David himself, too, had discovered that the capture of Mokwanpur would be the most that could be effected in this campaign, for he found that it would not be safe to keep the troops in that valley after the middle of March; this therefore was not the least powerful of the motives which influenced him in granting the terms.

The articles of the treaty were all punctually executed according to agreement. The Supreme Government, however, thought it would be a politic act to give up such part of the Terai as might not be required to form a straight and even frontier, in lieu of the portions stipulated in the treaty. The Marquis of Hastings, therefore, after every article had been executed, gave notice to the Raja that the Hon'ble E. Gardner was appointed Resident, and empowered to conclude a new arrangement[1] on this basis. This was subsequently effected after the boundary had been surveyed and laid down with pillars; this boundary constitutes the present frontier to the east of the Gandak.

The part of the Terai which skirted Oudh was retained and made over to the Nawab Vazir in extinction of a loan obtained from him during the war. This again came into our hands on the annexation of Oudh, and was restored to Nepal in 1860 for services performed by the Nepalese troops during the Mutiny. A treaty was also made with the Sikkim Raja by which we guaranteed him his possessions, thus shutting out the Nepalese from all means of aggrandizement to the east and circumscribing Nepal with British territory on three sides; this policy has no doubt done much to secure peace with Nepal since 1816.

[1] See Aitchison LV.

Of the other columns mentioned above, with which it was Lord Hastings' intention to invade Nepal, Colonel Nicolls was afterwards ordered to take command of a force of 6,617 men at Sitapur and penetrate into the provinces of Doti and Salena. Lieutenant-Colonel Adams from Kumaun was to co-operate by moving on the back of the Gurkha position. Major-General John S. Wood, with a force of 4,866 men, was to act as a corps of observation on the Gorakhpur frontier for the purpose of watching and overawing Butwal in the first instance, and eventually reducing and occupying such part of the Terai between the Gandak and the eastern limits of Bahraich as were not yet brought under subjection to the British Government. Captain Latter had command of a force of 2,445 men assembled at Titalia [1] with which to co-operate with the Raja of Sikkim.

The early termination of the war prevented the employment of either of the detachments assembled under the command of Major-General John S. Wood and Colonel Nicolls as well as the projected move of Lieutenant-Colonel Adams from Kumaun on the back of the Gurkha position. Those officers had respectively assumed command of their detachments, and were proceeding to the destined quarters in which their military operations were to be carried out, when information of the conclusion of peace was received by them. The corps composing those detachments were consequently dispersed to their several stations.

Captain Latter entered the hills with a portion of the troops under his command, in order to support the operations of the Sikkim Raja's troops, which had been continued with tolerable success, and to encourage the revolt of the Kirontis against the Nepalese Government. He advanced to within three miles of the fort of Nagar which the Sikkim troops had invested. In this position he received from Sir David Ochterlony intelligence of the conclusion of peace, and he accordingly directed a cessation of hostilities on the part of the Sikkim force and discontinued all the proceedings which he had commenced against the Gurkha Government.

Concluding remarks.

General Ochterlony's conduct of this campaign differs materially from that of his previous successful campaign against Umar Singh at Malaun. There he carried on his operations with the most extreme caution,

[1] Titalia is in the Terai, due south of Darjeeling.

leaving nothing to chance, and working as methodically as if he had been besieging a fortress, in which light, indeed, we may look on the naturally strong position of the enemy. There is no doubt that the chief reason for his extreme caution was the feeling that the Bengal sepoy was not equal to the task of coping with the Gurkhas on their native hills; he was consequently very careful not to expose them to the chance of a severe repulse, which might have had a bad influence on, if not entirely destroyed, their *morale*, and rendered ultimate success in the difficult task before him hopeless. In his second campaign we cannot but look upon his turning movement in the neighbourhood of Bichia Koh as a most hazardous one. A successful General has no criticism to fear, and this enterprise was doubtless prompted by urgent necessity, but had he not been aided by great good fortune it might have resulted in serious disaster. Its success, however, not only abridged the period of the campaign from months to weeks, but probably saved the army from an inglorious retreat at the beginning of the hot and sickly season, which was due in about a month. There can be little doubt, nevertheless, that a few men on the edges of the defile might have almost annihilated the brigade without exposing themselves to much danger. This brigade, on entering the deep and narrow ravine of Balu Khola, about a mile from Bichia Koh, had to march through in single file for five miles; the banks on either side were covered with trees, sometimes meeting overhead; at other times precipitous cliffs of great height rose on either side; fallen trees had to be removed here and there from the path; the final ascent was at least 300 feet, up which the men had to clamber with the assistance of the bushes. In face of any opposition the march was indeed a dangerous one, and such perilous enterprises are only justifiable when undertaken as a means of averting disaster, and when the saving of time is all-important.

In conclusion, we must notice the fact that the Gurkhas attempted to poison the water in the passes both in this campaign and in that of 1814-15. Sir David Ochterlony in his depatches reports the death of some elephants and horses from this cause, but no men appear to have suffered. This is probably because the water poisoned was in stagnant recesses between the first and second stockade of the Bichia Koh, and was probably not used by the men. The water was supposed to be poisoned with *mohoor* root, baskets of this being found in the vicinity. Precautions would have to be taken to guard against losing men from this cause.

---

*BIBLIOGRAPHY.*


*Political and Military Transactions in India*—Henry T. Prinsep .. .. .. .. 1825

*Official Papers relating to the Nepal War* .. .. 1824

*Treaties, Engagements and Sanads, Volume* II, Aitchison.. 1892

*Report on Nepal*—Brevet-Major E. R. Elles and Major Newnham Davis .. .. .. 1893

*Gurkhas*—Lieutenant-Colonel Eden Vansittart .. 1906

# APPENDIX.

## STRENGTH OF FORCE UNDER SIR DAVID OCHTERLONY, FEBRUARY 1816.

*Right Column, 1st Brigade—Colonel Kelly, 24th Foot.*

| | | |
|---|---|---|
| Her Majesty's 24th Foot .. .. | Rifles | 849 |
| 1st Battalion, 18th Native Infantry [1] .. | „ | 747 |
| „ „ 21st „ „ [2] .. | „ | 390 |
| 2nd „ „ „ „ [3] .. | „ | 437 |
| Chumparun Light Infantry .. .. .. | „ | 1,246 |
| Total | „ | 3,669 |

*Centre Column—Major-General Sir David Ochterlony.*

3RD BRIGADE—LIEUTENANT-COLONEL MILLER, 39TH FOOT.

4TH BRIGADE—COLONEL DICK, 9TH NATIVE INFANTRY.

| | | |
|---|---|---|
| Her Majesty's 87th Foot .. .. | Rifles | 876 |
| 2nd Battalion, 4th Native Infantry [4] .. | „ | 784 |
| „ „ 8th „ „ [5] .. | „ | 784 |
| „ „ 9th „ „ [6] .. | „ | 810 |
| „ „ 12th „ „ [7] .. | „ | 894 |
| „ „ 15th „ „ [8] .. | „ | 805 |
| „ „ 22nd „ „ [9] .. | „ | 860 |
| „ „ 25th „ „ [10] .. | „ | 815 |
| 1st „ 13th „ „ [11] .. | „ | 425 |
| Total | „ | 7,053 |

1 Became the 36th Regiment in 1824; mutinied at Jullundur in 1857.
2 „ „ 41st „ „ 1824; „ „ Sitapur in 1857.
3 „ „ 42nd „ „ 1824; now the 5th Light Infantry.
4 „ „ 23rd „ „ 1824; mutinied at Mhow in 1857.
5 „ „ 24th „ „ 1824; disbanded for disaffection in 1857.
6 Now the 1st Brahmans.
7 Became the 1st Regiment in 1824; mutinied at Cawnpore in 1857.
8 Now the 2nd Queen's Own Rajput Light Infantry.
9 Became the 44th Regiment in 1824; mutinied at Agra in 1857.
10 „ „ 50th „ „ 1824; „ „ Nagode in 1857.
11 „ „ 26th „ „ 1824; „ „ Mian Mir (Lahore Cantonment) in 1857.

*Left Column, 2nd Brigade—Lieutenant-Colonel Nicoll, 66th Foot.*

| | | | |
|---|---|---|---|
| Her Majesty's 66th Foot | .. .. | Rifles | 762 |
| 5th Grenadier Battalion[1] | .. .. | „ | 627 |
| 8th „ „ [1] | .. .. | „ | 688 |
| 1st Battalion, 8th Native Infantry[2] | .. | „ | 724 |
| 2nd „ 18th „ „ [3] | .. | „ | 744 |
| | Total | „ | 3,545 |
| | GRAND TOTAL | „ | 14,267 |

with 83 pieces of artillery.

1 Temporarily formed from the Grenadier companies of various native battalions.

2 Became the 9th Regiment in 1824; mutinied at Aligarh in 1857.

3 „ „ 37th „ „ 1824; „ „ Benares in 1857.

# PART II.

---

# SIKKIM.

# SIKKIM.

## CHAPTER III.

### *THE COUNTRY AND PEOPLE.*

THE territory known as Independent Sikkim, comprising an area of 3,600 square miles, lies south of the main Himalayan range, and between two of its great southern offshoots: one, a range culminating in the great mass of Kinchinjunga and tailing down into what is known as the Singalela ridge; the other, the Cho range. Thus, except on the south, Sikkim is entirely separated from its neighbours by a wall of giant mountains varying from 10,000 to 28,000 feet in height. It may be described as the catchment area of the upper Tista river. Westward lies Nepal; on the north and east Tibet, Chumbi, and Bhutan; and on the south the British district of Darjeeling.

The country may be conveniently classified under two headings: Northern and Southern; and Tangu may be taken as marking the dividing line of these two portions. The southern consists of forest-clad and extremely precipitous hillsides, sparsely cultivated, and affording but small space for camps or villages. The rivers are rush torrents, dangerous to cross at all times, and in the rains almost impassable. The villages are very few and far between. In the northern portion a more open and undulating country, partly pine forest and partly pasture, is found. In the extreme north this gives way to open grassy slopes. In this region, the Bhutiah population, nomads in the summer, gather into large villages in the winter.

The climate has corresponding variations. In the summer the valleys are damp, steamy, and pestilential. In the winter communication in the high levels is impeded by the rigorous cold and deep snow. The southern parts of Sikkim are subject to a very heavy rainfall, varying in normal years from 120 to 150 inches. The further one goes north, the less the rainfall becomes, until at last when the northern frontier is reached, the figures have dwindled to a minimum.

The population numbers about 59,000. Of this number the chief tribes are the Lepchas and Khambas. The Lepchas, a jungle folk, the oldest, and perhaps aboriginal inhabitants, call themselves Rong, and are found in Nepal, Sikkim, and Bhutan. They seem liable to be ousted by other tribes, and do not thrive in high cold places or beyond their own forests. The Khambas, called by us Bhutiahs, are immigrants from Tibet. Generally the people are very strong, hardy, unwarlike, good-tempered, and well-affected to white men.

Buddhism is the general religion of the country, which is priest-ridden to an incredible extent. Many thousands of men are cooped up in monasteries, leading lives of absolute sloth, and supported almost entirely by forced and voluntary contributions from the people.

Through Sikkim runs a trade high road between Bengal and Tibet. Along it there is a considerable traffic in live stock, musk, grain, yâk tails, and cloth. In 1899 the trade between Bengal and Sikkim amounted to a value of twenty-one lakhs of rupees. It is this high road which has largely brought about our relations with Tibet; of which later.

There is no standing army in Sikkim.

Outline of History.

Sikkim is governed by a royal family which is no doubt Tibetan by origin and by recent inter-marriage. In old days their country was much more extensive, but was surrounded by powerful neighbours and suffered at their hands. About the year 1700 the Bhutanese overran the country and retained some territory. Again in 1770 they overran all Sikkim east of the Tista; but this time they were driven out by a national rising. The Gurkhas next began to encroach upon Sikkim with varying success, and after the Nepal-China settlement in 1790 the Chinese authorities gave the Nepalese the country west of the Tista and appropriated the Chumbi valley as a part of Tibet.

First contact with British.

In 1814, in course of the Nepal war, the British Government, wishing to encourage the resistance of the Sikkim Raja to Gurkha aggression, sent a force under Captain Latter to the Purniah frontier: and in

1817, when we had confined the Gurkhas to their own territory, an Anglo-Sikkimese treaty[1] was concluded whereby the Sikkim Raja was confirmed in his own dominions. The main object of this treaty was to prevent the expansion of the Nepalese eastward. But even then the Sikkim Raja lost the country between the present boundary and the Tambar river.

In 1825, on the occasion of some internal troubles, a number of Lepcha malcontents fled to Nepal. These refugees made an inroad into the Sikkim Terai in 1834. Colonel Lloyd was sent to enquire into the disturbance, and, under pressure from us, the intruders withdrew. The opportunity was taken to secure the cession of Darjeeling,[2] the advantages of which as a sanatarium had been noticed by frontier commissioners in 1828. Our possession of Darjeeling soon became a source of constant jealousy and annoyance to the Sikkim authorities, offering as it did an asylum for escaped slaves. In retaliation the Sikkim *Dewan* frequently denied aid in capturing escaped criminals, and British subjects were occasionally kidnapped and sold into slavery. As compensation for the cession of this district, the British Government now makes the Sikkim Raja a yearly allowance. This was fixed at Rs. 3,000 in 1841 but subsequently was increased to Rs. 12,000.

Cession of Darjeeling, 1828.

In 1847 the Sikkim Raja was seized, while travelling in Tibet, by the Bhutanese, who hoped to extort from him some terms in a boundary dispute. We refused to help him, and he was eventually released by a Tibetan force.

The discontent against us culminated in the seizure, in 1849, at the instigation of Namguay, "the mad *Dewan*," of Doctor Campbell, the Superintendent of Darjeeling, and Doctor Hooker. These gentlemen were travelling in Sikkim with the consent of both Governments. Namguay hoped, by holding them as hostages, to extort concessions from the British Government. They were, however, soon released, and the treachery was punished by the annexation of the Terai and a large part of the Darjeeling District, and by the stoppage of the Raja's allowance.

For some years matters proceeded smoothly; but later the kidnapping of British subjects was resumed, and in 1860 the

[1] Aitchison LIV. [2] Aitchison LV.

Governor General resolved to occupy Sikkim territory, in order to enforce the restitution of the persons kidnapped and to ensure a correct attitude on the part of the Sikkim Durbar. The Superintendent of Darjeeling, Doctor Campbell, advanced to Rinchinpung, but was compelled to return, and a stronger force under Lieutenant-Colonel Gawler was despatched. After his successful operations a new treaty [1] was concluded. By it we were empowered to make a road through Sikkim; matters of trade and extradition were arranged; Sikkim recognized the suzerainty of Great Britain; and the Raja's allowance was continued.

1860 Expedition.

Up to this time the Tibetans appear to have taken no active interest in the affairs of Sikkim, and notwithstanding the Raja's close family connection with Tibet we had made no allowance for any possible claims to suzerainty on the part of that State.

Subsequent to the conclusion of the 1860 Treaty our relations with Sikkim became so friendly that in 1873 the Deputy Commissioner of Darjeeling, Mr. (afterwards Sir John) Edgar was deputed to "enquire into the condition and prospects of trade with Tibet and the advisability of making a road through Sikkim to the Tibetan frontier." He met the Sikkim Raja and some Tibetan officials from the Chumbi valley, but found that the latter regarded with suspicion any attempt to use the Sikkim Government and country in our efforts to open up trade with Tibet. He was also told that the Chinese Amban had warned the Sikkim Raja that he was bound to prevent Europeans from crossing the Himalayan frontier, and that if he continued to make roads for the English through Sikkim "it would not be well with him."

The road to the Jelap La [2] was constructed about this time.

In 1885 and 1886 events occurred, to which our subsequent difficulties with the Tibetans may be largely attributed. A Mission under Mr. Macaulay, having been authorized by the Chinese Government to pass through Tibet, was actually organized and ready to start, when, in deference to Chinese objections, it was abandoned. Exulting at the abandonment of this expedition, which they attributed to fear of themselves, the Tibetans became

The Macaulay Mission.

1 Aitchison LVI. 2 *La* means pass.

aggressive, and an armed party obstructed the Jelap La road at Lingtu; and in the course of negotiations during 1886 it was found that a treaty had been signed by which the Sikkim Raja declared that Sikkim was subject only to China and Tibet. Diplomatic efforts to secure the withdrawal of the force at Lingtu having

1888 Expedition.

proved unavailing, the Sikkim Expeditionary Force was despatched in March 1888. The Tibetans were expelled, and China recognized our suzerainty over Sikkim by the convention of 1890.[1]

On this a British Political Officer was appointed to Gantok, the capital of Sikkim, his duty being to advise the Raja in consultation with a Council of the chief men of the country. The Raja then refused to live at Gantok, and in 1892 he attempted to go to Tibet. He was, however, stopped by the Nepalese on the way, brought back, and placed under surveillance, and was only restored to his full powers in 1896.

The Tibetans did not accept the boundary as defined by our convention with China, and for some years kept an armed force at Giaogong, to obstruct the passage of unwelcome travellers. In order to settle this matter, a commission was nominated in 1895, consisting of Mr. Claude White, three Tibetan and two Chinese officials. None of these delegates met the British commissioners on the appointed date, but after a delay of some months the Chinese arrived at the Jelap La. Three boundary pillars were erected, which, however, were afterwards pulled down by some persons unknown, and the commission finally broke up in August of the same year with its objects still unaccomplished.

Again in 1902 Mr. White was sent to tour along the Sikkim frontier and exclude the Tibetans from the grazing grounds at Giaogong. Mr. White had the Tibetan blockhouses destroyed, and surveyed the frontier. The Tibetan officials whom he met repudiated the validity of the 1890 treaty.

The boundary question now becomes merged with the affairs of Tibet. Looking back there can be no doubt that the Tibetans have regarded the Sikkim Raja as a kind of vassal. A similar claim over Bhutan was advanced by the Tibetans to Warren Hastings when the latter was engaged in punishing some raids.

[1] Aitchison LVII.

In consequence of the persistent absence in Tibet of the eldest son of the Raja, notwithstanding the repeated injunctions of Government of India to return to Sikkim, the second son has been recognized as the heir-apparent. The administration now vests in the Maharaja and Council, the Political Officer being the arbiter in the event of any difference of opinion arising.

## CHAPTER IV.

*MILITARY OPERATIONS.*

### Expedition under Captain Barre Latter in 1814.

DURING the Nepal War of 1814[1] Captain Latter was furnished with 2,000 men, including his district battalion, for the defence of the Purniah frontier. He was ordered to open up relations with the petty Raja of Sikkim and, short of an actual advance of troops for the purpose, to give him every assistance to expel the Gurkhas from the eastern hills. The co-operation of the Raja was gained, negotiations having been opened by an overture on his part and a request for a few military stores. An attempt was made by the Gurkha Commander at Morung to cut off a British post stationed at Moodwanee, but Lieutenant Foord of the 9th Native Infantry repulsed their night attack after the assailants had succeeded in firing his tents and baggage. This little detachment had several killed and wounded and fought very pluckily, but as the position was evacuated the next day there was little to boast of in the victory. Subsequently Captain Latter was about to aid the Sikkim troops in their investment of Nagar when the news of the general cessation of hostilities arrived.

On the 10th February 1817 Captain Latter concluded a treaty[2] at Titalia with the Sikkim Raja.

### The 1850 Expedition.

The immediate causes of the expedition in 1850 are given in the preceding chapter. There are no military details to record of its progress, for our terms were agreed to without hostilities. The force crossed the river Ranjit in February 1850, but did not proceed far. Sir C. Napier concurred in the military report, which speaks of Sikkim in these terms:—

> In a precipitous and densely wooded country like this, where the track is with difficulty traced through an almost impenetrable jungle of brushwood and briars, with the largest forest trees on either side of it, the facility with

[1] See Chapter II. [2] Aitchison LIV.

which the best troops may be impeded, if not entirely stopped, by the felling of forest trees across a path, without any necessity of firing a shot, is so evident, that further remark is unnecessary. It is not a belt of forest to be passed through, or a pass to be forced; the whole country presents but this one feature.

### Lieutenant-Colonel Gawler's Expedition, 1860.

The causes which led to this expedition were briefly as follows:—In March 1860 some subjects of the Raja of Sikkim, who eventually turned out to be relations of the *Dewan*, kidnapped on various occasions, within British territory, subjects of the British Government. Restitution was demanded, but no satisfactory answer was returned. After several months the Government of India directed the occupation, for three months, of a strip of territory belonging to the Sikkim Raja, lying between the Great Ranjit and the Nepal boundary. If restitution were not made within that period, the strip was to be permanently annexed. Possession was taken of the country on the 1st November 1860 by the Superintendent of Darjeeling, Doctor Campbell, and a body of Sebundy Sappers under the command of Captain Murray. They cut roads and commenced to establish themselves at Rinchinpung,[1] the local people, and even the Sikkim authorities, helping them with supplies. On the 27th November, however, they were attacked by a mixed force of Tibetans and Sikkim Bhutiahs under the direction of the *Dewan*, and were compelled to retreat. They had received no notice of the impending attack; and had the Lepchas and Limbus proved hostile, they must have been cut to pieces. The roads were damaged on their line of retreat; they were waylaid, and rocks were rolled upon them. The Sebundy Sappers, who hardly knew how to use a gun, disappeared in all directions. The officers made their way to Darjeeling with only two attendants, and for the next few days men continued to come in; but ten men and a quantity of property, including seventy rifles, remained in the hands of the enemy.

It was now necessary to punish the State of Sikkim for its original aggression and subsequent opposition; also to counteract

[1] Colonel Gawler (April 9th, 1861) visited this place and did not think well of the position in which they had established themselves. But in any case such a small force would have been isolated.

the political effect of the captured plunder upon Tibet and Bhutan. Subjects of the former country had been employed against us ; and to the latter the *Dewan* held out a strip of territory (Dikeling) as a bribe for their assistance.

Colonel Gawler, an officer of considerable experience in jungle warfare, made the following remarks upon the country at that time :—

The rivers lie very deep, and the ascents out of them for the first hundred feet are almost precipitous, after which the slope is usually considerably less until near the summit of the range. The rivers are rapid ; the Tista is about eight yards broad ; there are fords, but not many. Rafts are constructed by coolies in a few hours ; or a cane bridge in about a week. The ranges are mostly covered with forest trees, which afford excellent firewood. There is no malaria, except in summer time in some of the river-beds.

Except the roads cut by Doctor Campbell on the west of the Ranjit, there are only footpaths in the country. There are two practicable paths for horses and cattle to Tumlong.

The country produces sufficient grain for its own consumption. There are a few cattle. There is no lack of timber or bamboo ; of the latter the natives speedily make, with a few strokes of their heavy knives, either chair, table, bed, bucket, or house.

The enemy are armed with bows and arrows and a few guns. Their home-made ammunition is scarcely serviceable, but they have 9,000 rounds captured from Doctor Campbell.

*Commanding*—Lieut.-Colonel J. C. Gawler.

| | |
|---|---|
| H. M. 6th Regiment[1] .. | .. 400 |
| 73rd Native Infantry[2] .. | .. 420 |
| Sikh Police .. .. | .. 290 |
| Convalescent Depôt .. | .. 120 |
| Sebundy Sappers .. | .. 190 |
| Artillery two 3-pr. guns. | |
| 2 Naval 12-pr. howitzers. | |

The Government having decided to despatch an expedition, assembled a force of 1,820 men, as per margin, and ordered the Hon'ble Ashley Eden to accompany the troops as Political Officer. Colonel Gawler's general plan was : to leave 400 men at Darjeeling ; move to Namchi ; establish there a camp guarded by 300 men ; and proceed to Tumlong either by Bhomsang or Took.

The enemy estimated at 800, including some Tibetans, were encamped at Namchi. They had a piquet of fifty or sixty men behind stockades at the crossing of the Ranjit river.

[1] Now the 1st Battalion, Royal Warwickshire Regiment.
[2] Disbanded in 1861.

The force left Darjeeling on the 1st February 1861 and the following dispositions were made to force the crossing of the river. A working party of sappers prepared a floating bridge ready to be thrown across the river, under the protection of a covering party of 250 men. The main body with all the baggage, under Major Maitland, 79th Highlanders, camped under cover near the crossing. A flanking party, four companies, British Infantry, went to a point two miles up stream, where a raft had been prepared for them. All were in position before dawn of the 1st. At daybreak the crossing was effected almost unopposed and Namchi was reached with the loss of one man wounded. After a reconnaissance on the 4th as far as Sillok Vok ridge, the artillery, baggage, and stores were pushed forward to Mikh. This advance was most difficult, through dense forests, along a mere footpath overhanging the *khud*, with an ascent varying from one-in-four to one-in-six. Some stockades at Namchi, weakly held, were carried by a reconnoitring party with a loss of one man wounded. On the 6th the main body advanced to Namchi unopposed, a flanking party being sent by the Cheadam road and a guard left at the Ranjit bridge. To circumvent the enemy at a difficult position at Sandoopchi, Colonel Gawler led a volunteer party round their flank by night, whereupon the enemy evacuated their camp in haste. At Namchi a blockhouse was constructed and an advanced depôt organized, garrisoned by a company 6th Foot and seventy Gurkha police.

The main body then advanced in three columns, one on Bermick and Temi, one on Mount Tendong and Temi, and the third on Neongong. The enemy withdrew east of the Tista river, and sent 100 men from Neh to oppose our advance at Temi. This party were surprised by night by No. 2 column and fled to the Tista, throwing away clothes and weapons.

As usual, the principal difficulties were those of commissariat and transport. The coolies employed were unreliable and lazy, the roads were execrable, and the poverty of the country rendered it impossible to obtain supplies locally.

At the request of the Special Commissioner a halt was made at Rungpadan until the 12th March. As resistance was expected at Neh, a position where the Gurkhas had been repulsed in 1789, or at the Samdong bridge over the Tista river, measures were taken to have both localities reconnoitred. A position commanding the crossing at Samdong was Seized by night, and a notable piece of work was carried out by the Sebundy sappers—a bridge eight feet in width and 212 feet in length over a foaming torrent being completed in twenty-eight working hours.

All opposition was now at an end. The force advanced to Kabbi, on the Tibet road, within an hour's walk of the palace at Tumlong. The young Raja arrived from Chumbi, and while negotiations were in progress Colonel Gawler visited the Cho La, where Dr. Hooker had been seized in 1849. By the 29th March the Sikkim authorities had agreed to our terms and a treaty was signed at Tumlong.

This ended the campaign and the withdrawal of the force was completed, without incident, by the 15th April.

The following general remarks by the Honourable Ashley Eden are worthy of record:—

> That the Europeans and natives of the Sikkim Field Force have conducted themselves in such a manner as to reflect credit on their country, I can with pleasure affirm. From the date on which they distinctly understood our position as regards the inhabitants, they passed through villages filled with men, women, and children, without doing the slightest injury to a single individual. One act of violence or ill-treatment would have deprived us of all transport; but the conduct of the troops was such that men who had been taught to consider them in the light of savages, soon learnt to mix with them and remain without apprehension in the camp. From the date on which the troops left Senchal to the date of their return, not a man has been under cover, except such as was afforded by boughs of trees. The men had neither tents nor greatcoats. They marched in several instances night and day, through a country which Brigadier Young, in 1850, pronounced impracticable for troops.

Lieutenant-Colonel Gawler throws some further light on the subject. He says:

> The British soldier can force his way wherever he can be fed, but you cannot carry on offensive operations and perform escort duty at the same time. My commissariat and transport give me considerable trouble and anxiety. The difficulties of the Commissariat Department are much increased by the bad transport. It is now apparent to every one that the hill coolies on monthly wages are not fit material for a transport corps. Starting with their loads they take their own time, and deliver them at their own convenience. Hill coolies,

I think, should be employed "tekha" at so much per maund for a certain distance, and paid on delivery.

## General Graham's Expedition, 1888.

The causes which led to the war of 1888 were as follows :—

By the treaty of 1861 the Sikkim Raja was bound not to spend more than three months of each year in Tibet. For years we strove in vain to induce him to fulfill the conditions subscribed to in that treaty, and in 1887, after residing in Tibet for almost two years, he declared himself unable to visit the Lieutenant-Governor at Darjeeling because he had been forbidden to do so by the Chinese representative at Lhasa. At the same time he plainly shewed that he had no intention of returning to Sikkim, by ordering the urgent collection and transmission of revenue to Chumbi. These acts pointed to the decline of our influence in Sikkim.

There was one great difficulty which interfered with the re-establishment of satisfactory relations. While measures were in progress for the despatch of the Macaulay mission to Lhasa in 1886, an armed party of Tibetans, 300 strong, crossed the Jelap La and took up a position at Lingtu, about thirteen miles within the Sikkim border. The abandonment of the mission, it was thought, would have led to these troops being withdrawn, the Government of Lhasa having made the proposed mission an excuse for the incursion. Instead of this being done, however, the Tibetans built a fortified gate house across the road constructed and maintained by the Indian Government, and showed every appearance of retaining a permanent garrison there. Their presence prevented all trade, and was a source of unrest to the people of Sikkim, and even to those in the Darjeeling district.

After some representations to China, the matter was delayed, at her request, until March 1888, when it became evident that any further dilatoriness on our part was liable to be mis-interpreted both by the people of Sikkim, and by the neighbouring states of Nepal and Bhutan.

In January 1888 the Government of India sanctioned the despatch to the frontier of the head-quarters and one wing of the 32nd Pioneers for the purpose of restoring the Rongli bridge and of repairing the road. Sanction was also accorded for the preparation of the camping grounds at Sevoke and Riang in the

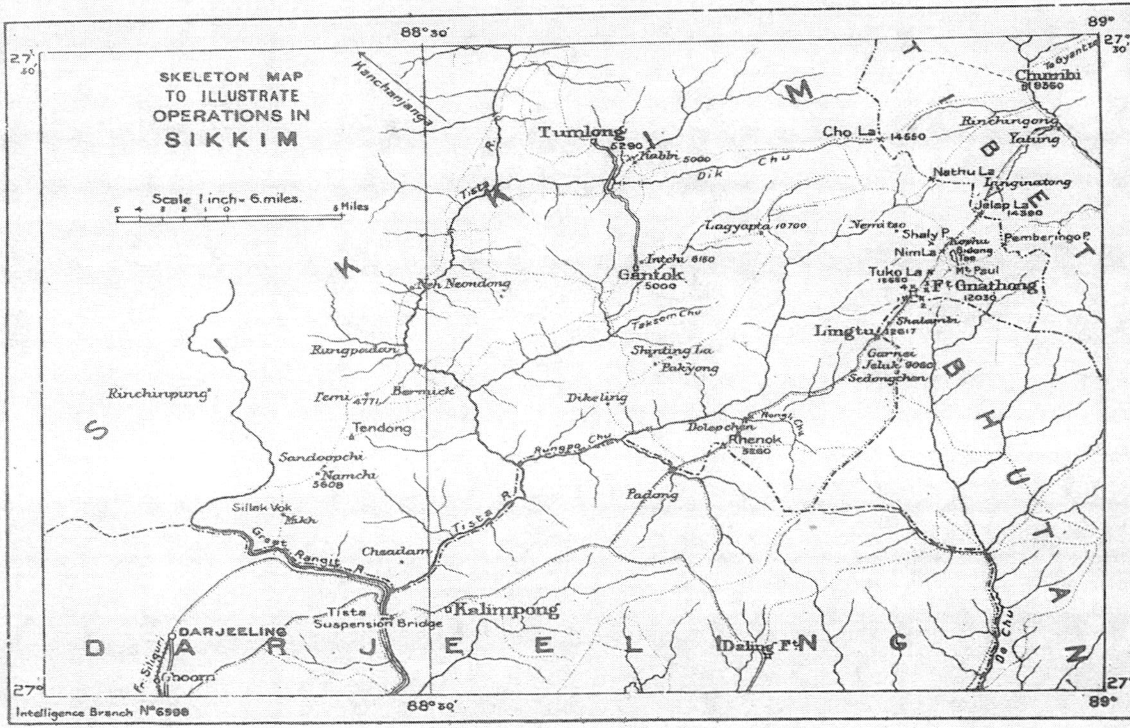
SKELETON MAP
TO ILLUSTRATE
OPERATIONS IN
SIKKIM
Scale 1 inch = 6 miles.
Intelligence Branch No 6998
Kanchanjanga
Tumlong
Gantok
5000
Cho La
14550
Chumbi
Rinchingong
Yatung
Nathu La
Jelap La
Lingtu
Ft Gnathong
Kalimpong
DARJEELING
Tista Suspension Bridge
Rhenok
Pakyong
Namchi
Dikeling
Padong
Tendong
Rinchinpung
Rungpadan
Tista R.
Great Rangit R.
Di Chu
Dik Chu
Rungpo Chu
Taksam Chu
Lagyapta 10700
Intchi 6150
Shinting La
Dolepchen
Daling Ft
Chaadam
Sandoopchi
Ghoom
Mt Paul
Tuko La
Nim La
Shaly P.
Pemberingo P.
Sedongchen
Jeluk 9060
Garnei
Shalambi
Linginatong
88° 30'
89°
27°
27° 30'

Terai. At the same time letters were sent to the Dalai Lama, and to the Tibetan Commandant at Lingtu, demanding the withdrawal of the Tibetan troops by the 15th of March.

On the 25th February 1888 the margially noted force under the command of Colonel T. Graham, R.A., was ordered to take the field, Mr. Paul being attached as Political Officer.

| | | |
|---|---|---|
| 9-1st Northern Division, R. A. | .. | 4 guns. |
| 2nd Bn., Derbyshire Regiment | .. | 200 men. |
| Hd.-qrs. wing, 13th Bengal Infantry [1] | .. | 400 ,, |
| 32nd Pioneers .. | .. | (about) 700 ,, |

With regard to the objects of the expedition the Government of India issued the following instructions:—

It should be explained to Colonel Graham, R.A.. the officer selected to command the force, that the object of the expedition is to advance upon Lingtu and turn the Tibetans out of that place, and thus to vindicate our treaty rights in Sikkim and over the road to the Jelap La pass. He should clearly understand that the expedition should not be pushed further than absolutely necessary to attain the end desired, and no attempt should be made to cross the Jelap La and invade Tibet. This instruction must not, of course, preclude him, if he is attacked, from pursuing his assailants across the border, but it must be explained to him that the Government of India are most desirous to confine their efforts to the vindication of their own rights, and to avoid anything approaching ulterior complications with the Government of Tibet or the Tibetans. The question of dividing the force into two columns—the one advancing direct on Lingtu, and the other to be posted at Gantok, the latter either to prevent the Tibetans raiding from Gyantse or Chumbi on the Sikkim villages and to protect Tumlong, or to move against the line of retreat of the Lingtu garrison, must be decided by the Officer Commanding, on the advice of the civil and political authorities on the spot, and under the orders of the Commander-in-Chief; but the desirability of protecting the exposed portion of the Sikkim frontier from reprisals must be borne in mind. As the object of the expedition is merely to turn out from a locality in which they have no business a Tibetan garrison who have not themselves been guilty of any hostile action outside of the post they have been occupying, it is to be hoped that their surrender or dispersion may be effected without loss of life on either side, and every endeavour should be made by the Officer Commanding to secure this result.

The base depôt was formed at Siliguri, a site which subsequently proved unsatisfactory from its unhealthy climate; and Colonel Graham selected Dolepchen for the advanced depôt. The whole

1 Now the 13th Rajputs (The Shekhawati Regiment).

force was assembled at Padong by the 14th March and was then divided into two columns, as per margin, the Lingtu Column under the command of Colonel Graham in person, and the Intchi Column under Lieutenant-Colonel Mitchell, 13th Bengal Infantry. The latter force, remaining halted at Padong, sent a detachment of 200 men to Pakyong and a party of 50 men to move carefully by Shinting La–Lagyap La. The last named party was, however, soon afterward recalled, the Political Officer being apprehensive that it might cause the flight of the Sikkim Raja to Tibet.

*Lingtu Column.*

2 guns, Royal Artillery.
100 men, Derbyshire Regiment.
300 Pioneers.

*Intchi Column.*

2 guns, Royal Artillery.
100 men, Derbyshire Regiment.
300 men, 13th Bengal Infantry.

The Lingtu column moved to Sedongchen, and next day drove the enemy from their positions. Colonel Graham thus describes the operations.

The force under my immediate command, reached Sedongchen, some seven miles from Lingtu, at midday on the 19th instant. A reconnaissance made that afternoon showed that the Tibetans had occupied a position about two-and-a-half miles from our camp, and close to the encamping-ground at Jeluk; that they had erected a stockade on the top of a very steep ascent, and barricaded the road with a stone breastwork. It was impossible to estimate their numbers, but from information supplied by the political officer it was unlikely that they were very numerous.

At 7 A.M. on the morning of the 20th instant, I advanced from Sedongchen with the force noted in the margin, the Pioneers forming the advance guard, with the Derbyshire in support. I further directed the two guns of 9-1st Northern Division, Royal Artillery, to follow us an hour later, their escort of fifty men of the Pioneers starting at the same time as the advanced party, in order to repair the road, which was very bad. The advance was slow, as, owing to the dense bamboo jungle through which the road ran, and also the steepness of the road itself and its many windings, great caution was necessary.

78 men, Derbyshire Regt.
100 men, 32nd Pioneers.

Attack on Jeluk stockade.

On reaching the spot where the enemy had been encountered the previous evening, shots were fired at the advance guard, but were not returned by the Pioneers until they were close to the enemy, when, after firing a few rounds, they charged with a cheer straight at the centre of the stockade, headed by Colonel Bromhead, who was himself the first man into the work. The place was carried after a short struggle, during which I moved up a section of the Derbyshire in support of the Pioneers. After carrying the stockade, Colonel Bromhead continued his advance for about a mile along the Lingtu road in pursuit of the flying enemy, and then halted.

Meanwhile, at his first advance, Colonel Bromhead had detached a party of his men under Captain H. R.W. Lumsden along the road which passed to the left of the stockade, and across which the enemy had built a stone breastwork. On advancing to within about ten yards of this wall, the party found that the road had been cut away, and that to approach nearer was impossible. The defenders of the breastwork, unaware, apparently, that the main work had been carried, continued to fire on this party, and I was obliged to send some of the Derbyshires down from the stockade, thus taking them in rear, before they were dislodged.

The enemy's position consisted of a strong stockade about 200 yards in length and seven feet high. It was constructed of large logs laid horizontally, whilst trees had been felled in front and formed a sort of abatis. It rested at either end on a precipice, so that it could not be turned; and as the approach to it was up a very steep—in fact, a precipitous—ascent, it formed a most formidable obstacle. The road ran round the left of the stockade, about thirty feet below it, and had been, as above stated, cut away and barricaded.

The enemy numbered about 120, armed with matchlocks, bows, and slings; during the attack many of the bowmen, ensconced in trees, discharged large numbers of arrows, so that it is singular that so few of our men were hit. Their loss was at the time supposed to be about twelve killed and twenty wounded, but I have since had reason to believe that it exceeded that number. One Tibetan was taken prisoner, the remainder escaping down the hills in different directions. On our side Captain Lumsden received a bullet wound in his left arm, and four sepoys of the 32nd Pioneers were slightly wounded.

After re-forming the force I proceeded along the Lingtu road as far as Garnei unmolested by the enemy; and though here within 1,700 yards of the Lingtu fort, I was unable to see the place owing to the mist. I reinforced Colonel Bromhead and directed him to remain where he was for the night. The Royal Artillery and detachment, Derbyshire Regiment, spent the night at Jeluk. I myself returned to Sedongchen.

Before leaving Jeluk, I directed Major J. Keith, R.A., who commanded there, to march to Garnei at daybreak with his two guns and the detachment, Derbyshire Regiment, and endeavour, if possible, to shell the fort at Lingtu.

After a short delay next morning, caused by the non-arrival of rations we reached Garnei about 9-30 A.M., and found that the Pioneers had bee undisturbed during the night. It was, however, so misty that nothing could be seen of the Lingtu fort. A Tibetan soldier, one of several fugitives who had endeavoured to get past Garnei during the night, had been captured by Colonel Bromhead, and corroborated the accounts which we had previously heard regarding the preparation of "booby traps," *i.e.*, large heaps of stones arranged over the road so as to fall on the heads of the attackers. On arriving at Garnei, the prisoner taken at Jeluk was at once despatched with a letter in the Tibetan character, stating that, if the fort was evacuated at once, the defenders would be allowed to retire unmolested, but that an immediate reply must be sent. This man was never seen again nor was any reply received.

The detachment of the Derbyshire Regiment arrived at 11 A.M. and we then moved on towards Lingtu. The advance guard was composed of fifty men of the 32nd Pioneers under Sir Benjamin Bromhead. The remainder of the column followed at an interval of 350 yards. The mist was so dense that it was impossible to see, as a rule, more than fifty yards; and owing to this, as well as to the steep and broken nature of the road, the advance was but slow. The snow, too, which was partially thawed, and which near Garnei was two or three inches deep, gradually increased in depth as we advanced, until at Lingtu it lay two feet deep even on the road.

Capture of Fort Lingtu.

At about 1-30 P.M. I heard the bugle of the 32nd Pioneers sound the charge, but without any firing; and word arrived from Colonel Bromhead thad he had reached the gate of the fort and, finding it open, had charged through it. When he entered, the place was occupied by some thirty Tibetans, who fled at his approach along the Gnathong road. A party of the 32nd Pioneers was at once despatched along this road, and proceeded some two miles, but without finding any trace of the enemy.

Although the fort of Lingtu was thus occupied without resistance, I desire to bring to His Excellency's notice the behaviour of the troops during this most trying march. They, one and all, made light of the discomforts to which they were subjected, and vied with one another in their anxiety to come to close quarters with the enemy. Both then and since they have had to put up with many privations, due to the wet and cold, as well as to the bad state of the roads and of the high altitude, 12,600 feet above the sea; but they have been at all times in the best of spirits, and anxious to make light of their troubles.

The fort, so-called, consists of a straight wall of loose stones some four feet thick and about 240 yards in length. Its average height is about twelve feet, but, as it is built in steps, it is in places much lower. There is a round tower some fifteen feet high and twelve feet in diameter at each end of the wall, and in the centre of the wall there is a wooden doorway through which the road runs. There are loopholes in the wall about every twenty feet, but they are so badly constructed that the fire from them would have but little effect; and there is no banquette of any kind, so that it would have been impossible for the defenders to fire over the top of the wall. There is complete cover to within a few yards of the fort at several points, and the wall itself does not extend to within some twenty yards of the top of the hill, so that had resistance been offered there would not have been the slightest difficulty in taking the work. There is one detached tower about 200 to 300 yards away, the same size as those at the end of the wall. The place is hardly worthy the name of a fort as it is quite incapable of defence.

The Tibetans now retreated over the passes into the Chumbi valley. The main object of the expedition, *viz.* the expulsion of the Tibetans from the Raja of Sikkim's territory, had therefore been effected, and it only remained to make the necessary dispositions to protect the exposed portion of the Sikkim frontier from reprisals. From a purely military point of view the most effectual means of gaining this end would have been to carry the war into the enemy's country, but the Government of India deemed it advisable to limit the operations as far as possible to Sikkim territory.

Accordingly the force settled down in an entrenched camp at Gnathong, an elevated plateau, 12,030 feet above sea level, some three or four miles north of Lingtu. Here the troops remained quietly erecting huts and making roads, while the Tibetans were known to be gathering beyond the Jelap pass.

On the 21st May the Lieutenant-Governor of Bengal arrived at Gnathong, and on the following day a determined attack was made by the Tibetans on the camp. As the fact of his visit was well known all over the country, there can be little doubt but that the Tibetan leaders were influenced by it in fixing on that particular day for their action. The enemy numbered about 3,000. They attacked about seven o'clock, but by ten o'clock were in full retreat. Our losses were three killed and eight wounded. The enemy's losses were thought to have amounted to 100 killed.

Attack by enemy on Gnathong.

Colonel Graham now wished to advance and inflict further punishment on the Tibetans across the Jelap La, but the Government would not give him the necessary permission.

After the attack on Gnathong all remained quiet at that place, and in June it was decided to send the British troops back to Darjeeling. Incessant rain [1] greatly added to the difficulties of transport, but the health of the troops does not appear to have been injuriously affected. Many of the mules, however, were sick, and many more were hardly able to carry their loads. The prevailing complaint among them was sore-feet, due to the hoofs getting worn away from working on the stony portions of the road after having been employed on the muddy ones.

Towards the end of July, while these movements were being completed, the situation changed. The enemy were observed to be gathering in considerable numbers, and to be building walls in the neighbourhood of the Chumbi passes; in consequence of which Colonel Graham applied for reinforcements. He had at that time but 500 men available for an offensive movement, after leaving a garrison at Gnathong; while the latest news at the disposal of the Government of Bengal showed that the number of Tibetans between Rinchingong and Kophu was 7,000; in reserve at Lingamathang, 1,000; with Shafi at Phari 500. Besides these, 1,500 were said to have gone to Nathu La, and many more reported to be on the way. Reinforcements were promptly sent,[2] and by the 25th August Colonel Graham had at Gnathong a total force of 1,691 men and four guns.

| | | |
|---|---|---|
| Derbyshires | .. | 386 men. |
| 32nd Pioneers | .. | 791 „ |
| 2–1st Gurkhas | .. | 514 „ |
| Royal Artillery | .. | 4 guns. |

Several insignificant encounters now took place in which some prisoners were captured and other small losses inflicted on the Tibetans. Meanwhile, communications were improved and blockhouses constructed at points on the road, and a road was constructed by the Intchi Column to the Taksom Chhu.

Attack of Tuko La.

At last the Tibetan General made a bold move. Some two miles north of Gnathong the road to the Jelap La crosses a low ridge by a pass known as the Tuko La. On the morning of the 24th September it was discovered that the Tibetans had established themselves on the Tuko La ridge, and had rapidly constructed a wall three

1 The average rainfall at Gnathong amounts to 140 inches, lasting from May to November.

2 Some of the Derbyshires arrived without warm clothing, which followed them, and the Gurkhas had to sleep in single fly tents which were utterly useless in the heavy rain of Sikkim.

or four feet in height and nearly three miles in length. General Graham[1] decided to attack, and his dispatch thus describes the proceedings:—

"At daybreak it could be seen from Fort Gnathong that the Tibetans had occupied in force the whole range of hill from the Tuko La peak on the west, past Mount Paul, to the Trigonometrical Point on the east, and had also placed an advanced post on an isolated hill in the Upper Gnathong valley. The greater part of this position, which is nearly three miles in length, appeared to be strengthened by a stone wall some three or four feet in height. The enemy announced his presence by loud shouts and the frequent discharge of *jingals* and also cannon of a larger size. Considering that the position could not have been occupied until some time after dark the previous evening, I estimate that at least 7,000 men must have been at work during the night.

"As it soon became evident that the Tibetans did not intend to advance nearer to Gnathong, I decided to assume the offensive. By 8 A.M. all was ready and the force advanced to the attack in three columns as follows:—

(1) The left column, under my personal command, was to advance past No. IV Blockhouse up the south of ridge, leading to the Tuko La peak, which was the key to the enemy's position, as from it the remainder of his line of defence could be enfiladed.

6 companies, 2-1st Gurkhas.
4 guns, 9-1 Northern Division, Royal Artillery.
3 companies, Derbyshire Regiment.

(2) The centre column under command of Lieutenant-Colonel Sir B. Bromhead, Bart., 32nd Pioneers, was directed to proceed up the main Tuko La road, keeping level with the left column, to which it was to act as a right flank guard.

3 companies, 32nd Pioneers.
1 company, 2nd Derbyshire Regiment.

(3) The right column, under command of Major H. Craigie-Halkett, 32nd Pioneers, was directed to proceed to the saddle-back north-east of Woodcock Hill, and hold its position there with a view to meeting any forward movement of the enemy's left, and also to deceive him as to our real point of attack.

2 companies, 32nd Pioneers.
2 fort guns (worked by Pioneers).

1 He had recently been given the temporary rank of Brigadier.

"Major T. H. Goldney, 32nd Pioneers, was left in command of the Fort with three companies of his regiment and small guards of the 2nd Derbyshire Regiment and 2-1st Gurkhas.

"At about 9-30 A.M. the guns of the right column came into action against the enemy's walls in the centre of the valley and made excellent practice. They were assisted by volleys from a section of the Derbyshire, and about 10 A.M. the occupants of the walls were seen retiring rapidly towards Mount Paul.

"The centre column next became engaged at about 10 A.M., having got somewhat ahead of the left column owing to having an easier road to traverse, and also to the mist, which covered the whole valley shortly after the advance began, rendering it almost impossible to maintain communication. About a quarter of an hour later Colonel Bromhead had made his way without loss to a point on the road some 300 yards from the Tuko La; here he halted, sending Lieutenant Holland with a small party to the top of the hills on his immediate left.

"At 10 A.M. the left column had reached a peak 800 yards from the Tuko La, and the guns fired two or three rounds at the enemy's fortifications, taking advantage of a transient glimpse of his position obtained through the mist. At 10-30 the Gurkhas of the advanced guard reached the hill occupied by Lieutenant Holland's party, and both they and the Pioneers on the road below opened a hot fire on the enemy, which was replied to vigorously all along their line of walls, but with little effect.

Capture of Tuko La peak. Flight of Tibetans.

"Ten minutes later, our men having recovered their breath, I directed Captain Robinson, who was in command of the three leading companies of Gurkhas, to storm the Tuko La peak, taking with him Lieutenant Holland's party of Pioneers. This was done in capital style, Colonel Bromhead's party at the same time advancing along the road straight at the pass itself. The Tibetans waited until our men were within fifty yards of them and then turned and fled, their walls being at once occupied by the Gurkhas and Pioneers, who opened a hot fire on the fugitives. On seeing their right turned, the remainder of the Tibetans apparently considered further resistance hopeless, and the flight became general along their whole line.

"The guns were at once brought into action on the Tuko La peak against the enemy who were retreating over the Nim La.

Colonel Bromhead with the Pioneers was directed to pursue along the main road, two companies of the Gurkhas being with him and the Derbyshires in close support, whilst Lieutenant-Colonel Rogers, with the remainder of the Gurkhas, took the direct road along the ridge towards Mount Paul, keeping one company in the valley on his left. The guns advanced as soon as their fire was masked by the advancing infantry, and by noon the whole of the centre and right columns was concentrated at the Nim La, with the exception of the Gurkhas under Lieutenant-Colonel Rogers, who had pursued the enemy over Mount Paul, to the entrance to the Pemberingo pass, where they had halted.

"I now despatched the Pioneers of the centre column, who were now commanded by Lieutenant Holland, owing to Colonel Bromhead having been severely wounded shortly after leaving the Tuko La, to join the right column, which had advanced to Mount Paul; I also directed Major Craigie-Halkett to send his company of Derbyshires to join me, and with the remainder of his force hold in check the Pemberingo Tibetans, whilst I attacked the Jelap pass. At the same time I signalled to Colonel Rogers to move to the north end of the Bidang Tso and halt until I joined him. A message was also sent to the detachment, 13th Bengal Infantry, at Shalambi, to join me as soon as possible.

"By 2 P.M. all necessary movements were completed, and I moved forward against the Jelap pass. As soon as the entrance to the Jelap valley was reached, the guns came into action, two on the spur on the left bank of the stream, and two on some high ground immediately below, firing first at the lower and afterwards at the centre Jelap wall. At the same time the infantry formed for attack in the valley itself, the Derbyshires on the left of the road and the Gurkhas parallel to them on the right. The Tibetans replied to the guns but feebly with *jingals* and matchlocks, and after a few rounds had been fired, I directed the infantry to advance. On their approach the enemy retreated rapidly and the lower and centre walls were occupied successfully almost without opposition. The force bivouacked in the pass, and as the baggage did not come up until after midnight and the rain came down heavily, the men passed an uncomfortable night.

"The next morning the pursuit was continued over the pass to Rinchingong, distance about ten miles. Little resistance was encountered *en route*, only a few long shots being fired at the advance guard, but our progress was much impeded by the rough and precipitous nature of the road. The enemy had, moreover, broken down three out of the seven bridges over which the road passes, thus causing additional delays. Rinchingong was reached at 4 P.M., and, beyond a few shots fired as soon as we came in sight, and replied to by the advance guard, it was undefended. The enemy's loss was four or five killed in the village, and several fugitives were also shot. The night was passed without molestation.

Advance to Chumbi, 26th September.

"The next morning the force proceeded to Chumbi, three miles up the Ammo Chu, the bivouack for the night being at Myatong (Yatung), two miles on the Jelap side of Rinchingong. The enemy appeared to be completely disorganized and thoroughly dispirited, not a single shot being fired at the force during the march.

"The day following, theforce returned to Gnathong, a long march of fifteen miles, the ascent to the summit of the Jelap pass being particularly trying both for men and animals, and the difficulties of the road being much increased by the pouring rain.

"The number of the enemy opposed to us on the 24th was, so far as can be ascertained, about 11,000, of whom some 8,000 advanced to the Tuko La ridge. They possessed about twenty *jingals* and small cannon, but these were withdrawn early in the fight and either hidden or carried away, and frequent search parties, subsequently sent out, have failed to discover them. One 6-pounder brass smooth-bore field gun, complete with carriage, was captured and brought to Gnathong. Large quantities of powder, arrows, and other warlike stores were destroyed at Rinchingong.

"The Tibetans' loss may be estimated at 400 killed and at least as many more wounded. About 200 prisoners remained in our hands, but many of those captured across the passes, being wounded, were released. Our loss was Lieutenant-Colonel Sir B. Bromhead, Bart., Commanding 32nd Pioneers, and three sepoys, wounded."

This concluded the fighting, and thereafter the Tibetans kept to their own side of the frontier at the Jelap La,

In the meantime an advance on Gantok was deemed necessary, owing to the mischievous activity of the Tibetan party at that place, and the collapse of the leading men in the British interest. Colonel Mitchell with 150 men, 13th Bengal Infantry, accordingly moved to Gantok on the 23rd September, but the Raja decamped prior to their arrival. On the 29th Colonel Mitchell left for Tumlong with a party of sixty men, and Mr. White, Political Officer. They were well received and Colonel Mitchell wrote :—

> As a political move there is no doubt that this marching of troops to the capital of Sikkim has had a beneficial effect ; the cordiality with which we have everywhere been greeted, and the hospitality received, show that friendly relations have been established.

This party returned to Gantok on the 4th October.

An uneventful period followed. The troops were employed in road making and hutting, and a road was carried over to the Tibetan side of the Jelap La. The Tibetans seemed completely disheartened, and the Chinese appeared the more active in negotiations. As the winter weather set in the troops began to suffer from bronchitis, and by the middle of December all, save 400 Derbyshires and 200 Gurkhas, were withdrawn from Gnathong to Rhenok Bridge, Padong, and Pakyong.

On the 21st December the Chinese Amban, after innumerable delays and evasions, arrived at Gnathong, and negotiations began. They, however, came to no satisfactory conclusion, and the Amban returned to Rinchingong, there to wait, by the orders of the Chinese Government, the arrival of Mr. T. H. Hart, of the Chinese Imperial Customs Service, who finally reached Gnathong on the 22nd March 1889. After a long exchange of views, an Anglo-Chinese convention [1] was signed at Calcutta on the 17th March 1890. The Tibetan claim to suzerainty over Sikkim was abandoned, but perhaps not forgotten, and our boundary was defined. Trade matters were to be settled subsequently.

The troops were not withdrawn until 1895, when fifty Military Police were left in Gnathong and two companies, native infantry, at Gantok. In 1896 the former were withdrawn and the Gnathong fort dismantled.

[1] Aitchison LVII.

The chief military difficulties encountered by the expedition of 1888 appear to have been—

1. The unhealthy climate of Siliguri, the base depôt. Captain Mansfield, Assistant Commissary General, wrote:—"Siliguri is a most unhealthy spot when once the heat begins, and neither Europeans or natives will keep in health." The Government afterwards sanctioned the removal of the base depôt to Ghoom.
2. The sickness among the transport mules. Originally, for a force of 1,600 men, there were provided 1,500 mules and 2,000 coolies. As soon as the wet weather set in the number of sick mules rapidly increased, until, in August, 53 per cent. were out of action.

The variety and rigour of the climate in Sikkim, while it caused the troops, especially at Gnathong, the greatest discomforts and hardships, does not appear to have materially affected their health. The sickness among British troops was highest (7·6 per cent.) in March 1889, and among native troops (5·68 per cent.) in June 1888.

---

*BIBLIOGRAPHY.*

*Political and Military Transactions in India*, 1825.—Henry T. Prinsep.

*Sikkim*, 1873.—Lieutenant-Colonel J. C. Gawler.

*Treaties, Engagements and Sanads, Volume II.*—Aitchison.

*Report on the Sikkim Expedition*, 1890.—Lieutenant C. J. Markham.

*Gazetteer of Sikkim.*—H. H. Risley.

*Report on the Sikkim–Tibet Boundary*, 1903.—Major H. A. Iggulden.

# PART III.

# TIBET.

# TIBET.

## CHAPTER V.

*THE COUNTRY AND PEOPLE.*

OF the vast territory, known to us as Tibet, which lies in the heart of Asia, neither the area nor the population can be stated with any approach to accuracy. The former has been estimated at 500,000 square miles, and the latter at from three and a half to five millions. The boundaries are for the most part undefined. On the north and east lie the Chinese provinces of Turkistan, Mongolia, Kan-suh, Ssu Chuan and Yünnan, while on the south and west are Assam, Bhutan, Sikkim, Nepal, Kashmir, and other districts of British India, and states under British protection. England and China are thus the only countries whose territories adjoin Tibet.

Tibet has always been a *terra incognita* to most of the outside world. That this should have been possible is chiefly due to the remarkable systems of mountain ranges by which it is enclosed. On three sides lie the Himalaya, Karakoram, and Kuen-lun ranges. These isolate Tibet from the deserts of Chinese Central Asia and from the plains of India, and support between them the lofty tablelands which constitute the greater part of the country; and the drainage of these uplands to the sea has cut their eastern slopes into a series of crests and gorges trending south and east, which are also a very effective barrier. They culminate in the great Yung Ling or Yeddo range, which is the natural eastern boundary of Tibet, though some provinces on the west of it are administered directly by China. It has been, however, from the east that any external influence has penetrated the country.

Tibet falls naturally into three great physical divisions. They also correspond to the districts of government.

The Chang Tang.

The first of these includes the Chang Tang, a great, dreary plateau, scourged by tearing winds, dotted with innumerable salt lakes which have no outlet to the sea, and standing at an elevation above the sea nowhere less than 15,000 feet. This expanse is such a remarkable feature of the world's surface that it is worth recording some of the impressions made upon the minds of the few travellers who have visited it. Captain Wellby in four months saw no vegetation of a higher order than an onion; for fourteen weeks he came across no sign of mankind. M. Grenard,[1] who travelled with the ill-fated Dutreuil de Rhins, says "it was a rough experience; and this journey in the midst of such desolate and infinite solitudes was one of inexpressible melancholy. Each day we traversed arid valleys . . . we skirted blue lakes, and we surmounted passes laden with snow . . . all nature was robed in silence, except for the rushing of the wind which blew furiously, as if it wished to roll aside the impassable summits of the mountains. This pitiless wind which was accompanied by a cold of 35° below freezing point, penetrated into us even to the marrow, and peeled the skin from our faces and our hands." Captain Rawling[2] is more cheerful: he writes "The depressions in the surrounding land seemed to be the empty beds of great lakes, which had dried up at no very remote date; they had a horrible deathlike appearance, not a blade of grass or any *boortsa* growing, not a beast nor a bird moving; desolation and stillness reigned supreme. On the ridges, however, grass grew freely, hares scurried about, and kiang roamed hither and thither, while in the dips the mighty yaks slowly made their way over the rich young grass. . . . The surrounding country was teeming with animal life, and yaks and gazelle were seen in abundance; sand grouse were also plentiful."

As Captain O'Connor reports, this great expanse is practically a desert; for although it produces a fair and in some parts a luxuriant vegetation, and thus supports immense herds of wild animals, it is nevertheless to all intents and purposes uninhabited and uninhabitable. What pasturage there is is too remote from winter quarters.

Were the Chang Tang more under the influence of the monsoon, no doubt the level of perpetual snow would be lower than it is, 19,140 feet, and a great part would be a glacier region.

[1] M. F. Grenard, *Dutreuil de Rhins. Mission scientifique dans la Haute Asia.*
[2] Captain C. G. Rawling, *The Great Plateau.*

The inhabitants consist of a few wandering shepherds, and of one or two small settlements by Dangra Yum Tso and Kyaring Tso. The government is vested in two jongpens who reside at Sanja Jong, a meeting place of trade routes.

Kham.

The second division consists of the wild rugged regions of Eastern Tibet, known as the province of Kham. Little beyond the trade routes are known to Europeans—in fact our knowledge of it is extremely meagre. Prjevalsky encountered great privations and hardships in the north: while in the south Captain Bower saw "deeply cut, well cultivated valleys, and steep wooded hillsides." "The country," he says, "bears a great resemblance to many parts of Kashmir." The Kong-ba Derge and Po-med districts are spoken of by natives as being the richest in Tibet. "They carry on a great trade, principally with China." The region is divided into small states, of all degrees of independence. China claims a suzerainty over the whole country, but in one or two cases tribes maintain an absolute independence both of her and Lhasa. In many parts it is a veritable no man's land infested by robbers and bad characters of all kinds.

The government of these small states is of all kinds—from republicanism and rule by independent chiefs to direct administration from Lhasa or China. Important trade centres are Jye Kundo, Ta-Chien-Lu, Batang,[1] Chiamdo, and Hsining.

Tibet Proper.

The third division is the valley of the Tsanpo or Brahmaputra and the upper drainage areas of the Sutlej and Indus rivers. This is Tibet proper and with it we are chiefly concerned, bordering as it does upon our own settled frontiers and containing the centre of religious and temporal power. It is divided into the three administrative districts of Ngari Khorsum, Tsang, and U.

The province of Ngari Khorsum or Teu comprises all the land from the frontiers of Ladakh to about 86° 30′ east Longitude, a distance of 600 miles. The government is in the hands of two *jongpens* at Gartok, the centre of trade. Most of the land lies at too great an elevation for cultivation.

[1] Ta-Chien-Lu and Batang are in Chinese territory.

The province of Tsang consists roughly of the Tsanpo valley between the province of Teu and the Lhasa district. It contains Shigatse the head-quarters of the Penchan Rimpoche, or Tashi Lama, the second ecclesiastical dignity of Tibet. Its chief towns, Shigatse and Gyantse, are very important trade centres.

U is the province surrounding Lhasa, the seat of the Dalai Lama and the supreme government of the country. Both these provinces as a whole are rich and thickly populated and offer the greatest possible contrast to the Chang Tang. From very early times their prosperity and fertility have impressed travellers. Turner thought in 1783 that the valley of Gyantse possessed "every natural advantage of space, climate, and fertility"; it was "extremely rich in abundant crops of ripe corn, and extremely populous." He was also very greatly attracted by the climate; he complains, it is true, of the dust vortices, but adds: "nothing else obscures the extreme purity of the atmosphere; from the dawn of light until darkness, not a vapour intercepts the sight to the most distant edge of the horizon. It is a clearness, bordering upon brilliancy, which dazzles and fatigues the eye." Save for the continual strong winds, the climate in all the southern districts of Tibet may be described as perfect from June to December.

Manning, who visited Lhasa in 1811, leaves us a graphic picture of the Brahmaputra valley where the Lhasa road crosses it. "The valley," he says, "was wide, a lively stream ran through it, houses and villages were scattered about. The place was not destitute of trees, nor of arable land, and an air of gaiety was spread over the whole, and, I thought, over the faces of the people."

This part of Tibet possesses the advantages of water transport. For 135 miles below Lhatse the Tsanpo is wide and navigable, and goods and men are transported by boats covered with leather.

The traffic is considerable. Near Lhasa in 1882 Sarat Chandra Das[1] saw "the road alive with travellers, mostly grain dealers, on their way to the city with trains of yaks, ponies, mules, and donkeys." It is capable of further extension, for Mr. White, when accompanying Colonel Younghusband's mission in 1903, thought that "in these broad, well-watered valleys, thousands of acres

[1] Sarat Chandra Das, *Journey to Lhasa and Central Tibet*. 1902.

might easily be cultivated if there were only more population for the work."

The most promising district of Tibet, however, is evidently that which lies along the Brahmaputra valley, east of the longitude of Lhasa. This, as Captain O'Connor writes, may be called the garden of Tibet. All the native explorers who have visited this region unite in praising its climate and scenery. The river flows in an open valley, with well-wooded sides; and the main and side valleys are thickly populated and well cultivated.

The explorer K-p, who went further down this river, speaks of every kind of cultivation along it, till at last, as he nears British territory in Assam, he finds cotton fields, mangoes, and plantains.

The provinces of U and Tsang fall naturally into two types of land—arable and pasture. Up to a height of 13,000 feet it is cultivated. Above that succeeds a belt of grazing land. Captain Rawling reports in 1905:—"as the country rises" (in the Dingri valley) "grass grows still more freely, and is of the fine and nutritious variety; and here immense herds of sheep and goats graze all the year round. The sheep are large and of good stamp, the wool they produce being the largest and some of the finest in the world."

The main trade routes flow: eastward, through Hsining and Ta-chien-Lu; westward through Rudok to Leh; and southward to India by the various Himalayan passes. Of these latter the most important routes are: by Tawang to Odalguri; the Jelap La; by Kirong to Khatmandu; and by Spiti to Simla. In old days the trade with Hindustan was considerable. The first check which it received was due to the conquest of the independent Nepalese kingdoms in 1768. The ambitious military policy of the Gurkhas necessitated increased revenue, and the trade was consequently injured by excessive duties.

The Gurkha kings were again indirectly the cause of the second check to southern trade: for it was only subsequent to the Gurkha-Chinese war in 1792 that the suspicious and exclusive policy of Tibet was enforced, which culminated in a wall being built across the main trade route in 1886.

Chinese trade with Tibet has meanwhile continued to flourish in spite of the length and difficulty of the roads, and is reckoned to amount to a value of several millions sterling, while that of India was worth only £200,000 in 1903. It will be noticed that this proportion is in inverse ratio to the proximity and accessibility of the countries.

Tibet produces notably musk, yak tails, live stock, gold, and wool. She imports silk, lace, and carpets from North China; leather, sheep, and horses from Mongolia; tea, cotton goods, and porcelain from Sze Chuan; rice, indigo, spices, and Indian wares from Bhutan and Sikkim; saffron, silk, and Indian produce from Ladakh.

Wool is really her most valuable product. Immense quantities might be produced on her vast plains, and as to the quality, all who know the best Kashmir shawls can testify. What may attract more immediate attention are the mining possibilities.

Gold mines have long been worked in Tibet. Both in the eastern and western ends of the country all travellers have remarked upon them, and the riches of the monasteries are proverbial. The most precise account of the gold workings is given by the Pandit Nain Singh. He visited the Thoke Jalung gold-fields in 1865 and described the primitive methods of the workmen. These methods result in the export to Ladakh of some Rs. 20,000 worth of gold annually—Rockhill [1] says that "the famous Gork gold-fields" yielded 10,000 ounces in two years. These are only two out of the many fields to be found in many parts of Tibet. Deposits of other minerals are also known to exist, especially in the south-east. In that part fuel, almost entirely wanting in the upper country, is found in the form of quantities of timber, so far untouched. The one part of Tibet, however, which has been explored by an English geological expert, namely U-Tsang, is reported to be poor in minerals.

The inhabitants of Tibet are of a Turko-Mongol stock. They have as a rule made a very favourable impression upon travellers. Bogle admired them enthusiastically. They are "much better bred and more affable than their southern neighbours, and their manners are, in general, very engaging." The ruling class specially impressed him. Of the Tashi Lama he says "the expression of his countenance is smiling and good humoured. His disposition open, candid, and generous. He is extremely merry and entertaining in conversation. I endeavoured to find out, in his character, those defects

[1] W. W. Rockhill, *The Land of the Lamas.*

which are inseparable from humanity, but he is so universally beloved that I had no success, and not a man could find it in his heart to speak ill of him." When Turner talked to the Tashi Lama of his time, "In the discussion of geographical topics his mind took a very extensive range, and scarcely left any quarter of the world untouched." Bower too thought some Lamas who came to meet him "a strikingly able and intellectual set of men." But the men of the provinces did not make a good impression upon him. "The Chang Tang nomads are all much the same—greedy, faithless, and suspicious": and the men of South-East Tibet resemble the nomads. "Faithless, immoral, cowardly, and untruthful; to those they are afraid of they are servile, but to others insolent."

Physically these men of the south-east are well developed, and they can stand any amount of cold and hunger. The Chang Tang nomad too is well inured to privation; but he is a small man, averaging less than five feet in height. No Tibetan ever washes.

Faithlessness and suspicion are commonly noticed by travellers as a national fault. "They are not only suspicious of strangers but of each other," says Turner. They are also obstinately shy of intercourse with travellers; but this is more the result of national policy than of character. Colonel Younghusband writes from Khamba Jong in 1903: "the two delegates from Lhasa have strict orders to hold no personal intercourse with us, and they thoroughly follow out their orders. These people are too excessively suspicious." He, however, continues "this shy exclusiveness, this suspiciousness, this faithlessness, and this belief in superstitions, are, however, traits which are very common in Asiatic peoples, especially among hill races. And what is equally noticeable in the Tibetan is his geniality and politeness when once he does meet strangers; and the kindness and general brightness of his nature. . . . They certainly have many of the attributes of gentlemen, and are eminently a people to whom Europeans would take."

Women occupy a position of distinct consideration among them. Both polyandry and polygamy exist.

The Tibetans are an eminently religious people. Bogle speaks of his stay at Tashi Lhumpo as "monastic to the highest degree. Nothing but priests. Nothing from morning to night but the chanting of prayers, and the sound of cymbals and tabors." Nor is this confined to the monks. Turner says that, at Lhasa "in the evening, just as the day is verging on its decline, all the Tibetans stay business, and meet together, men, women, and children, according to their sex and age, in the principal parts of the town, and in the public squares. As soon as the groups are formed, every one kneels down, and they begin slowly and solemnly in undertones to chant prayers." Intense reverence is paid to the great Lamas. Up to 1903 the Tale Lama held supreme temporal as well as civil power. In fact, religion takes a very large part in the national life. They are an intelligent race. The fact that they were able to impress their religion on the conquering Mongols; that they have for centuries been able to keep up their religious authority over that race to such an extent as to make successive Chinese emperors feel the necessity of keeping on good terms with the Lama; and that they have been able to keep themselves together, a compact nation acting in unfaltering obedience to the Tale Lama; is sufficient to show that they have no mean intellectual capacity. They possess, too, a vast literature, and for many generations have practised the art of printing. The intellectual level of the Tibetans would probably be a good deal higher than it is, if it were not stifled by the iron rule of the monks and their gross superstitions. The abbot at Dongtse who befriended Sarat Chandra Das and studied English and such books as "Ganot's Physics" was punished in the most barbarous manner.[1]

The common people of Tibet live a rough life, of course; but Colonel Younghusband thinks their condition compares favourably with those of other Himalayan hill tribes. They wear home-made cloth and sheepskins. The higher classes wear "tunics of satin," brocaded or plain, lined with sheep and lambskins of Siberian furs; a round cap faced with fur, and crowned with a silk tassel; and "Bulgar" hide boots.

The buildings of Tibet, monasteries and forts, are more remarkable for their strength and solidity than for their beauty. The size of the monasteries is immense, several containing from 3,000 to 10,000 monks. Many rooms in them are well decorated. The upper classes have good houses; for instance in the house where the Mission lodged in 1904 in Lhasa "all the best rooms

[1] He was beaten and drowned, and his servants mutilated.—(*Official papers.*)

have glass windows and are richly painted and gilded, and some have silk ceilings . . . this house is a particularly good one, but there are many others hardly less luxurious . . . all filled with rich clothing, silks, and European and Chinese knicknacks."[1] Having no desire for personal cleanliness, the Tibetans naturally keep their streets filthy.

Government.

Unfortunately the wealth is accumulated in the hands of the few privileged classes, and the labour and resources of the country are required not only to support a large class in idleness, but also to accumulate reservoirs of treasure about them. This does not appear to be in any way resented by the outsiders. "These people are organized," says Colonel Younghusband, "into what we cannot but acknowledge as a very solid nation." From 1640 to 1903 the supreme power was in the hands of "a sovereign Lama, immaculate, immortal, omnipotent, omniscient . . . the viceregent of the only God, the mediator between mortals and the supreme." The mortal part of the *Gyalwa Rinpoche* or Dalai Lama, as we call him, is subject to death. When he departs, disgusted with the sins of this world, his reincarnation is sought for in the person of some infant; and during the minority of the child a regent, or *Peu Gyalpo,* is appointed to act for him. In practice it is noticeable that few Dalai Lamas attain their majority. The Dalai Lama is assisted, and to a certain extent controlled, by a council, the *Ka-sha Lhen-giye,* consisting of four laymen, called *Ka-lon* or *Shape,* with sometimes a fifth, an ecclesiastic, called the Ta Lama. These ministers are elected for life and sit daily in the Council House at Lhasa to transact political, judicial, and administrative business.

The country is divided, for administrative purposes, into *jongs,*[2] each governed by one or two *jongpens.* The official communication between them and the central government is carried on through the channel of a number of civilian and ecclesiastical officials termed *Dung-Kor* and *Tse-dung.* The chief military officials are six generals called *Depon.* Their military duties are nominal. On important occasions a national assembly, the

1 Official papers.

2 Properly Dzongs, so called after the forts which are their centres. There are said to be fifty-three of these districts.

*Tsongdu Chembo,* meets. The chief voices in it are those of the abbots of the three great monasteries of Sera, Gadan, and Debung, who are men of light and leading, and are each fortified by a backing of several thousand sturdy monks. The ecclesiastical influence is supreme in the *Tsongdu,* and hence, it follows, in the whole range of Tibetan politics.

Since the withdrawal from Lhasa in 1904 of the Tale Lama, the temporal power has remained in the hands of the Council at Lhasa. The Tashi Lama of Shigatse, head of the church in the province of Tsang, and, by his adherents, deemed more holy than the Dalai Lama, has since then occupied an ill-defined position as head of the church. He has carefully abstained from any interference with the civil government: nor would the Lhasa authorities have accepted any.

The Army.

The Tibetan army nominally numbers 6,000; but in the 1888 campaign 11,000 men took the field, and in 1904, 16,000. There are, of course, a large number of able-bodied monks in the country, who occasionally come out to fight. The men are armed with swords, bows and arrows, matchlocks, and a few modern rifles. Some of the latter have been imported, some are made in the country.[1] A few cannon have also been made in the arsenal. The military value of the army is negligeable.

The Chinese Amban is in command of the Tibetan troops, although his power over them is uncertain. He also has charge of all foreign negotiations, and the definition of his duties drawn up in 1792 gives them a considerable amount of internal interference. The Tibetans profess to regard him merely as the representative of a friendly country. It is impossible to estimate the precise value of his influence.

Exclusive Policy.

This brings us to the question of the origin of the exclusive policy of Tibet. Turner and other writers have put it down to our unfortunate policy in 1792, when the Chinese were convinced that we were backing the Gurkhas. But it must be remembered that Bogle in 1774 was not allowed to visit Lhasa, and that he gives as his opinion that the

[1] This manufacture has been carried on since the 1888 campaign. The rifles are of Martini-Henry pattern, and carry a heavy hollow bullet 1,000 yards. Several thousand of these had been made in 1903.

admission of Europeans to Tibet was "a thing simply impossible." The attitude of the Tibetans at that time, however, was certainly not so decided as it subsequently became when they refused to receive communications of any sort from India. The people individually are friendly enough to Europeans, and few travellers have met with anything but kindness at their hands.[1] "It is palpable," writes Littledale, "that the common people bear strangers no ill will, and that all the trouble springs from Lhasa." It was by the orders of the Amban that Huc and Gabet were expelled from Lhasa. Opinions vary as to the source of the obstruction: Brian Hodgson thought it originated in the Tibetan officials' jealousy for their trade monopoly; Captain O'Connor says that China is a very convenient stalking horse behind which the Tibetans can shelter their invincible distrust of Europeans; Colonel Younghusband is of opinion that the obstruction proceeds from the monks, who foresee that intercourse with the outer world will tend to the decline of their influence.

Outline of History.

The early history of Tibet, or Bot as it is called by its inhabitants, the Bot-pa, is still obscure. That the country has long enjoyed a settled government is indicated by the remains found recently by Dr. Stein at Khotan,[2] which show the existence in Turkistan of an Indian civilization in the eighth century. For the purpose of this work we need go no further back than the conquest of Tibet by the great Mongol Jenghiz Khan in 1206, and the adoption by Kubilai Khan of Lamaism about 1250, events which have an important bearing on the subsequent position of Tibet. Kubilai actively promoted the interests of Buddhism in China and Mongolia; and thus, while the Mongols and Chinese mastered the Tibetans by force of arms, the latter appear to have effected a spiritual conquest over their masters, and to the present day the state of affairs, thus inaugurated, continues. The physical mastery rests with the Chinese; the spiritual influence, especially over the Mongols, remains with the Tibetans. The Mongols recognized a grand lama of the Tibetan church, and one of them, who built the great monastery of Tashi

1 Dutreuil de Rhins was not killed by Tibetans but by Kalmaks. Walter Savage Landor's accounts of his sufferings have been thrown into considerable doubt by the subsequently proved inaccuracy of his observations.

2 See M. A. Stein, *Archæological exploration in Chinese Turkistan*, 1901.

Lhunpo in 1445, inaugurated the system of perpetual reincarnation. The sixth reincarnate lama in succession was one Dgang-wang-Lo-Zang. When the Mongols under Yusri Khan overran Tibet in 1640, they dethroned the petty princes and installed this Lama as head of a central government. He took up his residence at Lhasa, and built the Potala palace there; in 1650, he visited Pekin, where his position was recognized by the Manchu Emperor. These events show clearly the mutual dependence of Tibetans, Mongols, and Chinese.

Towards the end of the seventeenth century internal troubles induced the Chinese to send an army to Lhasa. They withdrew in 1703, but since that time a large part of Eastern Tibet has remained under direct Chinese administration. In 1717 the Chinese were again in Lhasa, where they came to drive out an army of Dzungarians, who had made a marvellous march from Khotan under Sereng Dondub. This time the Chinese secured the maintenance of their influence in Lhasa by leaving there two Ambans or representatives. In 1732 the Chinese encroached further upon Eastern Tibet; and in 1749 when the Ambans had murdered the Regent, and had been subsequently massacred themselves by the populace, a Chinese army again appeared at Lhasa, and still further increased Chinese influence.

First relations with British.

We now come to Tibet's first contact with the Government of India. Warren Hastings had sent an expedition into Bhutan to punish some irregularities committed by the Bhutanese, and his object had been accomplished, when a letter of mediation on behalf of the Bhutanese was received by the Governor General from the Dalai Lama. It is noticeable that Bhutan is spoken of as "dependent on the Dalai Lama." Warren Hastings improved on the occasion by sending Mr. George Bogle in 1774 to try to open up friendly relations with the Tibetans and encourage trade between Bengal and Tibet. He was very well received at Shigatse and grew much attached to the Tibetans. Evidently they also liked him; for the Tashi Lama, who shortly afterwards visited China, suggested to the Emperor that Bogle too should be invited. But he was not allowed to visit Lhasa, and obtained only verbal promises of support from the Tashi Lama and the Bhutanese Durbar. Unfortunately both the Tashi Lama and Bogle died soon after. Captain Samuel Turner, however, who was sent by Warren Hastings to congratulate the new Tashi Lama, also gained the affection of the Tibetans, and, while he was not allowed to go beyond Shigatse, he obtained an agreement from the Tashi Lama that natives of India, recommended by the Governor General, should be allowed to visit and live at that place. This agreement was carried into effect and many natives from Bengal visited Shigatse.

In 1792 occurred the Gurkha invasion of Tibet already related.[1] While the Chinese were driving out the invaders at the invitation of the helpless Tibetans, the Dalai Láma wrote and warned the Governor General not to interfere on behalf of the Nepalese. Lord Cornwallis replied proposing mediation, and sent Colonel Kirkpatrick to Khatmandu. Kirkpatrick arrived late on the scene, and the Chinese appear to have suspected that we had given secret aid to the Gurkhas. The Indian Government lost all the good results of the policy of Warren Hastings and the friendship of the Lamas; they excited the jealous suspicion of the Chinese Government and the scorn of the Nepal Durbar; and were despised by all. The immediate consequence was that all the passes into Tibet were closed to natives of India. In spite of this, Manning succeeded in making his way to Lhasa; but his visit, while producing some interesting information, led to no solid result.

In 1841 the Chinese again came to the rescue of the Tibetans. Gulab Singh of Jammu, who a few years before had conquered Ladakh, now sent a Dogra army of 5,000 men, who occupied the Manasarowar country. A Chinese army of 10,000 men advanced over the Mariam La, utterly defeated the Dogras,[2] and subsequently advanced to Leh. They, however, could not stay there, and the former boundary was re-established.

In 1844 a Chinese mission was sent to Lhasa to intervene in some alleged misconduct of the Regent, and the latter was banished by the Chinese.

In 1854, on the pretext of some alleged ill-treatment of Nepalese merchants in Lhasa, the Gurkhas again invaded Tibet. In the early spring 1,800 men seized Kirong and Jonkha Jong, and were shortly joined by reinforcements completing a total of 27,000 men, with thirty-six guns and eight mortars. The Tibetans

[1] See *ante*, page 4.

[2] The month was December, and the battlefield 15,000 feet above the sea. Two Dogras survived. (*Markham.*)

attacked them and achieved some temporary success, but soon met with two severe reverses, and in 1856 they agreed to pay an annual subsidy of ten thousand rupees to the Nepal Durbar and to allow a Nepalese trading station and agency to be established at Lhasa.

In 1863 some disturbances broke out in Eastern Tibet between the two small states of Derge and Nyarong. The Lhasa authorities came to the aid of Derge and subjugated Nyarong. Meantime the Chinese seized upon Gyarong, a district on the western border of Ssu-Chuan, which they have since held.

About 1865 geographical authorities turned their attention to Central Asia, and a number of explorers began to visit Tibet. Most of them encountered little opposition, so long as they did not persist in attempting to reach Lhasa.

After the lapse of nearly a century the Government of India again took up the question of trade with Tibet. In 1873 Mr. Edgar, Commissioner at Darjeeling, was deputed to enquire into the position and prospects of trade with Tibet, and the advisability of making a road through Sikkim to the Tibetan frontier. He met some Tibetan officials from Chumbi and found that they were just as seclusive as ever, and very jealous of our relations with the Sikkim Government. The proposed road was made a few years later, and in 1886 Mr. Colman Macaulay of the Bengal Civil Service was allowed to organize a mission to Lhasa. He had been sent during the previous year to the Sikkim frontier to enquire into a trade route into Tsang, and had made friends with some subordinate Tibetan officials. He had then visited Pekin, and obtained a passport for a mission to visit Tibet. The members of the Tsungli Yamen, however, were very averse to giving this passport, and stated that the idea had met with great opposition in all parts of Tibet. Eventually we abandoned the project in deference to Chinese wishes, and in return for a much needed concession in Burma. Meantime the mission was actually organized and ready to start, and its abandonment was the signal for an outburst of aggression on the part of the Tibetans. In the autumn of 1886 they built a stone wall barring the Jelap road, some miles within Sikkim territory. We expected that the Chinese would be able to cause their withdrawal, but in this we were disappointed; and in

March 1888, when further delay was evidently inadvisable, a force was sent up which drove the Tibetans from Sikkim territory with severe losses, and advanced to Chumbi.[1]

It has subsequently been ascertained that the Tibetans do not acknowledge that they were beaten on this occasion. On the contrary, they say that it was only the intervention of the Amban which prevented their sending an army of 7,000 invincible monks to swallow up the British. It is known that in attacking at all the Tibetans positively disobeyed the Amban's orders.

In another part of the country some aggression was shown by the Tibetans. In 1889 it was reported that they were encroaching on the Niti district in Kumaun and ill-treating British subjects there. A small expedition was despatched in November 1889 and cleared out the intruders.

After the advance on Chumbi the Government of India proceeded to negotiate peace with China. We have seen that the Tibetans thought they had a claim to Sikkim. In the course of negotiations it was found that the Chinese were very loath to abandon it, although they apparently recognized the extreme forbearance which had been shown to the Tibetans. The British terms comprised—

(1) The recognition of the long-established frontier between Sikkim and Tibet;
(2) the acknowledgment of exclusive British supremacy over the Sikkim State.

It must be owned that these terms were moderate. Nevertheless it was not until 1890 that a convention was at last signed in which the Chinese recognized these claims and also gave certain trading facilities. Although there was pretty conclusive evidence at the time that the Chinese had no control over the Tibetans, still the fact that the latter took no part in the negotiations was not remarked upon.[2] It was natural that the Government of India should negotiate with China as suzerain. From a consideration of Tibetan history it is evident that that country owes much to the Chinese. The Lhasa authorities have invariably appealed

[1] See page 50.

[2] Colonel Younghusband was informed by the Nepalese representative in June 1903 that the National Council had seen the 1890 convention before the Amban signed it.

to Pekin when threatened by a national danger, and in 1886 it was only due to Chinese diplomatic intervention that severe punishment by the British Government, and perhaps occupation of the Chumbi valley, was averted.

This attitude of the Chinese demands a little consideration. Why are they so magnanimous ? All they appear to get in return is a yearly tribute mission and a shadowy suzerainty over the country. Perhaps the best answer is to be found in a remark by the Abbé Huc, who was as well acquainted with China and Mongolia as with Tibet. "The Tatar Manchu Dynasty," he says, "saw from the commencement of their elevation the great importance of conciliating the friendship of the Dalai Lama, whose influence is all powerful over the Mongol tribes." In Manning's time the Chinese exercised a real influence in Tibet. Sir Frank Younghusband found that they still seem to assume a superiority, but only in ceremonial matters, and that they have little real influence.

From the very first it was evident that the Tibetans had no intention of observing the convention of 1890. The barrier across the road at Lingtu no longer existed, but another had been erected in the Chumbi valley, on the Tibetan side of the new trade mart at Yatung; passage was still refused to all traders, and a duty was levied. In 1894 Mr. White found that the Tibetans claimed that they had nothing to do with the treaty. In 1895 a commission was appointed to enquire into boundary and trade matters. Mr. White, the English member, found that the Chinese representatives came forward most reluctantly and the Tibetans not at all. The boundary pillars erected were immediately pulled down by the Tibetans. Various attempts to communicate with the Dalai Lama were made, but without success. All letters were returned, though it was evident that one had been opened and read. Another commission was sent up a few years later to delimit the frontier and exclude the Tibetans from some Sikkim territory. This territory was the valley of Giaogong, to which the Tibetans seemed to attach importance, and which, though on the south side of the Himalayan watershed, is more easy of access from Tibet than from Sikkim. The party excluded the Tibetans, surveyed the boundary, and returned.

This remote and minor dispute, and the refusal of the Tibetans to enter into external relations, would not have led to any action on the part of the British Government, but a new factor had meantime been introduced into the situation. It now became apparent that Russia was taking an increasing interest in Tibetan affairs. She had turned her eyes to Lhasa many years before, Turner having been told that "many efforts had been made on the part of Russia to extend her commerce to the internal parts of Tibet." Soon after 1870 a series of military scientific expeditions began. These accomplished much useful exploring work, but in common with all travellers, they one and all failed to reach Lhasa. It was otherwise with various Siberian Buriats, Asiatic Russians who profess Tibetan Buddhism. In 1899 some of these men began to visit Lhasa, which proved quite open to them. The most noticeable was one Dorjieff who travelled more than once between Lhasa and St. Petersburg, and who, at the latter place, in 1901, attended by a suite of Tibetans, was officially received in audience by the Czar as "Envoy Extraordinary of the Dalai Lama of Tibet." Count Lamsdorff assured the British Ambassador at St. Petersburg that this mission could not be regarded as having any political or diplomatic character. This, however, was not the impression left upon the Tibetans, for as early as 1899 the Chinese Amban spoke of the Tibetans falling back "on the support of Russia, who had already offered them assistance." Russia assured Britain that there was no convention about Tibet, that the Russian Government had no agents in the country, nor any intention of sending agents; but, as Colonel Younghusband remarks, "in remote Asiatic countries private European travellers are almost invariably regarded as agents of Government," and when a traveller is received, in the presence of Tibetans, in audience by the Czar, one must admit there is some ground for such belief. A more solid foundation for the impression on the mind of the Tibetans was the arrival in Lhasa of a large number of rifles from the north, said by them to be sent by Russia. The effect of all this upon our negotiations with the Tibetans is readily pictured, and, as Colonel Younghusband remarks, was "a sufficiently mischievous result for merely unofficial travellers

Influence of Russia.

to have brought about." A curious misapprehension arose about this time. It seems to have been accepted that Russian territory adjoins Tibet. This is not the case. The nearest Russian territory is in the Pamirs and is distant about 330 miles from a remote and uninhabitable part of Tibet—the Aksai Chin desert. The distance from the Russian province of Transbaikalia, past Urga, the centre of the Mongolian Buddhists, is some 800 miles.

Such was the situation when in February 1903 the Government of India announced that "circumstances have recently occurred which throw upon us the obligation of placing our relations with the Government of Lhasa on a more satisfactory footing."

The 1903 Mission.

In June 1903 the Viceroy of India accepted the invitation of the Chinese Amban to a conference on the subject of frontier matters. He deputed Major Younghusband[1] and Mr. Claude White, Political Officer in Sikkim, as British Commissioners, and named Khamba Jong, the nearest inhabited spot on the Tibetan side of the disputed frontier, as the meeting place. The Maharaj Kumar of Sikkim, heir to the Maharaja, accompanied the Commissioners, who were escorted by 200 men of the 32nd Pioneers and supported by 300 more at Tangu. The Commission assembled at Khamba Jong about the middle of July 1903. From the outset negotiations were impossible. The Chinese Commissioners were uninfluential and of inferior rank; the Tibetans unapproachable. They refused to receive any communications, said they could not negotiate on Tibetan ground, and finally shut themselves up altogether. It was learned in September that the *Tsongdu*[2] had decided to fight, and two British subjects, natives of Sikkim, were seized, ill-treated, and detained by the Tibetans at Shigatse, despite the protests of the British Commissioner. Representations to China produced no effect, and in November the Government of India ordered that the Chumbi valley should be occupied and negotiations resumed at Gyantse.

The Mission achieved no more at Gyantse than it had at Khamba Jong. It entered the Chumbi valley on the 12th of December, and halted at Thuna pending military preparations.

1 Now Colonel Sir F. E. Younghusband, K.C.I.E.
2 The National Assembly.

When these were completed, the Mission moved forward about the end of March and reached Gyantse on the 11th of April, its advance having been opposed. The Tibetans then said they could only negotiate at Khamba Jong, and their attitude, after the Mission had halted, rapidly became most aggressive. A representative from the Lhasa Council, nominally coming to negotiate, was known to be recruiting; some servants of the Mission were barbarously murdered; and finally an attack was made on the Mission on the 5th of May. In spite of this the Mission waited patiently at Gyantse. Its patience, however, was severely tried by a continual fire from the walls of the jong, and when some Tibetan officials arrived in July to negotiate, they were told the jong must be evacuated. This was not done and the place was taken by assault on the 6th of July.

It was now considered:—

that these officials had no wish nor power to negotiate;
that the settlement could only be binding if concluded at Lhasa;
that a demonstration of force at Lhasa would have a very salutary effect on the Lhasa officials in the future.

Accordingly the Mission advanced on the 14th of July, only delayed by the Tibetans entreating them to discuss things at Gyantse. Lhasa was reached on the 3rd of August.

Many reasons for the impossible attitude of the Tibetans had now been ascertained. Besides their original belief in their own invincible and sacred persons, they had also been sustained by the recent presence of the Buriat, Dorjieff, in their midst. This individual appears to have acquired a great ascendancy over the Dalai Lama; to have made him most extravagant promises of Russian support, which were corroborated in the minds of the people by the arrival of arms from the north; to have negotiated a treaty between Russia and Tibet [1]; and to have represented that the Czar was desirous of conversion to Buddhism.[2] The monks he conciliated by large subsidies: originally a poor traveller, he had, on his last visit to Lhasa distributed to the monasteries between four and five lakhs

[1] A draft of this treaty was shown to Colonel Younghusband in Lhasa.

[2] This is not the occasion to discuss the foundation for these statements, or even the truth of Dorjieff having made them. The essential fact is that they were widely known and universally accepted in Tibet, Nepal, and Bhutan.

of rupees. Shortly before the arrival of the Mission, the Dalai Lama departed northward in company with Dorjieff.

At first the negotiations made no progress. There was no one to take the lead in the *Tsongdu*; every man fearing his neighbour, and all the absent Dalai Lama. Eventually, however, the Ti Rimpoche [1] was recognized as Regent by the *Tsongdu*, and on Colonel Younghusband threatening an immediate renewal of hostilities [2] a treaty [3] was eventually signed on the 7th September 1904 in the Potala, in the presence of the *Tsongdu*, by the British Commissioner, the Amban, the Regent, the Shapes, and the representatives of the monasteries.

Convention, 1904.

Soon after the conclusion of the treaty, the Mission withdrew to India, leaving only a force in occupation of the Chumbi valley, and a British Commercial Resident [4] with an escort at Gyantse.

A remarkable feature of relations with the Tibetans during the Mission to Tibet was the friendly attitude of the common people; and after the conclusion of the negotiations that attitude also extended to the chief men, who showed marked cordiality on our departure from Lhasa. The attitude of the Governments of Nepal and Bhutan also calls for comment. The Bhutanese delayed some time before accepting the invitation of the Government of India, given in October 1903, to a meeting with the Commissioner of Rajshahi. But as soon as they understood from the occupation of the Chumbi valley that the Government of India were serious, they sent messages of goodwill and offers of supplies. The Nepalese were throughout most friendly to India. They addressed an early letter of remonstrance to the Lhasa authorities, of which they sent a copy [5] to the Government of India, and they offered transport animals for the British force. Both the Bhutanese and Napelese representatives were of the greatest service to the British

1 The head of the Gaden Monastery.

2 This threat was most opportune. The time for the necessary departure of the troops was approaching, and three days after the conclusion of the treaty the Amban received orders from Pekin not to sign. We could have dispensed with his adherence, but his action would certainly have influenced the Tibetans.

3 See Appendix 4.

4 Captain W. F. O'Connor, R.G.A., C.I.E.

5 See Appendix 3.

Commissioner during the negotiations. Colonel Younghusband thought that they were both impressed by the strength and moderation of the British attitude.

The Dalai Lama.

The Dalai Lama, we have seen, fled northward on the approach of the British force, in company with Dorjieff. He had sent at least two urgent messages to Russia since the arrival of the Mission at Khamba Jong, and it was to Russian territory that he now turned. On arrival at Urga, however, he was met by the news of the events in Manchuria,[1] and he then halted. Up to the present time (1906), in spite of many rumours as to his return to Lhasa, he appears to have remained in the north, and was at Urga in the autumn of 1905.[2] It appears that the relations between him and the Taranath Lama of Urga are not cordial. The common people in Lhasa seem to have lost some of their love for the Dalai Lama, mistrusting his Russian intrigues, but they still fear him and resent Chinese interference; for when the Amban, who had, in September 1904, denounced the Dalai Lama to Pekin as the source of the troubles in that year, posted a proclamation in Lhasa deposing him, it was torn down by the populace.

Ever since Europeans first crossed the Himalayas the authorities at Shigatse have been better disposed to travellers from the south than have those at Lhasa. This seems to have kept the Tashi Lama always under the suspicion of the Dalai Lama, and between Shigatse and Lhasa the relations have not always been cordial. The fact of the Tashi Lama being held in the highest veneration by many Buddhists probably accounts for much of this feeling.

In 1905 the Tashi Lama accepted the invitation of the Government of India to visit the Prince of Wales, then touring in India. He was present at a large review at Rawal Pindi, was twice received by the Prince of Wales, and visited several places held holy by Buddhists. His visit had no political character, the Chinese Government being assured that the Indian Government considered him solely as a holy personage.

1 The Russo-Japanese war.

2 The latest news of the Dalai Lama is that he was at Gumdum in November 1906.—(*Editor.*)

Disturbances in Eastern Tibet, 1905.

There were considerable disturbances in Eastern Tibet in 1905. Of these we have as yet no precise particulars.[1]

The relations between India and Tibet remain good. The officials at Lhasa have made one or two protests against the occupation of the Chumbi valley, but the country people and officials have been most friendly. Three expeditions to Tibet have been sanctioned by the Government of India since the conclusion of the Treaty. Captain Rawlings was sent in 1904 to establish a trade mart at Gartok. Mr. Sherring, Deputy Commissioner of Almora visited Western Tibet in 1905, and in 1906 Captain FitzGerald visited Shigatse, and made a small tour on his way south. All were everywhere well received.

China early objected to the 1904 convention, as impairing her sovereignty over Tibet; and delayed its ratification until April 1906. The Government of India, on the other hand, consider that the position of China in Tibet has, on the contrary, been considerably improved. It was certainly quite clear between 1886 and 1904 that the Tibetans completely disregarded the Chinese, and the treaties concluded between Nepal and Tibet in 1854 were made regardless of Chinese approval.

The policy of the British Government towards Tibet is concisely summed up in the declaration more than once made: that "As long as no other power endeavours to intervene in the affairs of Tibet, we will not attempt either to annex it, to establish a protectorate over it, or in any way to control its internal administration."

1 The operations were between the Chinese and the semi-independent Tibet tribes on the Tibet-Chinese frontier, in the neighbourhood of Batang. Severe fighting took place especially in the neighbourhood of Siang-Chen, but the tribesmen were defeated and brought under control in June 1906, and a Chinese Viceroy has now been established in these parts, his jurisdiction extending along the Yünnan and Ssu-Chuan borders.—(*Editor.*)

# CHAPTER VI.

*MILITARY OPERATIONS.*

## The Niti Expedition of 1889.

THE first operations to be noted are those of the Niti Expedition of 1889. The force was composed of 209 men of the 3rd Gurkhas with six British officers, Major C. Pulley commanding. It moved up to the Tibetan frontier in November 1889. At Barahoti, where the Tibetans were reported to have encroached, their traces, but no signs of life, were found. The only difficulties encountered were the height of Marichak pass (18,000 feet) and the twenty-five degrees of frost at Barahoti. The party returned to India without incident.

## The Tibet Mission, 1903-04.

The causes which led to the despatch of the Tibet Mission of 1903 may be briefly summarized as follows :—

1. The breach of treaty obligations by the Tibetans in thwarting trade.
2. The occupation by them of Sikkim territory, and the destruction of boundary pillars.
3. The seizure of British subjects.
4. The Tibetans' refusal to receive communications.
5. The dilatoriness of China in the matter.
6. The military preparations of Tibet.
7. The obvious breakdown of the lenient policy of the Government of India of 1888 and subsequently.

32nd Pioneers.
23rd "
2 companies, 10th Jats.
No. 4 Company, 2nd Sappers and Miners. About 1,800 men.

When the success of the Mission at Khamba Jong seemed doubtful, it was decided to improve the communications in Sikkim towards the Chumbi valley. Troops for this purpose were sent up at different times during 1903 and set to work on the roads. There were also present in Sikkim the Escort to the Mission and the ordinary garrison at Gantok.[1] Colonel J. R. Macdonald, C.B., R.E., was in command, with the temporary rank of Brigadier-General, and Major Iggulden, Derbyshire Regiment, was his Staff Officer.

Two guns, No. 7 Mountain Battery.[2]
Two 7-pr. R. M. L. guns.[2]
Two maxim guns.[3]
No. 3 Company, 1st Sappers and Miners.
8th Gurkhas.
Field Hospital.

On the 9th November 1903 the mobilization of additional troops was ordered, and the occupation of the Chumbi valley was decided on, with a view to negotiations at Gyantse. The force was made up to 3,000 men; transport corps were organized for this number; and special clothing was issued to the troops in view of the coming movements in trying altitudes.[4] The head-quarters reached Gnathong on the 7th December. At that time the enemy had collected a considerable body of troops to watch the Mission at Khamba Jong, and every effort was made to encourage them in the idea that our main advance was to be made from there. Thus when the Mission withdrew into Sikkim on the 13th December, simultaneously with the main advance into the Chumbi valley, it appears that a number of the enemy's levies, seeing the former movement and not knowing of the latter, disbanded and could not be again collected in time to resist the advance up the Chumbi valley.

The altitude of Gnathong and the Jelap La, and the intense cold experienced there, were very trying to all, but caused no casualties.[5] In this and subsequent periods of the expedition the greatest difficulties were occasioned by the unusual trials experienced by the transport.

1 2 companies, 10th Jats.

2 No. 7 Mountain Battery was armed with 10-pr. B. L. mountain guns. At first these were only provided with shrapnel; but on the need of common shell being experienced, 300 experimental 10lb common shell which were at Cossipore were sent up in May 1904. These proved satisfactory and the supply was continued. The section of No. 30 Mountain Battery was armed with 7-pr. R. M. L. guns of 200lb, provided with a double common shell, which were effective. The Gurkha guns (7-pr. R. M. L. of 150lb) could only be employed with shrapnel at ranges up to 2,000 yards, and their fire with double common shell was most erratic, from irregular bursting of the shell. The Tibetans had several pieces in Gyantse which ranged well over the Mission enclosure—distant 1,800 yards. They fired mostly a 3lb solid round ball.

3 The water in the maxim gun jackets froze and was replaced by a mixture of water, rum, and kerosine. It was also found necessary to remove all oil from the locks of rifles and maxims, as it froze hard. The arms were used without any lubricant.

4 To each man a long sheepskin over-coat, a quilted rug, fur-lined gloves, two lambskin vests, quilted overalls, extra socks, felt knee boots, comforter, and goggles.

5 The minimum temperature at Gnathong was 21° Fahr.

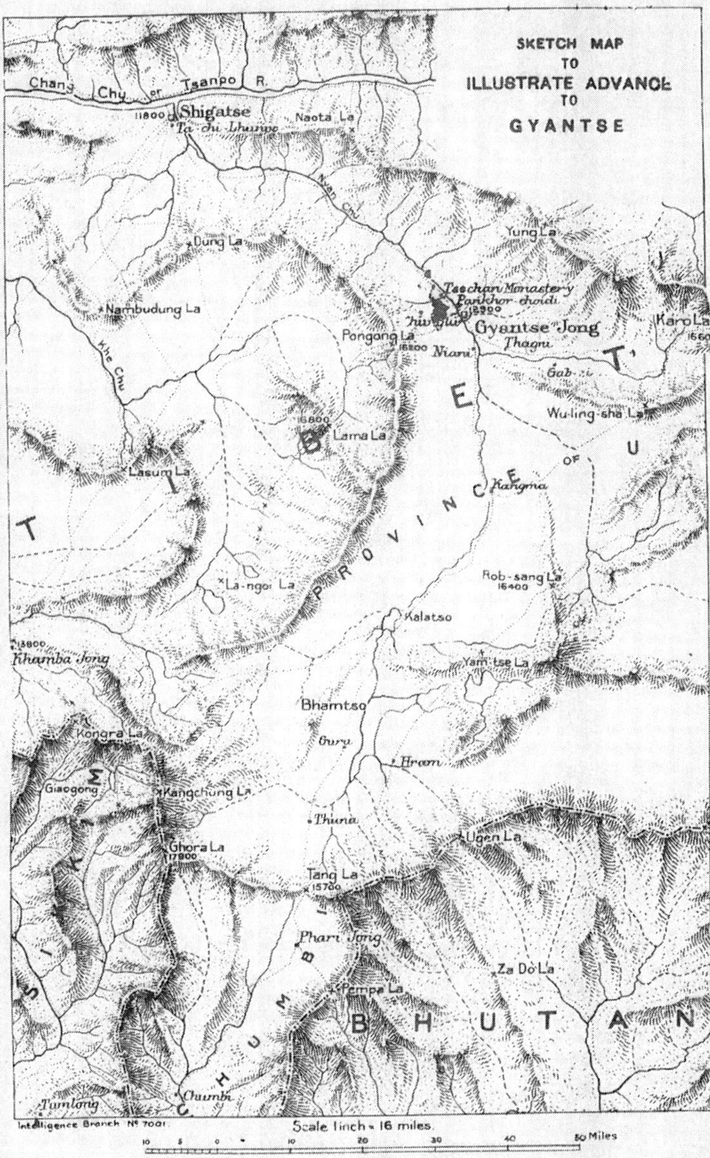

SKETCH MAP
TO
ILLUSTRATE ADVANCE
TO
GYANTSE
Chang Chu or Tsanpo R.
11800 Shigatse
Ta-chi-Lhunpo
Naota La
Nyan Chu
Dung La
Yung La
Nambudung La
Tsechan Monastery
Palkhor choidi
Gyantse Jong
Karo La
15600
Pongong La
16200
Niani
Thagu
Khe Chu
Gob-si
T
E
16800
Lama La
Wu-ling-sha La
B
U
Lasum La
OF
Kangma
T
I
PROVINCE
Rob-sang La
16400
La-ngo La
Kalatso
13800
Khamba Jong
Yam-tse La
Bhamtso
Guru
Kongra La
Hram
Giaogong
Kangchung La
Thuna
Ghora La
17900
Ugen La
Tang La
15700
Phari Jong
Za Do La
Pempa La
BHUTAN
CHUMBI
SIK
Tumlong
Chumbi
Intelligence Branch No 7001.
Scale 1 inch = 16 miles.
10 5 0 10 20 30 40 50 Miles

The Mission Escort crossed the Jelap La in separate bodies, the first consisting of 1,200 fighting men with three days' supplies and 1,400 transport animals. Chumbi was occupied on the 15th December, and a flying column of 800 pushed on and seized Phari Jong on the 20th, thus securing the Chumbi valley. It was fortunate that this advance was unopposed, for the Chumbi–Phari road is a most difficult one, part of it winding along rocky gorges, where a few resolute men could effectively delay an advancing force. Phari Jong is an important post on the line of communication to Gyantse. It was found to contain a large store of grain, but no garrison of any consequence. Phari itself is a filthy and comfortless place where fifty degrees of frost were not unusual. The local supplies were quite insufficient, and consequently everything, including fodder and fuel, had to be brought up from the base. Between Phari and Gyantse lies a barren tract of 100 miles where no supplies at all were available. To maintain the force and provide for a future advance large supplies had to be collected at the former place, and the forwarding of them in mid-winter over the passes from Sikkim was a work of great difficulty. The difficulties of transport and trouble occasioned by the coolies will be alluded to hereafter. In addition the roads were execrable, and their improvement, when the soil was frost-bound, was a work of extreme labour. General Macdonald speaks of the succeeding three months as a period of grim strain. Meantime the Commissioner was at Thuna. He wished to be within Tibetan territory proper, in order to meet the expected Chinese Amban, and was installed, on January 8th, in a walled enclosure outside Thuna village, under the escort of four companies, 23rd Pioneers, one 7-pr. gun, and some mounted infantry, who protected the Mission against the 2,000 or 3,000 Tibetans assembled at Guru. During the halt at Chumbi a company of mounted infantry [1] was raised, under Captain Ottley.

The preparations for the advance were completed by the 24th of March, and on that day the force began to advance from Chumbi. By that time the Commissioner had come to the conclusion

[1] In all there were three companies, each 100 strong, employed with the force. The 1st was composed of men of the 23rd and 32nd Pioneers and 8th Gurkhas. The remaining two were raised in India and were composed of Pathans and Punjabis. General Macdonald says they proved invaluable. Besides purely military duties they carried mails, and in this work suffered great hardships from exposure. The pluck and endurance of the men received high praise.

that the Tibetans had a contempt for the small British force, and that the Indian Government "had not one ounce of prestige in Tibet." The Tibetans were reported to have 3,000 men at Guru, guarding the Gyantse road ; 2,000 at Hram, east of the Bhamtso, guarding the Lhasa road ; and 2,000 in réserve.

The column was concentrated at Thuna on the 29th March. Two days later the Tibetans commenced hostilities at Guru. A body of troops moved forward from Thuna on the 31st March 1904 with the object of establishing a supply depôt at Guru, preparatory to a general advance of the British force. Some Tibetan officials met the column and endeavoured to persuade the British to return to Thuna, and threatened trouble when informed that the Commissioner would only negotiate at Gyantse.

Encounter at Guru.
4 guns, Machine Gun Section.
9 companies infantry.
200 Madras „

The column continued its advance, and presently found the Tibetans occupying some *sangars* on a rocky ridge west of the Bhamtso, and a wall, easily outflanked, on the flat. The troops moved forward in attack formation, it appearing that the Tibetans intended to defend their walls. The British soldiers, however, had received orders that they were not to fire a shot unless first attacked, but were to try to persuade the Tibetans to leave their defences. The 23rd Pioneers and 8th Gurkhas now proceeded to clear the *sangars*, and these the Tibetans gave up readily enough, some of them staying in a body on the hillside, but most gathering with the defenders of the wall on the flat. With the evacuation of the *sangars* it was assumed that all danger of hostilities was at an end.

It was, however, impossible for the British column to advance with this large armed force encamped right across the road. The Tibetans were accordingly informed that they must either retire or give up their arms. They showed no intention of doing either, and, in an attempt to disarm some of them, some scuffling now ensued. The Lhasa Depon exhorted his men to resist, and presently fired his pistol in the face of a sepoy. Thereupon, with a yell, a number of Tibetans dashed forward with swords upon the nearest Englishmen and sepoys, and others discharged their matchlocks at point-blank range. Major Wallace Dunlop, 23rd Pioneers, and Mr. Candler, Press correspondent, who were among the Tibetans at the moment, received several severe sword cuts, and ten sepoys were wounded. The British, recovering from their momentary surprise, opened a magazine fire on the mass of the Tibetans, who, surrounded on three sides, now fell into the greatest confusion and beat a precipitate retreat, leaving the ground strewn with dead and wounded. Some of them made a stand in Guru village, which was shelled and carried by assault, and the pursuit was continued for ten miles by Captain Ottley's mounted infantry.

The Tibetans numbered 2,000, half of whom were regular soldiers, armed with matchlocks. They left 628 killed and wounded on the field, and 222 prisoners. The British casualties were 12 wounded.[1] The enemy's wounded were, to their great astonishment, treated in the British Hospitals. The force returned to Thuna the same day, leaving a small garrison at Guru. The Hram force of the enemy retreated immediately to Kalatso.

4 guns.
4 Machine guns.
10½ companies, 23rd and 32nd Pioneers and Gurkhas.
Field Hospitals.
1,850 mules.
700 yaks.
600 coolies.
70 ekkas.

The forward movement was resumed on the 4th April, the composition of the column being as shown in the margin. The advanced guard came under fire on the 6th at the village of Samanda, but no serious opposition was encountered until the enemy were found in position in the Lamdang, or Red Idol Gorge, on the 10th, when an action ensued which lasted eight hours. The Lamdang gorge is a winding and constricted valley, much encumbered with broken rock, and overlooked by crags and high ridges. The Tibetans, about 2,000 in number, were posted in *sangars* and behind rocks, and they had mounted several *jingals* on a crag. A flanking force, consisting of two companies of the 8th Gurkhas, were despatched to turn the enemy's right, and a long wait ensued, for they had some distance to climb. The guns opened and cleared the enemy from the nearer ridges, and presently the 32nd Pioneers were sent forward into the gorge, just as the Gurkhas were advancing along the enemy's western flank.

Action at Lamdang, 10th April 1904.

The Tibetans fought fanatically at close quarters, but their weapons were inferior and their fire most erratic. Consequently

[1] Mr. Candler, Press correspondent, lost his hand.

the British advance, though slow, was continuous, and the enemy suffered severely. Once through the gorge, the mounted infantry took up the pursuit, and carried it on for some miles. The enemy lost 500 killed, wounded, and prisoners, while the British casualties were 3 men wounded.

Next day the British force reached Gyantse, and the fort was handed over without opposition. Gyantse Jong is a strong place built on a rock 600 feet high, in the middle of a richly cultivated plain. The water-supply, however, is external, and the perimeter was thought inconveniently large. Accordingly the entrance gate of the jong was demolished, and the hamlet of Chunglu, 1,500 yards from the jong, selected for occupation by the Mission. Chunglu is a large walled enclosure, which was subsequently loopholed and provided with abatis. Here the Mission was established, protected by the marginally noted escort, while the main body returned to Chumbi, leaving one company at Kangma and one company at Kalatso.

Lt.-Colonel Brander, 32nd Pioneers.
6 companies infantry.
Two 7-pr. guns.
50 mounted infantry.
2 maxims.

This ended the first phase. Gyantse, the objective named by the Government, had been reached.

All went smoothly at Gyantse for two or three weeks, but at the end of April information was received that the Tibetans were gathering at Karo La, forty-six miles distant, on the Lhasa road. There is a short cut to Kangma from this place, so that this force threatened the Gyantse communications. Lieutenant Hodgson, 32nd Pioneers, was sent off with a party of mounted infantry to reconnoitre, and found a strong *sangared* position three miles beyond the Karo La. No Tibetans were visible, but on his approaching the position with a small party the enemy opened a sudden fire, fortunately without inflicting any casualties.

Action at Karo La.

*Troops.*
3 cos., 32nd Pioneers.
2 „ 8th Gurkhas.
2 maxims.
Two 7-pounders.
50 mounted infantry.

The party then returned to Gyantse; and on the 3rd May Colonel Brander moved out and attacked the enemy in position. They held the entrance to a gorge, flanked by precipitous mountains, which they had closed by a wall 600 yards long and strengthened by *sangars* on the hillsides. The issue was for a short time doubtful. The frontal attack received a check at 500 yards, and Captain Bethune and three men were killed at the very foot of the wall in an attempt to storm it. Meanwhile the flanking movements were not making great progress. The gun and maxim fire did not touch the enemy in their intrenchments, and the Gurkhas and Pioneers had to advance over grassy slopes devoid of cover. Finally, however, the flanking parties secured the extreme flank *sangars*, and, after four hours' fighting, the enemy withdrew, pursued for ten miles by the mounted infantry. Their numbers were estimated at 3,000, a considerable proportion being armed with breech-loading rifles effective up to 1,100 yards. Their losses were about 450. The trenches in the position were skilfully placed and constructed, each man being provided with head-cover, and cut off from his neighbour by a traverse. The engagement was fought at an altitude of 16,000 feet in a cutting wind. The British casualties amounted to five killed and fourteen wounded.

Attack on Mission at Gyantse.

During Colonel Brander's absence the Mission Escort at Gyantse was reduced to 160 rifles, and the enemy, taking advantage of the opportunity, moved up 1,600 men from Shigatse and assaulted the post at dawn on the 5th May. The attack was, however, expected, and the issue was at no time doubtful. Eight hundred of the enemy attacked, and a few succeeded in penetrating into the enclosure; but they were soon driven out, and the assault was repulsed with a loss of 250 killed and wounded, the British loss amounting to only 4 men wounded.[1]

When Colonel Brander returned to Gyantse on the 9th May he found the jong occupied by a strong force of the enemy, who had repaired its defences. He was not strong enough to attack them, but proceeded to so occupy their attention as to keep his communications free. Reinforcements of 160 rifles and two guns reached him, and several encounters took place, such as the assault of a house, afterwards known as "the Gurkha post," 600 yards from the enclosure; the capture of Tagu village; and the assault and occupation of Palla, where the enemy offered a stubborn resistance for eleven hours. These minor operations so occupied the Tibetans that

[1] It was subsequently ascertained that the Chinese General Ma was aware of the impending attack. Several Mission servants were brutally murdered that night in Gyantse.

they made no attempt on the communications until the 7th of June, when they attacked Kangma in considerable strength, but were easily beaten off by the garrison of 200 men. In all these actions the enemy's losses were heavy; those of the British amounted to sixty-eight, including Lieutenant Garstin, R.E., killed in the breach at Palla.

During the month of May General Macdonald was busy accumulating supplies at various points on the lines of communication preparatory to a further advance. The situation had now changed. The attack on the Mission, directed by Lhasa officials and known to General Ma, the murders of Mission servants, and the practical investment of Chunglu, had convinced the authorities that vigorous action was necessary. Reinforcements were consequently sent to General Macdonald, and the Tibetans were informed on the 12th May that if representatives did not arrive at Gyantse to treat by the 25th June, the Mission would advance to Lhasa.

*Reinforcements.*
4 companies, Royal Fusiliers.
4 „ 40th Pathans.
4 guns, No. 7 Mountain Battery, Royal Artillery.
4 guns, No. 30 Native Mountain Battery.

The main body, strength 8 guns, 125 mounted infantry, 2,950 infantry, 2,150 followers, and 4,000 animals moved forward from Chumbi on the 12th of June.

The Tibetans had by this time concentrated some 16,000 fighting men, together with some thirty *jingals* and 800 breech-loading rifles, besides matchlocks. Their force was distributed in strongly fortified positions as follows:—At Gyantse, 8,000; at Niani, 800; at Niru, 800; at Gobshi, 1,000; at Tsechen, 1,200; at Doogtse, 2,500; and moving up from Lhasa, 1,500. The fact of their being so scattered was probably due to the difficulty of obtaining supplies.

On the advance of the British force the Tibetans at Niru hastily withdrew to Niani, where they stood and were attacked by General Macdonald. Niani is a monastery on the Gyantse road, surrounded by a solid masonry wall, forty feet high and eight feet thick, with only two entrances. These are a gate on the east side, and a narrow mud ramp on the other. There is also a small fort of solid masonry. The Tibetans fired upon the reconnoitring party on the afternoon

Attack on Niani, 26th June 1904.

of the 25th from this position, and killed one man. Next day Niani was attacked. Colonel Brander co-operated by holding the ridge east of the monastery, and also the Lhasa road. The attack began by shrapnel fire from Colonel Brander's guns, while No. 7 Mountain Battery breached the south face of the monastery wall. At noon the 40th Pathans secured a lodgment in the monastery, where they were joined by some of the 23rd and 32nd Pioneers, and a hand-to-hand fight ensued. The enemy then concealed themselves in the buildings and cellars within, whence, for want of guncotton, their ejection was not completed. For the same reason they were left in possession of the village, but this was well shelled, and the enemy's fire silenced. The British column resumed its march to Gyantse at 3 P.M., and next day the enemy abandoned Niani. Their casualties at that place were estimated at 200, while the British lost 2 killed and 13 wounded. The force reached Gyantse on the 16th June, and camped about a mile south-east of the Mission post. A heavy fire was opened upon them as they passed the jong, but no damage was done at the range—2,500 yards.

Operations about Gyantse.

General Macdonald immediately proceeded to clear the Gyantse valley of the enemy, by which the communications of the jong with Shigatse were cut, and the valley opened up to foraging parties. Operations began before dawn on the 28th. Four companies of infantry were sent down the right bank of the Nyan Tsu to occupy the attention of the defenders of Gyantse, while the main body operated on the left bank. The enemy were found in some villages two or three miles from the jong, one of which, Gobshi, they held in some strength. The artillery opened upon them, and this fire was so demoralizing that the Tibetans withdrew and joined the garrison of Tsechen monastery. This, with its attendant village, forms a very strong position at the northern end of an extremely steep, isolated hill, the crest of which, crowned with two forts and several *sangars*, was strongly held by the enemy. The position was attacked at 5 P.M. by the 8th Gurkhas, 40th Pathans, and 1st Sappers and Miners, a company of the 8th Gurkhas making a flank attack along the south-western end of the ridge. Both infantry attacks were carried out with the greatest dash and gallantry, and were admirably supported by No. 7 Mountain Battery, which kept up an exceedingly accurate fire on the *sangars* on the top of the hill, and on the houses and towers which were seen to be held by the enemy. To the excellent work of this battery was due the small numbers of casualties incurred in taking a difficult position. The enemy held their ground until driven out at the point of the bayonet, in spite of a heavy shell, maxim, and rifle fire; they also defended a large tower in the monastery until the gates were blown in. The fighting lasted till dark. The enemy's losses were not known, but the British lost Captain J. C. P. Craster, 46th Punjabis, killed, and eight men wounded.

These two decisive actions demoralized the enemy, who now sent in a flag of truce. Futile negotiations followed and hostilities were suspended until noon on the 5th July, when a demonstration was made against the north-west face of the enemy's stronghold in Gyantse, the Pulchior Choide monastery. The troops pushed in and occupied some houses at the foot of the hill, and held them until dark, when they withdrew, leaving fires burning. At midnight on the 5th the troops for the real attack, on the south-east side, moved off. They were in position by 3-30 A.M., formed up in three columns, each consisting of a party of Sappers with explosives, a company of infantry, and a company of Pioneers, with a reserve of two companies. The three columns were to attack the points marked A, B, and C on the plan. The Tibetans, subsequently estimated at 6,000, occupied the whole town, Jong, and monastery. They had fortified their position on every side, existing walls were all loop holed, the elevated position D to E was occupied by a continuous wall, and strong *sangars* were erected on the points E, F, G, and H. The roofs of the houses in the jong and town were provided with head-cover made of bags of wool. The sky was clear and the moonlight disclosed the attack to the enemy, who opened fire a few minutes before four o'clock at about 300 yards' range. The columns pressed

Assault of Gyantse Jong.

*Commanding.*—Lieutenant-Colonel Campbell, D.S.O., 40th Pathans.

*Assaulting columns.*

3rd and 12th Company, Sappers and Miners.
1 company, Royal Fusiliers.
1 „ 32nd Pioneers.
2 companies, 23rd „
1 company, 40th Pathans.
1 „ 8th Gurkhas.

*Reserves.*

1 company, Royal Fusiliers.
1 „ 32nd Pioneers.
1 „ 23rd „
1 „ 40th Pathans.
2 companies, 8th Gurkhas.

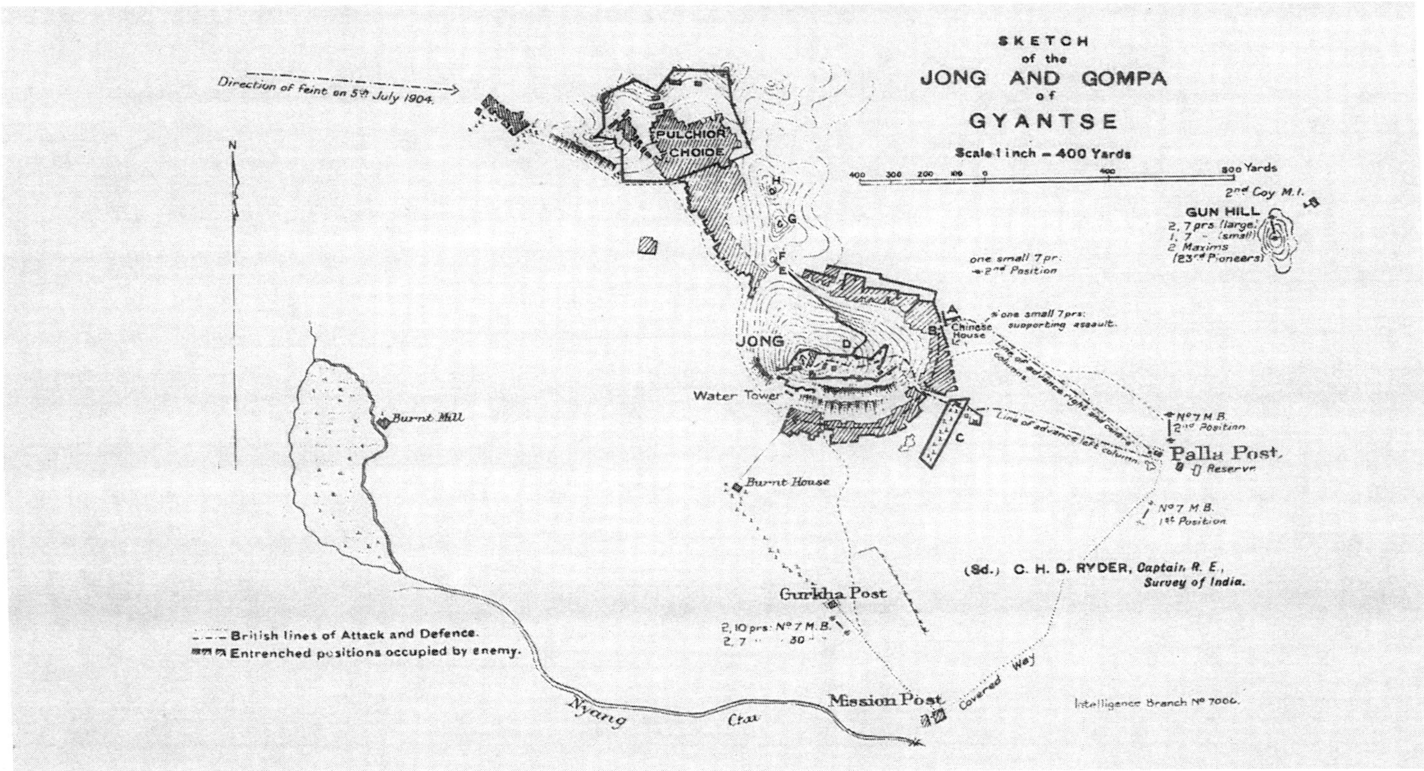
SKETCH
of the
JONG AND GOMPA
of
GYANTSE
Scale 1 inch = 400 Yards
400 300 200 100 0 400 800 Yards
Direction of feint on 5th July 1904.
N
PULCHIOR CHOIDE
H
G
F
E
JONG
D
A
B
C
Chinese House
Water Tower
Burnt Mill
Burnt House
one small 7 pr. 2nd Position
one small 7 prs. supporting assault.
Line of advance right and centre columns.
Line of advance left column.
2nd Coy M.I.
GUN HILL
2, 7 prs (large)
1, 7 " (small)
2 Maxims
(23rd Pioneers)
No 7 M.B. 2nd Position
Palla Post
Reserve
No 7 M.B. 1st Position
(Sd.) C. H. D. RYDER, Captain R. E.,
Survey of India.
Gurkha Post
2, 10 prs: No 7 M.B.
2, 7 " 30 "
Covered Way
Mission Post
Nyang Chu
Intelligence Branch No 7006.
British lines of Attack and Defence.
Entrenched positions occupied by enemy.

## RECONNAISSANCE SKETCH FROM THE PALLA VILLAGE

(*Sd.*) N. V. L. RYBOT, *Lieut.*,
*28th P.*

Lettering corresponds to that on plan.
X is point where breach was made and entry effected.

⊙ Position of Palla Post.

Intelligence Branch Nº 7003.

forward, doors and walls were blown in, and a lodgment had been effected at all three points before dawn. As soon as it was light the troops were able to find their way through the intricate mass of houses, and by 8 A.M. the whole town, from B to its south-west corner, was taken. At daybreak, too, the artillery posted on Gun Hill and Palla opened a fire on the jong, and the infantry replied to the very heavy fire opened from the walls and *sangars* by the enemy.

At 2 P.M. their fire had slackened and an assault on the jong was ordered. The guns of No. 7 Mountain Battery were directed upon a weak spot at the east corner of the jong, and by 3-30 P.M. the 10-pr. common shell had made a practicable breach in it. A company of the 8th Gurkhas, led by Lieutenant Grant, and backed up by a company of the Royal Fusiliers, now began to clamber up the precipitous slope. They were met with showers of stones and a heavy musketry fire, but took no denial,[1] and scrambling through the breach, one at a time, took possession of a tower close by. This was the climax of the day. The Tibetans, offering no further organized resistance, at once began to retire to the monastery and western part of the town, and by 6 P.M. the British troops were masters of the jong.

The enemy still maintained a fire from the monastery, and preparations were made to take it next day. On the morning of the 7th, however, it was ascertained that the Tibetans had evacuated the place and withdrawn from Gyantse. The British losses in this fighting were four killed[2] and thirty-three wounded.

Advance to Lhasa.

200 mounted infantry.
1,900 infantry and sappers.
8 guns.
6 maxims.
2,000 followers.
3,900 animals.
23 days' rations.

After the capture of Gyantse Jong and the retreat of the enemy, supplies were collected from the Gyantse valley and the marginally named column was got ready to escort the Commissioner to Lhasa.

The advance on Lhasa began on the 10th July. At Karo La some slight resistance was met with, but Nagartse Jong and Pete

[1] Lieutenant Grant was hurled back some distance by stones, but scrambled up again. He was subsequently awarded the Victoria Cross for his gallantry during the assault. Havildar Kabir Pun received the 1st class of the Indian Order of Merit.

[2] Including Lieutenant G. P. Gurdon, 32nd Pioneers, an officer who had done excellent work on several occasions during the campaign.

Jong were undefended, and the force reached the Tsanpo on the 24th. The Tsanpo was then a rapid river, 150 yards wide. The mounted infantry had captured two large native boats, and with them and the Berthon boats[1] carried by the column, the crossing of the river was completed in seven days.

Lhasa was reached without incident on the 7th of August. The town was not defended, and beyond some skirmishing operations, which cleared the Tibetan troops away from the neighbourhood of Lhasa, and a demonstration against the Debung monastery, which at first refused to furnish supplies, no other military operations took place.

The force left Lhasa on the 23rd September, and withdrew without further incident to India.

Transport.

The difficulties met with by the Supply and Transport Corps may be said to have been the greatest obstacle encountered by the expedition. From Siliguri, the base depôt, to Gyantse is a distance of 225 miles: to Lhasa 145 miles more. Commencing in the unhealthy Tista valley, the route crosses four passes of from 14,000 to 17,000 feet in height, before arriving at the Tsanpo, itself a formidable obstacle. The greater part of the country traversed is quite barren; the climate most rigorous; the soil for the greater part of the year frozen hard. Such were the physical difficulties. There was also from the first an astonishing prevalence and variety of disease among the transport animals.[2] The yaks which came from Nepal were already permeated with anthrax; they lost condition from the heat of the Tista valley, and still more from want of grazing; and of the thousands which started few survived.[3] The bullocks suffered from rinderpest and foot-and-mouth disease; the mules, which proved the most reliable of all the transport animals, from glanders and epizootic lymphangitis; and the ponies from pneumonia, consequent on the excessive cold. Great trouble was also experienced among the coolies. Many at first deserted from fear

1 These boats were first joined together to make rafts. One of them capsized and an officer and four men were drowned. General Macdonald says that the loss of Major G. H. Bretherton, D.S.O., Chief Supply and Transport Officer, one of those drowned, was the cause of "the intense regret of the whole force, and a great loss to the service."

2 *Vide* Report on the working of the Army Veterinary Department with the Sikkim Tibet Mission, 1904.

3 Of the 3,500 which left Nepal 400 reached Chumbi, and of these only 30 or 40 survived the attacks of pneumonia.

of the Lamas, and cholera subsequently broke out among them. Altogether the extraordinary difficulties of climate, locality, and disease with which the Supply and Transport Corps had to cope may be said to have been most successfully overcome.

## *BIBLIOGRAPHY.*

C. R. MARKHAM.—"*Narratives of the Mission of George Bogle to Tibet, and of the journey of Thomas Manning to Lhasa,*" 1875.

CAPTAIN S. TURNER.—"*Account of an Embassy to the Court of the Teshoo Lama,* 1800."

CAPTAIN W. F. O'CONNOR, R.G.A.—"*Report on Tibet,*" 1903.

*Official Despatches, Diaries and Memoranda.*

GRAHAM SANDBERG.—"*The Exploration of Tibet,*" 1904.

# APPENDIX I.

*TOTAL FORCE EMPLOYED WITH THE TIBET MISSION*, 1903-04.

No. 7 Mountain Battery, Royal Garrison Artillery, 10-pr. guns—*Major Fuller.*
1 section, No. 30 Mountain Battery, 7-pr. 200-lb guns—*Lieutenant Marindin.*
1 section, No. 27 Mountain Battery, 10-pr. guns—*Lieutenant Field.*
2 7-pr. R. M. L. guns, Gurkha detachments—*Captain Leeke.*
Maxim Gun Section, 1st Battalion, Norfolk Regiment—*Lieutenant Hadow.*
Maxim Gun Section, 1st Battalion, Royal Irish Rifles—*Lieutenant Bowen Colthurst.*
1st Company, Mounted Infantry—*Captain Ottley.*
2nd Company, Mounted Infantry—*Captain Peterson.*
3rd Company, Mounted Infantry—*Major Rowlandson.*
4 Companies, 1st Battalion, Royal Fusiliers—*Colonel Cooper, D.S.O.*
23rd Sikh Pioneers, with maxim guns—*Lieutenant-Colonel Hogge.*
32nd Sikh Pioneers with maxim guns—*Lieutenant-Colonel Brander.*
19th Punjabis—*Major Herbert.*
40th Pathans—*Lieutenant-Colonel Campbell, D.S.O.*
8th Gurkha Rifles—*Lieutenant-Colonel Kerr.*
Maxim Gun Section, 9th Gurkha Rifles.
No. 3 Company, 1st Sappers and Miners—*Captain Sheppard, D.S.O.*
No. 12 Company, 2nd Sappers and Miners—*Major Heycock.*
13 Sections, Field Hospital.
1 Base Hospital.
10,000 transport drivers.
8,000 Supply and Transport coolies.
10,500 mules and ponies.
400 donkeys.
9,225 bullocks and yaks.
230 British officers.

# APPENDIX II.

*ABSTRACT OF CASUALTIES.*

*Tibet Mission Escort*, 1903-04.

| Date. | Place. | Nature. | KILLED. British Officers. | KILLED. British Rank and File. | KILLED. Native Officers. | KILLED. Native Rank and File. | KILLED. Followers. | WOUNDED. British Officers. | WOUNDED. British Rank and File. | WOUNDED. Native Officers. | WOUNDED. Native Rank and File. | WOUNDED. Followers. | Total. | Percentage of loss of fighting men engaged. |
|---|---|---|---|---|---|---|---|---|---|---|---|---|---|---|
| 7th January. | Phari .. | Fracas .. | .. | .. | .. | .. | .. | 1 | .. | .. | 1 | 1 | 3 | |
| 31st March.. | Guru .. | Action .. | .. | .. | .. | .. | .. | 2 | .. | 1 | 10 | .. | 13 | 1·25 per cent. |
| 7th April .. | „ .. | Explosion .. | .. | .. | 1 | 4 | .. | 1 | .. | .. | 2 | 4 | 12 | |
| 10th „ .. | Zamdang .. | Engagement .. | .. | .. | .. | .. | .. | .. | .. | 1 | 2 | .. | 3 | |
| 15th „ .. | Gyantse .. | Explosion .. | .. | .. | .. | .. | .. | 1 | .. | .. | 13 | .. | 14 | |
| 5th May .. | „ .. | Defence post .. | .. | .. | .. | .. | 1 | .. | .. | .. | 4 | 1 | 6 | 2·25 per cent. |
| 6th „ .. | Karola .. | Action .. | 1 | .. | .. | 4 | .. | .. | .. | .. | 13 | .. | 18 | 5·00 „ „ |
| 12th „ .. | Gyantse .. | Jong's fire .. | .. | .. | .. | .. | 1 | .. | .. | .. | 1 | .. | 2 | |
| 19th „ .. | „ .. | Sortie .. | .. | .. | .. | .. | .. | .. | .. | .. | 3 | .. | 3 | 1·50 per cent. |
| 19th „ .. | „ .. | Defence Mails .. | .. | .. | .. | 1 | .. | .. | .. | .. | 2 | .. | 3 | |
| 19th „ .. | „ .. | Jong's fire .. | .. | .. | .. | .. | .. | .. | .. | .. | 1 | .. | 1 | |
| 20th „ .. | „ .. | Capture of Tagu | .. | .. | .. | 2 | .. | 1 | .. | .. | 3 | .. | 6 | 2·00 per cent. |
| 26th „ .. | „ .. | „ „ Palla.. | 1 | .. | .. | 3 | .. | 3 | .. | .. | 9 | .. | 16 | 3·70 „ „ |
| 4th June .. | „ .. | Jong's fire .. | .. | .. | .. | .. | .. | .. | .. | .. | 1 | .. | 1 | |
| 5th „ .. | „ .. | „ „ .. | .. | .. | .. | .. | .. | .. | .. | .. | 1 | .. | 1 | |
| 7th „ .. | Kangma .. | Defence post .. | .. | .. | .. | 1 | 1 | .. | .. | .. | 6 | .. | 8 | 3·80 per cent. |
| 8th „ .. | Gyantse .. | Jong's fire .. | .. | .. | .. | 1 | .. | .. | .. | .. | .. | .. | 1 | |
| 9th „ .. | „ .. | „ „ .. | .. | .. | .. | .. | .. | .. | .. | .. | 2 | .. | 2 | |
| 25th „ .. | Niani .. | Skirmish .. | .. | .. | .. | .. | .. | .. | .. | .. | 1 | .. | 1 | |
| 26th „ .. | „ .. | Action .. | .. | .. | .. | 5 | .. | 1 | .. | 1 | 9 | .. | 16 | |
| 28th „ .. | Tsechen .. | „ .. | 1 | .. | .. | .. | .. | .. | .. | .. | 7 | .. | 8 | |
| 5th July .. | Gyantse .. | Demonstration .. | .. | .. | .. | .. | .. | .. | .. | .. | 1 | .. | 1 | |
| 6th „ .. | „ .. | Capture of Jong.. | 1 | .. | .. | 3 | .. | 7 | 3 | 1 | 22 | .. | 37 | 2·30 per cent. |
| 7th „ .. | „ .. | Explosion .. | .. | .. | .. | .. | .. | .. | 8 | .. | .. | .. | 8 | |
| 12th „ .. | „ .. | Demolition .. | .. | .. | .. | .. | .. | .. | .. | .. | .. | 5 | 5 | |
| 18th „ .. | Karola .. | Engagement .. | .. | .. | .. | 1 | .. | .. | .. | .. | 2 | .. | 3 | |
| 25th „ .. | Chaksam .. | Crossing river .. | 1 | .. | .. | 3 | .. | .. | .. | .. | .. | .. | 4 | |
| 18th August | Lhasa .. | Attack by fanatic | .. | .. | .. | .. | .. | 2 | .. | .. | .. | .. | 2 | |
| 20th „ .. | Chaksam .. | Crossing river .. | .. | .. | .. | .. | .. | .. | .. | .. | .. | 4 | 4 | |
| | | Total .. | 5 | .. | 1 | 28 | 3 | 19 | 11 | 4 | 116 | 15 | 202 | |

# APPENDIX III.

From—His Excellency Maharaja Chandra Shamsher Jang, Rana Bahadur, Thong-Lin, Pimma, Kokang Wang-Syan, Prime Minister and Marshal of Nepal,

To—The Honourable the Four Kazis of Lhasa.

*After compliments.*—Here all well; hope same there. From information received from my officials at the frontier and also from various newspaper reports, it appears that the Commissioners deputed by the British Government to see to the enforcement of the terms of the Anglo-Tibetan Convention of 1890 and 1893, which have not been observed and carried into effect by the Tibetan Government, have been staying at a place called Khamba Jong, and that in the absence of fully-empowered Commissioners from Tibet to deal with the matters in dispute, and owing to the indifference of the local officials of the place, no settlement could be arrived at, and the British Commissioners are being unnecessarily detained there. But your complete silence on this subject makes me anxious. The friendly and fraternal relations of long-standing between the Nepal and Tibetan Governments induce me on the present occasion to enlighten you with my views concerning this matter, which I am confident will prove beneficial to you (if acted on).

Some time ago I had the occasion to enquire of you in my letter of Bhadra Badi 8th, Friday, Samvat 1958, whether there was any truth in the rumours that were current regarding certain secret arrangements made between your Government and that of Russia, when I received a reassuring reply, dated Marga Sudi 5th, Monday, Samvat 1958, to the effect that the rumours had no foundation in truth, and that they were being circulated in the newspapers with a view to bring about a rupture between the Governments of Nepal and Tibet, and this reassurance, coupled with the conviction that such revolutionary steps could never be taken by men of your intelligence, led me to allow our friendly relations to continue as before.

Now again, although it is long since the British Commissioners arrived at Khamba Jong with a view to discuss and bring about a settlement satisfactory to both parties of all matters relating to the aforesaid Convention, yet your omission to depute any Commissioners vested with full authority, and your neglect or failure to bring about a reasonable settlement so long, compel me to think that such unjustifiable conduct on your part might lead to grave consequences, and fill my mind with serious misgivings.

It is laid down in the treaty concluded on Chaitra Badi 3rd, Monday, Samvat 1912, between the Governments of Nepal and Tibet, that this Government will assist Tibet in case of an invasion of its territory by any foreign Rajas. Consequently, when a difference of opinion arises between you and any one else, it is incumbent on me to help you to the best of my power with my advice and guidance in order to prevent any troubles befalling you from such difference; and the manner in which you have managed this business not appearing commendable, the assistance to be rendered to you by me at this crisis of your own creation, consists in giving you such advice as will conduce to the welfare of your country. The said advice is given below, and I am fully confident that you will, after due deliberation, lay it before the Potala Lama and come to a speedy conclusion to act according to it. Should you fail to follow my advice, and trouble befall you, there would be no way open to me to assist you in any other way in the troublous situation brought about by you without listening to my advice and following a wayward course of your own. Understand it well; for the British Government does not appear to have acted in an improper or high-handed manner in this matter, but is simply trying to have the conditions of the treaty fulfilled, to which everybody has a right; and it is against the treaty, as well as against all morality or policy, to allow matters to drift, and to regard as enemies officers of such a powerful Government who have come to enforce such rights. Besides, when His Majesty the Emperor of China has, for your good, posted Ambans of high rank, it is a serious mistake on your part to disregard even their advice, and neglect to carry on business with the British Commissioners.

## Advice.

1. You are fully aware of the greatness of the British power. It is against all policy to disparage and to behave as if you had no concern with the Commissioners deputed by such a powerful Government to discuss the terms of the treaty concluded between two Governments.

2. It is the bounden duty of everyone to abide by a treaty made by oneself. It will be a serious failure of duty on your part if a calamity befalls your country through your not acting in a straightforward and reasonable manner with the powerful British Government, which is actuated simply by such lawful motives.

3. It is said that you refuse to be bound by the Anglo-Tibetan Treaty of 1890 on the ground that it was not concluded by you, but by the Chinese. If this report is correct, then you have acted very improperly. You and we have from a long time held in high respect His Majesty the Emperor of China, as is quite clear from the wording of the Treaty of 1912 between Nepal and Tibet. It is improper to declare that the aforesaid Convention, having

been made by the Chinese, is not binding upon you, since whatever was done was done on your behalf. It is against reason for you to say so.

4. I may point out here that, since the conclusion of the treaty of Samvat 1872 between the British and Nepal Governments, Representatives of both the Governments have resided in the two countries, and the due observation of the terms of the treaty has been continually advantageous to the Government of Nepal, nor has any religion suffered in any way. The advantages derived from such arrangement are too many to enumerate. Since the treaty was made, the British Government has on different occasions restored to us territories lost by Nepal in war and producing a revenue of many lakhs of rupees. This fact should also be known to you.

5. You must bear in mind that the Government you are to deal with are not a despotic, but a constitutional, one, and this will be corroborated by the fact that they have helped us to maintain the autonomy of our country up to so long a time, whereas they might have easily deprived us of it if they had a mind to behave to us in a despotic and unjust manner. The most notable feature in our relations with the British Government is that they sacredly observed our religious and social prejudices. Hence if you can even now take time by the forelock to settle the hanging questions and behave with them as your true friends hereafter, I am sure Tibet will derive the same benefit from such alliance as Nepal has hitherto done. I need not mention here how happy I should be if your relations with the British Government were as cordial as those of mine.

6. That the British Government have any evil designs upon Tibet does not appear from any source. It is well known that the sun never sets upon the British dominions. That the sovereign of such a vast Empire entertains designs of unjustly and improperly taking your mountainous country should never cross your mind.

7. Tibet is the great home of Buddhism. There should not be the least suspicion of the English meddling with that religion, for it is not their rule to interfere with other people's religion. On the contrary, their interest for Buddhism is apparent from the fact that, after consulting old religious books, they fixed upon the site of Kapilavastu, the birthplace of Buddha, as being situated in the Butwal district of Nepal, and when, upon the strength of this information, we traced the place and dug it up, foundations of old buildings were discovered, and we found out also the ancient image of Buddha with his mother situated in the Lummini garden.

8. Thinking that to bring about unnecessary complications with the British Government is like producing headache by twisting a rope round one's head when it is not aching, I have written to you my views, and I see it clearly that, if you disregard my advice, a serious calamity is likely to overtake you.

9. I am in hopes that I shall soon have reassuring news of you.

## APPENDIX IV.

*CONVENTION BETWEEN GREAT BRITAIN AND TIBET.*

**Whereas** doubts and difficulties have arisen as to the meaning and validity of the Anglo-Chinese Convention of 1890 and the Trade Regulations of 1893, and as to the liabilities of the Tibetan Government under these agreements; and whereas recent occurrences have tended towards a disturbance of the relations of friendship and good understanding which have existed between the British Government and the Government of Tibet; and whereas it is desirable to restore peace and amicable relations, and to resolve and determine the doubts and difficulties as aforesaid, the said Governments have resolved to conclude a Convention with these objects, and the following articles have been agreed upon by Colonel F. E. Younghusband, C.I.E., in virtue of full powers vested in him by His Britannic Majesty's Government and on behalf of that said Government, and Lo-Sang Gyal-Tsen, the Ga-den Ti-Rimpoche, and the representatives of the Council, of the three monastries Se-ra, Drepung, and Ga-den, and of the ecclesiastical and lay officials of the National Assembly on behalf of the Government of Tibet:—

I.

The Government of Tibet engages to respect the Anglo-Chinese Convention of 1890 and to recognize the frontier between Sikkim and Tibet, as defined in Article I of the said Convention, and to erect boundary pillars accordingly.

II.

The Tibetan Government undertakes to open forthwith trade marts to which all British and Tibetan subjects shall have free right of access at Gyantse and Gartok, as well as at Yatung.

The Regulations applicable to the trade mart at Yatung, under the Anglo-Chinese Agreement of 1893, shall, subject to such amendments as may hereafter be agreed upon by common consent between the British and Tibetan Governments, apply to the marts above mentioned.

In addition to establishing trade marts at the places mentioned, the Tibetan Government undertakes to place no restrictions on the trade by existing routes, and to consider the question of establishing fresh trade marts under similar conditions if development of trade requires it.

III.

The question of the amendment of the Regulations of 1893 is reserved for separate consideration, and the Tibetan Government undertakes to appoint fully authorized delegates to negotiate with representatives of the British Government as to the details of the amendments required.

IV.

The Tibetan Government undertakes to levy no dues of any kind other than those provided for in the tariff to be mutually agreed upon.

V.

The Tibetan Government undertakes to keep the roads to Gyantse and Gartok from the frontier clear of all obstruction and in a state of repair suited to the needs of the trade, and to establish at Yatung, Gyantse, and Gartok, and at each of the other trade marts that may hereafter be established, a Tibetan Agent who shall receive from the British Agent appointed to watch over British trade at the marts in question any letter which the latter may desire to send to the Tibetan or to the Chinese authorities. The Tibetan Agent shall also be responsible for the due delivery of such communications and for the transmission of replies.

VI.

As an indemnity to the British Government for the expense incurred in the despatch of armed troops to Lhasa, to exact reparation for breaches of treaty obligations, and for the insults offered to and attacks upon the British Commissioner and his following and escort, the Tibetan Government engages to pay a sum of pounds five hundred thousand, equivalent to rupees seventy-five lakhs, to the British Government.

The indemnity shall be payable at such places as the British Government may from time to time, after due notice, indicate, whether in Tibet or in the British districts of Darjeeling or Jalpaiguri, in seventy-five annual instalments of rupees one lakh each on the 1st January in each year, beginning from the 1st January 1906.

VII.

As security for the payment of the above-mentioned indemnity, and for the fulfilment of the provisions relative to trade marts specified in Articles II, III, IV and V, the British Government shall continue to occupy the Chumbi valley until the indemnity has been paid and until the trade marts have been effectively opened for three years, whichever date may be the later.

VIII.

The Tibetan Government agrees to raze all forts and fortifications and remove all armaments which might impede the course of free communication between the British frontier and the towns of Gyantse and Lhasa.

## IX.

The Government of Tibet engages that, without the previous consent of the British Government—

(*a*) no portion of Tibetan territory shall be ceded, sold, leased, mortgaged or otherwise given for occupation, to any foreign Power;

(*b*) no such Power shall be permitted to intervene in Tibetan affairs;

(*c*) no representatives or agents of any foreign Power shall be admitted to Tibet;

(*d*) no concessions for railways, roads, telegraphs, mining or other rights shall be granted to any foreign Power, or the subject of any foreign Power. In the event of consent to such concessions being granted, similar or equivalent concessions shall be granted to the British Government;

(*e*) no Tibetan revenues, whether in kind or in cash, shall be pledged or assigned to any foreign Power, or the subject of any foreign Power.

## X.

In witness whereof the negotiators have signed the same, and affixed thereunto the seals of their arms.

Done in quintuplicate at Lhasa, this 7th day of September in the year of Our Lord one thousand nine hundred and four, corresponding with the Tibetan date, the 27th day of the seventh month of the Wood Dragoon year.

# PART IV.

# BHUTAN.

# BHUTAN.

## CHAPTER VII.

*THE COUNTRY AND PEOPLE.*

BHUTAN is an exceedingly mountainous country, lying in the heart of the Eastern Himalayas. It is bounded on the north by the Tibetan province of U; on the north and north-west by the Chumbi valley, also a part of the same province; on the south and south-west by the Darjeeling district in Bengal; on the south by the districts of Jalpaiguri and Goalpara in Bengal, and by that of Kamrup in Assam; and on the east by the State of Tawang, subject to Tibet. It is about 190 miles in its extreme length from west to east, and some 90 from north to south. From a physical point of view it can be divided roughly into three belts or zones —

(1) that which is coterminous with Tibet;
(2) that which forms the centre of Bhutan;
(3) that nearest the plains.

Northern Zone.

The northernmost zone consists for the most part of high, bare, rugged mountains rising from an elevation of 12,000 to 24,000 feet. As the greater part of this zone lies above the limit of cultivation, it is sparsely inhabited. During the summer months, when the lower slopes are covered with beautiful grass, a limited number of grazier families migrate into the country to take advantage of the splendid grazing. Their herds, which are not very numerous, consist mostly of yaks. The general aspect of this country is that of a series of parallel and confined valleys running between precipitous spurs thrown out by the main range, generally in a southerly direction. These valleys form the beds of impetuous mountain torrents. The slopes are usually devoid of any kind of vegetation above an elevation of about 16,000 feet.

The central zone is about thirty miles in breadth, and consists of a series of wide and parallel valleys. The torrential career of the mountain streams flowing southward is here checked and their velocity is much diminished. The mountain slopes are not nearly so precipitous, and, owing to a moderate rainfall, are clothed with the vegetation of a temperate climate, such as firs, pines, junipers, oaks, etc. The valleys ascend from an elevation of approximately 3,500 to 10,000 feet, and often contain level bottom lands which sometimes attain a width of two or three miles, such as near Paro and Byagha. These valleys contain the bulk of the population of the country and are usually highly cultivated. The ranges which divide the main valleys are continuations of the spurs thrown out by the main Himalayan chain.

Middle Zone.

The zone nearest to the plains of India is about twenty-five miles wide, and consists of a series of short broken ranges, separated from one another by deep precipitous gorges. The country is covered with impenetrable tropical vegetation. The valleys are narrow, and the streams, now swollen into considerable rivers, flow at the bottom of deep precipitous gorges, and are subject to sudden and great rises in their level. The mountains vary in height from 4,000 to 16,000 feet, and in consequence catch the moisture-laden monsoon current as it rushes up from the Bay of Bengal across the plains. The valleys are narrow, unhealthy, and thinly populated. As a means of penetration into Bhutan, its rivers are useless for military purposes.

Southern Zone.

The climate is naturally different in these three zones. The southern portion of Bhutan has a very heavy rainfall, and owing to its proximity to the plains it is affected by the great heat which reigns there during the summer months. European life is almost unbearable there for any prolonged period. We have no regular records of the interior of the country, but from the character of the vegetation found there it may be judged to be temperate. From all accounts very little rain falls in the northern zone. Above 10,000 feet the land is covered with snow for four months in the year. A marked peculiarity about Bhutan in general is the prevalence of a violent wind which blows up all the main valleys every afternoon and evening.

The routes in Bhutan can scarcely be dignified with the name of roads. There is one route of great importance. It commences in the Chumbi valley and, crossing into Bhutan, traverses the whole of the country from west to east, from Ha-Tumphiong to Tashigong Jong and on to Tawang. Along it lie the principal places and centres of population, and from it numerous arteries strike off to the *Duars*, or passes. All these roads are only passable for animal transport in places.

The bridges are numerous and very well constructed; if strength, simplicity of design, and adaptation of local material be taken into consideration, it may be doubted whether we could evolve anything superior to the constructions met with in every part of Bhutan, across almost every stream.

The people.

Previous to the annexation of the Assam and Bengal *Duars* by the Government of India they were held and occupied by the Bhutanese, who made a practice of carrying off into slavery a certain portion of the inhabitants of those tracts. In this manner numbers of Bengali and Assamese men and women were introduced in course of time into the heart of Bhutan, and have naturally intermingled with, and been gradually absorbed by, the Bhutanese, thus introducing new strains of blood in the population of the country.

It is also quite probable that owing to the proximity of that group of aboriginal tribes, represented by the Daphlas, Abors, Miris, etc., who inhabited the track of country immediately to the east of Tawang, and to the north of the Brahmaputra, and who are considered, according to the latest theories, to belong to the Tibeto-Burman group of the human race, yet another cross has been implanted on the aboriginal Tephoo and Tibetan stock.

With such an admixture of races it can hardly be said that there is a distinctive type of Bhutanese. It takes more than the three centuries that have elapsed since the Tibetans first made their appearance in the country to evolve one. In fact, in any mixed crowd, such as amongst the retainers of some high official one sees men of fine stature, six feet and over, with well developed limbs, side by side with pigmies of five feet and under, whose physical development is just the reverse, each representing a distinct type. There is also a great diversity in their features. As a race they are ugly. Nevertheless they have broad, strong and open countenances, which are often very pleasant. Their disposition is cheerful and mild, often approaching stolidity, yet seldom running into moroseness.

No favourable opinion of their moral qualities was expressed by those who visited the country previous to 1905. Both Griffiths and Ashley Eden called them immoral, rapacious, untrustworthy, and drunken. But during Mr. White's Mission in 1905 none of these characteristics were evident. It may be that peace and quiet, and freedom from internecine wars for over twenty years, have wrought a wonderful change in the character and habits of the people. Certainly they are now different to what they were described to be in Pemberton's time or even in that of Ashley Eden, and are neither better nor worse morally than other Asiatics who profess the Buddhist faith.

Physically the Bhutanese, taken as a whole, are a fine robust people, who compare very favourably either with their neighbours of Tibet, Sikkim, or of the plains. They are active and capable of enduring hardships, are good walkers, and can cover on occasions immense distances in their own hills. They are, however, wanting in energy and initiative, given to bullying those weaker than themselves, and blustering. Those who live in the higher altitudes, where cold is intense in winter, are exceedingly dirty in their person and habits; but those who form the immediate *entourage* of the officials were found to be fairly clean and respectable in their outward appearance.

The population is unquestionably on the decrease, and the country rapidly relapsing into waste. For miles not a trace of an inhabitant can now be seen where there are unmistakable signs of villages having prospered, and of the land having once been cultivated. To a slight extent this can be attributed to the nomadic instinct, inherent in certain hill people who constantly shift their abodes and the sites of cultivation, but the Bhutanese are exceptional in this respect. They keep from generation to generation to the same field, and the people themselves declare that the population is dying out. They say that no children are now born. This constant decrease in the population may be principally attributed to four causes :—

(1) Bad Government and oppression by the governing class.
(2) Annexation of the *Duars* (passes), which furnished the bulk of the revenue, and whence numbers of slaves were drafted into the mountainous regions to cultivate the soil.
(3) Internecine wars in the past.
(4) Lamaism.

The last cause acts in two ways :—directly, by sucking the blood of the people, who have to work and till in order to feed a lot of idle monks ; and indirectly, by a certain portion of the male population becoming monks and taking vows of celibacy.

The population of Eastern Bhutan is roughly 200,000. There is no reason why Western Bhutan, which also possesses numerous wide and well populated valleys, should not possess nearly as many, and therefore an estimate of 300,000 to 400,000 as the total population would not be very much over the mark.

The dress of all classes consists of a long loose robe wrapped round the body and across the stomach. In the day time it is hitched up in front and secured in position by a belt round the waist, thus forming a sort of pouch all round the body. Among the upper classes this robe is usually made of *tussah* silk ; the lower classes wear cotton or blanketing. The pouch formed by looping up the robe is used as a pocket or receptacle where everything from a dagger to a *pan* box is kept.

Unlike the Tibetans, the Bhutanese crop their hair short.

Religion.

The Bhutanese nominally profess the Buddhist religion, which they brought from Tibet ; but in point of fact their religious exercises are confined to the propitiation of evil spirits and the mechanical recital of a few sacred sentences. The priesthood are a privileged class, whose numbers, avowed celibacy, and utter idleness, constitute a crying evil ; the best and most favoured sites are studded with their monasteries and dwellings, which are distinguishable by being whitewashed. The time of the priests is divided between the mummery of religious worship, the occasional celebration of festivals, eating, and sleeping. In addition to their religious duties the lamas are charged with the medical care of the people. The main feature of their medical treatment is, of course, exorcism.

The Dharma Raja is the supreme pontiff and spiritual head of the Bhutanese, as well as being theoretically their ruler. He is supposed to be a reincarnation of the head or spirit of the original *Guru* Rimpoche. When he dies an interregnum of three years takes place before the incarnation re-appears. During this period the Lam Thepoo, the head of the Lamas, becomes Regent, and carries out the duties of the Dharma Raja, who is also known by the titles of Lam Teekoo, Noya Namjee, and Lam Suddoon. Next to the Lam Thepoo is the Lam Kempoo; and then a number of abbots of the various monasteries.

Trade.

What trade there is, is carried on with India on one side and with Tibet on the other. It is quite insignificant, both in value and in volume. From all accounts it must at one time have been much greater, but a prolonged period of internal turmoil, which only terminated some twenty years ago, the oppression and ignorance of those in power, the scarcity of communications, and the bad condition of those in existence, have inevitably led to the present state. For many years there was a considerable trade to Rangpur, as the Indian Government kept up regular accommodation at that station for the Bhutan trader, but it has almost entirely ceased. There is no doubt that the country is considerably richer in natural products than it was at first believed to be. With a stable and wise government, and a settled state of affairs, commerce would certainly increase with leaps and bounds.

Bhutan is essentially an agricultural country, in that the bulk of its inhabitants live by tilling the soil. Unfortunately for the people the rapacity of the official has been a dead weight against any progress. The Bhutanese cultivator lays out his fields in a series of terraces, levelled from the side of the hill, and often supported by a strong revetment of stone, sometimes of considerable height. The spots most generally selected for cultivation are contained in a zone extending from 4,000 to 9,000 feet above the sea, and it is at this altitude that most of the population resides. Only sufficient land is kept under cultivation to fulfil the actual requirements of the people, with a little margin to pay the regular and authorized demands of the Government; for any balance that is over is immediately seized on some pretext or other by the petty officials.

Administration.

Bhutan is, in theory, an ecclesiastical state, ruled over by the Dharma Raja, who is supposed to be a reincarnation of Dupgein Sheptun, the first Dharma Raja. He is not only the spiritual but, in theory, also the secular, head of the state. One of the successors of Dupgein Sheptun, considering that temporal and spiritual powers were incompatible, confined himself entirely to the latter, and appointed a *Dewan* to wield the former. This *Dewan* by degrees became the Deb Raja, and is theoretically the temporal ruler of Bhutan. He is supposed to be assisted by a council called the *Lenchen*, composed of the following members :—

(1) Lam Zimpon, Chief Secretary to the Dharma Raja.
(2) Donna Zimpon, the *Dewan*.
(3) Thimbu Jongpen, the Governor of Tashichhu Jong.
(4) Punakha Jongpen, the Governor of Punakha.
(5) Angduphorang Jongpen, the Governor of Angduphorang.
(6) Deb Zimpon, the Chief Secretary to the Deb Raja.
(7) Zung Donnyer, Master of the Household.

In addition to the above there are three extraordinary members who attend the council when they happen to be present at the Durbar, and who are liable to be called on to attend in cases of emergency. These are the Tongsa, Paro, and Taka Penlops. Their collective title, according to Eden, is the *Chenlah*.

In summer the seat of the government is in Tashichhu Jong, and in winter at Punakha.

The Deb Raja is in theory elected by the council, and holds his office for three years. At one time he wielded a certain amount of power, but is now to all intents and purposes merely a puppet, the nominee of the most powerful Penlop or Jongpen for the time being. For the last fifty years or so the Penlops of Tongsa have had the most influence in the nomination of the Deb Raja ; in fact, Deb Nago, who was Penlop of Tongsa at the time of the Eden Mission, and responsible for its hostile reception, was Deb Raja on several occasions.

The nearest translation of the word *Penlop*[1] is probably governor, and that of *Jongpen* commander or general. The principal Penlops, such as those of Tongsa, Paro, and Taka, and the Jongpens are in theory nominated by the Deb Raja and his council. Eden describes how they arrived in his time at their positions in the following words :—

> In practice they fight their way to power. They begin life as common soldiers, and, by distinguishing themselves in treachery, fraud, and murder, gradually rise through the various grades till they reach the office of Zimpon to the Penlop. In that position they have the Penlop so thoroughly in their hands that they can always compel him to arrange that they shall succeed him. If a Penlop is hard pressed by his brother Penlop, he very commonly promises his Zimpon that if he will get him out of the trouble, he will within a certain number of years retire in his favour. If the Zimpon finds no other way of getting promotion, he either murders or deposes his master.

The Penlops and Jongpens pay a certain amount of revenue every year to the Durbar, but, according to Eden, rather from a superstitious dread of the consequences of starving the Lamas than from any sense of duty. The Penlops exercise authority of life and death, but it must not be inferred from this that there is anything like a judicial system in the country. If a murder or a serious robbery is committed in which any man is concerned whom it is expedient to get rid of, he is seized, all his property confiscated to the Penlop, and, his hands and feet being tied together, he is thrown into a deep river, generally from some bridge. If, on the other hand, it is not desired to get rid of him, he is confined until he surrenders all his property. There are no laws except the will of the Penlops and Jongpens, and there are no police. If an offence is committed, and is heard of by the district officer, the parties concerned are seized and kept at the fort until sufficient money is squeezed from them; and any amount of injustice can be procured by the offer of a bribe. There is no one to make inquiries or to give redress, and an insurrection is the only remedy for an unjust decision.

Most of the sub-divisions of the district are under Jongpens. A number of minor officials are attached to the court of each

[1] Penlop—the final *p* is hardly pronounced.

of the two great Penlops, and also to those of the principal Jongpens, such as of Punakha, Tashichhu Jong, and Angduphorang.

Pemberton summarized the system of government in the following words :—

> The form of government is in itself, if fairly administered, sufficient to produce far more favourable results to the people than are now perceptible; but as the removal of officers occupying the most responsible situations is so frequent, and they receive no fixed salary, every successor endeavours to amass as much property as possible during his tenure of an office, which he is aware is likely to be of short duration; and as the removal of the superior is generally attended by the dismissal of every subordinate under him at the same time, the incentive to peculating industry exists in every grade, and the unfortunate cultivator is the victim of a system which not only affords no protection to the weak against the injustice of the powerful, but systematically deprives industry of the rewards of its labour.

The existing state of affairs is hardly any better; although the country enjoys freedom from internal troubles, and frequent changes of its principal officials, the subordinates are still as rapacious as ever.

From the earliest times the little that is known of the history of Bhutan presents one long record of revolution and internecine struggles. Every British Mission which has penetrated into the country, with the exception of the last, conducted by Mr. White, has witnessed an outbreak of some kind or other. The probable causes that contribute to this almost chronic state of anarchy are, in the opinion of Major F. Rennick,—

(1) The central government is too weakly constituted. There is no special military force at its disposal to enforce its decrees. Such troops as exist belong to the Penlops and to the more important Jongpens, who, if they feel themselves strong enough, are able to defy the Deb Raja and his council. The Dharma Raja is merely a puppet, with very little actual authority.

(2) The great Penlops and Jongpens are practically endowed with autocratic powers in their own jurisdictions, and each has a considerable military following of some kind or another. The Deb Raja is, in theory, only appointed for three years. The nomination of his successor causes much rivalry, which has often broken out in the past into open hostilities.

(3) The shortest road to high office is often by treachery and murder. If a man is successful in disposing of his rival or his superior, and is able to maintain himself in the position acquired, the central government has not the power, even if it had the inclination, to oust him.

(4) Lastly, the minor Jongpens, or custodians of the numerous little jongs or forts dotted about all over the country, are often only the nominees or adherents of the Penlops or the major Jongpens. As a natural consequence, every change of the important or head officials is immediately followed by a change of all the minor officials subordinate to them.

There is no doubt that the Bhutanese are now beginning to see the folly of these recurring rebellions and are attempting some radical change in the form of government. Recently the Lam Thepoo, the Regent in the absence of the Dharma from the world, was appointed Deb Raja, and thus wields both secular and temporal power. The Tongsa Penlop, who commands the services of the largest body of fighting men in Bhutan, numbering about 4,000, has been appointed Prime Minister. Any measures receiving the imprimatur of his and the Deb Raja's assent are bound to be carried through without opposition or bloodshed, and if the Bhutanese could now devise some laws to regulate the succession to the Penlopship of Tongsa without bloodshed, Bhutan might conceivably enjoy a period of peace and prosperity.

Military Forces.

According to Sir Ugyen Wang Chuk, the present Tongsa Penlop, the fighting strength of the Bhutanese is as follows:—

| | |
|---|---|
| Tongsa Penlop .. .. .. .. | 4,000 |
| Paro Penlop .. .. .. .. | 1,500 |
| Thimbu Jongpen .. .. .. | 1,500 |
| Punakha Jongpen .. .. .. | 300 |
| Angduphorang Jongpen .. .. .. | 400 |
| The Deb Raja .. .. .. .. | 200 |
| Tagha (Taka) Penlop .. .. .. | 300 |
| Dukgye Jongpen .. .. .. | 100 |
| Ha Jongpen .. .. .. .. | 300 |

| | |
|---|---|
| Byagha (Biaka) Jongpen .. .. .. | 300 |
| Deb Zimpon .. .. .. .. | 100 |
| Paro Don-nyer .. .. .. .. | 200 |
| Paro Nyerchen .. .. .. .. | 150 |
| Zung Don-nyer .. .. .. | 100 |
| Others .. .. .. .. | 500 |
| Total .. | 9,950 |

It is impossible to state whether in peace time any kind of regular organization exists—probably not; but undoubtedly during war some attempt would be made to organize the numerous retainers into regular formed bodies under the most capable of the immediate personal attendants and orderlies of the various Jongpens and Penlops. It would appear that these personal attendants and orderlies are changed from time to time. A man serves for a stated period and then retires to his home and may be again employed or not, according to the whim of his Jongpen. The orderlies perform multifarious duties, from settling disputes in outlying districts to taking part in archery contests.

According to tradition each Penlop and Jongpen is supposed to conduct his retainers in person into the field. In an attack his place is at the head of his troops. Notwithstanding that our experience of Asiatics points to the contrary, instances are not wanting of Bhutanese high officials having led their men in person. Such was the case with the present Tongsa Penlop, who owes his ascendancy over Aloo Dorzi in 1885 to this fact.

Arms.

According to the experience of the last Bhutan war, 1864 and 1865, the arms of the Bhutanese consist of matchlocks, bows and arrows, slings, stones, and short single-edged swords without guard to the hilt; they also use catapults and indulge in various kinds of booby traps, and delight in the hidden dangers of *panjis*.[1] Their matchlocks are wretched, clumsy weapons, many of them being too heavy for one man to fire, and they consequently use them by

[1] A "*panji*" is a sort of "crow's foot" made of pointed bamboo, and hidden in the grass. They are very fine at the points and as sharp as knives; they are hardened by fire.

resting them on a wall, tying them to a tree, or putting them on a comrade's shoulder. The bullet is a bit of iron or lead, roughly beaten into a circular shape. These matchlocks, however, carry a great distance, an instance having occurred at Dewangiri, during the campaign of 1865, of a man being killed at 800 yards range. They are always effective up to 400 yards. The Bhutanese, however, cannot be called good shots, because the scarcity of ammunition is so great that they never practise. It would be very difficult to find a Bhutanese who has fired 100 shots in his life.[1] With their bows and arrows they make much better practice; the former are somewhat long and strong in the pull, and as their arrows are sharpened to a fine point, their penetration is sometimes very great, and would easily transfix a man. As usual, it has been asserted that the arrows are poisoned; but this was satisfactorily refuted during the operations in 1864, for though many men were wounded, none of the wounds ever showed symptoms of being affected by poison. Many of them are however barbed, and as the head of the arrow is always purposely placed on very loosely, if it penetrates beyond the barb it sticks in the wound, and can only be extracted with difficulty and after considerable incisions. It was the opinion of MacGregor that, all things considered, the bow and arrow was, in the hands of a Bhutanese, a more formidable weapon than the matchlock, for they practise a great deal more with the former, and though the latter does carry further, it is after all but seldom that a chance for a long shot can be got among these forest-clad mountains. The Bhutanese have no idea of using a sword; those which they carry are extremely cumbersome and awkward, and they scarcely ever use it except as a jungle knife. They are said to use the sling, and it is evident that this and the use of stones in defending a hill position is not altogether to be despised. In the last campaign several men were killed with stones.

Methods of fighting.

With regard to the Bhutanese methods of fighting they are said to display a certain skill in the erection of field works, but as these generally only provide against a frontal attack they are not, as a rule, hard to turn. In the war of 1865—the only time we have had a real opportunity

[1] Pemberton says their powder is of the most inferior description, very inferior to the worst manufactured by the natives of India.

of observing their fighting qualities—they rarely withstood a determined attack, while on the offensive they were very unenterprising. As regards their valour Sir C. MacGregor expressed himself as follows :—

> A favourable opinion cannot, I am afraid, be passed on the Bhutanese qualities as soldiers, for they are wanting in the first and most necessary quality—courage.

This last opinion, however, is undoubtedly biassed and misleading. MacGregor appears to have lost sight of the fact that the Bhutanese put to flight a force consisting of 10 British officers and 800 rank and file, with a loss of 2 guns, baggage, sick, and wounded; that in the final defence of Dewangiri 150 Bhutanese barricaded themselves in a blockhouse and fought to the bitter end. There is one quality, which redounds much to their credit as soldiers: they are a singularly humane people, not a single instance of mutilation of the dead, or ill-treatment of prisoners, having occurred throughout the whole of the operations.

Outline of History.

There is no reliable history and very little tradition regarding the origin of the Bhutan Government; what knowledge does exist is derived from old manuscripts in the Tibetan monasteries. Unfortunately the records kept by the Bhutanese themselves were destroyed at Tashichhu Jong and Punakha by fire and during the earthquake in 1897. According to Eden the Bhutanese have not possessed Bhutan for much more than two centuries; before which time it belonged to a tribe called Tephu by the Bhutanese. About the middle of the seventeenth century some Tibetan sepoys were sent from Kampa (Khams), a district of Tibet, by order of the Lhasa Government to look at the country. A fight ensued, and the Tephus gave way and retreated to the plains, with the exception of a few who remained in a menial capacity with the Bhutanese, and whose descendants are to be found still holding the lowest offices about the forts, their appearance clearly indicating their plains origin. The Kampa sepoys took such a fancy to the country that they refused to return, and formed a colony without organization or government. After a time they were visited by a travelling Lama, Sheptun La-pha, who having acquired great influence was eventually made king under the title of Dharma Raja. He was a good and wise ruler, kept the country in good order, was beneficent to his subjects and was supported entirely by voluntary contributions. Having occasion to travel, he appointed as his minister one Desi Amgea [1] who was the first Deb Raja.

There is no further trace of the history of Bhutan till about the year 1770, when a certain Deb Jeedah distinguished himself by his aggressive foreign policy. He was a man of great ambition and some ability. He rebuilt the palace at Tashichhu Jong, and invaded and took Sikkim, and held possession of it for six or seven years, during which time it was administered by a Bhutanese governor. The Sikkim Raja fled to Lhasa, and in course of time returned, when the Bhutanese retired ignominously to their own country on the approach of his messengers. It was in the time of this Deb Raja that the Bhutanese obtained possession of the large tract between the present Sikkim border and the Tegong pass, by the treacherous friendship of the Sikkim minister. It was also probably in the time of Deb Jeedah that in 1772 the Bhutanese set up a claim to Kuch Behar, and invaded that state. The retributive measures of the Company's troops were so little to their taste that they were constrained to invoke the aid of the Tibetan Government at Lhasa. In consequence of their mediation, the Bhutanese received lenient treatment, on condition of their restoring the captives and respecting the original boundaries. Since that time the Bhutanese have not transgressed their own frontiers except in 1883, when Tinle, Paro Penlop, attacked Phari, in Tibet, and seized the Jongpen.

The internal history consists of a succession of revolutions, completed or attempted. The last disturbance was in 1884 when quarrels broke out between the Tongsa Penlop (Ugyen Wang Chuk), and Aloo Dorzi, the Timbhu Jongpen, on account of the latter withholding the Tongsa's share of the British subsidy. The Tongsa gained the upper hand, and, not long afterwards, the whole power. Since then Ugyen Wang Chuk seems to have consolidated his position, and Bhutan has enjoyed a period of peace and freedom from internal broils.

1 "Desi Amgea" is really a title.

In the past the Bhutanese have more or less held aloof from foreign intercourse, and restricted their foreign relations to the countries immediately on their borders, *viz.*, Tibet, Nepal, Sikkim, and British India. In their relations, however, with Tibet, they have naturally come into contact with the Chinese. Three causes have contributed to this isolation :—

Foreign relations.

(1) The lofty mountain ranges of which Bhutan is composed, which, with their indifferent communications, have presented a barrier difficult of penetration.

(2) The suspicious nature of the Bhutanese themselves, who have in the past regarded every foreigner as a possible enemy to their independence.

(3) The violent antipathy of the ignorant *Gyelongs* or Buddhist monks.

Owing to the identity of religion, languages and origin, the political relations of Bhutan with Tibet are first in importance. In the dim past, when Bhutan was originally conquered or absorbed by Tibetans, the relations between the two countries must have been most intimate. In fact there is a tradition current in Bhutan that it was once ruled by Tibetan officers, resident in it, and that all the principal jongs or forts were originally constructed by Chinese or Tibetan architects for the accommodation of the provincial governors appointed from Tibet. But after holding the country for some time and finding it totally unprofitable, the officers were withdrawn, and the Bhutanese left to their own devices. The Bhutanese, however, agreed to pay an annual tribute and to recognize the continued supremacy of the Dalai Lama in spiritual matters. There is no doubt that these relations are still maintained, or were so until lately.

Relations with Tibet.

The relations between the Bhutanese and Tibetans have not always been of a friendly character. The earliest mention we have of the two countries being engaged in warfare was in the time of the first Shabdung, when Duk-gye Jong, at the head of the Par valley, was the scene of an encounter in which the former were victorious and succeeded in repelling an invasion by the latter. The existence of strong forts (mostly demolished by the earthquake of 1897), with large garrisons, near where the main routes enter the country from Tibet, is a proof that the Bhutanese at one time feared Tibetan aggression. In fact, as late as 1888 the Tibetans crossed the frontier and constructed a fort just below the Phew (Linsghi) La in Bhutanese territory. On the other hand, some kind of treaty or agreement exists between the two countries, whereby each undertakes to aid the other in war time. In 1773, when aggression in Kuch Behar had brought the Bhutanese into contact with the British, it was the Tashi Lama, then regent for the Dalai Lama, who successfully interceded for them, and in his letter to the Governor General, Warren Hastings, he characterized Bhutan as a dependency of Tibet.

The Bhutanese aided the Tibetans in their wars against the Nepalese. For their participation in these they were deprived by the latter of a considerable portion of the revenue the Dharma Raja used to receive from certain monastery lands in Nepal. It is said the Lhasa authorities promised them compensation by the cession of the tributary state of Meu Towang, a promise which has never been redeemed, and which now forms a source of irritation between the two countries.

A Tibetan contingent was undoubtedly present with the Bhutanese, and took part against us in the operations which culminated in the re-capture of Dewangiri on 3rd April 1865. Nevertheless, in 1883, Tinle, who was Penlop of Paro, attacked Phari in Tibet and seized the Tibetan officials there. This outrage led to the Mission of one of the Tibetan Shapes from Lhasa, and of a Chinese delegate, to Paro in July 1885 which resulted in the Bhutanese making complete restitution. On the other hand, some Bhutanese assisted the Tibetans against us at Gnathong in 1888.

Again in 1904 Tibetan envoys were sent to implore Bhutanese aid against us, but according to Sir Ugyen Wang Chuk, the latter answered to the effect " that if the Tibetans could not keep out the British, when they had only one gate to defend, how could the Bhutanese keep them out when they had twenty doors to keep closed ? "

Relations with China.

Through their connection with Tibet the Bhutanese came into contact indirectly with China. The Chinese authorities do not, however, appear to advance any claim to exercise any direct control in the government of the country.

Relations with Nepal.

From the existence of Bhutanese monasteries near Mount Everest, it would appear that, previous to the consolidation of Nepal into one kingdom by the Gurkhas, Bhutanese influence was considerable in the eastern portions of that country. Owing to the want of records it is impossible to say exactly what the relations were, but the two states appear to have come into open conflict when the Gurkha army invaded Sikkim in 1788. The Raja of that state, severely pressed by the enemy, supplicated assistance both from Tibet and Bhutan, and the combined forces of Sikkimese and Bhutanese appear to have compelled the Gurkhas to retire. The Bhutanese, however, soon withdrew, whereupon the Sikkimese submitted. The success of the Gurkhas caused serious alarm both at Lhasa and in Bhutan, and application was made to the Emperor of China for assistance. Before, however, a reply could be received, the Bhutanese sent an embassy to Khatmandu offering to purchase their safety by the sacrifice of that part of Bykantpur, in the plains of Bengal, which had been ceded to them by Warren Hastings; but the necessity of this concession was saved by the Chinese invasion of Nepal, whereby the pride of the Gurkhas was humbled and they were compelled to purchase an ignominious peace by an acknowledgment of vassalage.

The British invasion of Nepal indirectly affected the relations of that country with the Bhutanese. By 1815 the Nepalese had overrun Sikkim as far eastward as the Tista river. It was the object of the British Government to give every possible assistance to the Maharaja of Sikkim to expel the Gurkhas, and, on the conclusion of the Nepal war, the country between the Mechi and the Tista, which had been wrested from the Nepalese by us, was made over to him by the treaty of Titalia,[1] in 1817. The main object of this treaty was to shut out the Nepalese from carrying out any views of aggrandizement to the eastward. Thus the bold policy

[1] Aitchison LVIII.

of the Marquis of Hastings, had, by stiffening the petty state of Sikkim, placed a barrier which secured Bhutan from Nepalese aggression. It cut off the possibility of invasion by Gurkha troops except by a hostile movement through either British or British protected territory. To this arrangement alone Bhutan owes its existence as an independent state.

Relations with British.

The first intercourse of the British Government with Bhutan commenced with the expedition sent in 1773 for the relief of the Raja of Kuch Behar. The Bhutanese had invaded that state, and carried off the Raja and his brother, and had placed on the throne a Raja of their own, whereupon the Kuch Behar family solicited the aid of the Government of India. This was at once accorded, and a detachment of four companies of sepoys with two guns was despatched under Captain Jones, who drove the Bhutanese beyond the frontier, and so pressed them that they were compelled to invoke the aid of the Tibetan Government at Lhasa. The Tashi Lama, then Regent of Tibet, addressed the Government of India on their behalf. The application was favourably received, and a Treaty of Peace was concluded on the 25th April 1774, by which the Bhutanese agreed to pay to the British Government an annual tribute of five *Tangan* horses, to deliver up the Raja of Kuch Behar, and never to make any incursions into British territory, or molest the *ryots* in any way.[1]

Captain Jones' Expedition.

From that time, with the exception of two partially commercial Missions in 1774 and 1783,[2] there was little intercourse with Bhutan, until our occupation of Assam, which connected the British and Bhutan frontiers. With the annexation of Assam there commenced a continued series of aggressions by the Bhutanese on British territory, followed by reprisals on the part of the British Government, and by the British occupation of the *Duars*, which lie at the foot of the Bhutan hills.

In 1837 Captain Pemberton was sent on a Mission to the Deb and Dharma Rajas, but his deputation failed to secure any effectual or permanent settlement.

1 Aitchison LIV.

2 Those of Mr. Bogle and Captain Turner, who passed through on their way to Tibet.

In 1841, in consequence of renewed aggression and of the increasing disorganization of the country, the seven Assam *Duars*, comprising some 1,600 square miles in area, were annexed by the British Government, and it was agreed that a sum of Rs. 10,000 should be annually paid to the chiefs as compensation. No written agreement was made regarding this arrangement. These *Duars* are now under the control of the Lieutanant-Governor of Eastern Bengal and Assam.

These measures proved effectual as regards the country lying under this portion of the Bhutan hills. But along the section of the *Duars* which was formerly under Bengal, outrage followed upon outrage. At length in 1854 the Durbar sent a rude intimation that the compensation paid for the loss of the Assam *Duars* was insufficient and must be increased. The natural refusal of the Government of India to listen to this demand was followed by Bhutanese raids on Assam. Lord Dalhousie intimated to the Durbar that in future all property plundered by the Bhutanese would be deducted from the annual payment on account of the Assam *Duars*, and that further outrage would lead to the permanent annexation of the *Duars* on the Bengal side. These threats, however, produced no lasting effect; acts of kidnapping and plunder continued; and in 1859-60 the territory known as the Ambari Falakata, to the east of the Tista, which was held in form from Bhutan, was taken possession of, the terms under which it would be restored being fully explained to the Deb Raja.[1] As these outrages did not cease, and as the usurpation of frontier officials made it doubtful whether letters to the Bhutan Government were not intercepted, the Deb and Dharma Rajas were informed that a Mission would be sent to explain the demands of the British Government, the consequences of not acceding to them, and the terms of the treaty with the Raja of Sikkim, whom the Bhutan authorities had threatened to attack under the pretence that the Ambari Falakata rents had been withheld owing to the rupture between him and the British Government. After a year's delay caused by the evasive replies of the Bhutan Government, the Mission started in December 1863. The Envoy, the Honourable Ashley Eden, reached the capital, Punakha, on the 13th March 1864, where he found

[1] Aitchison LX.

the Deb and Dharma Rajas puppets in the hands of the Tongsa Penlop, the successful head of an insurrection which had lately taken place. By this man, who refused to treat, except on condition of the restoration of the Assam *Duars*, the Mission was subject to gross outrage and insult. With difficulty they obtained permission to return after the envoy had signed under compulsion an agreement that the British Government would readjust the whole boundary between the two countries, restore the Assam *Duars*, deliver up all runaway slaves and political offenders who had taken refuge in British territory, and consent to be punished by the Bhutan and Kuch Behar Governments acting together if they ever made encroachments on Bhutan.

British Envoy insulted.

The engagement, which had been extorted from the Envoy, was at once repudiated by the British Government; and, as a punishment for the treatment to which the Mission had been subjected, the Ambari Falakata was declared [1] to be permanently annexed to the British dominions; the payment of revenue to Bhutan from the Assam *Duars* was stopped for ever; and the Bhutan Government were informed that if the demands of the British Government were not complied with by the 1st September 1864, such further measures as might appear necessary would be adopted to enforce them. No steps having been taken, the Bengal *Duars* were permanently annexed to the British territory, and the districts were occupied in force by British troops.

Expedition, 1864.

Within a few months the Bhutan Government made overtures for peace and asked for a restoration of the *Duars*. They were informed that the *Duars* could not be restored; that if they were sincerely desirous of peace and would consent to the conditions laid down by the British Government, peace would be granted; but if they delayed and an advance to Punakha became necessary, much more stringent terms would be exacted. Preliminary negotiations were accordingly opened, and during their continuance hostilities were suspended. The principal conditions offered to the Bhutan Government were that they should surrender all British subjects, and all subjects of Kuchar Beh and Sikkim, detained in

[1] Aitchison LXI.

Bhutan against their will; that they should subscribe articles for the mutual extradition of criminals, the maintenance of free trade, and the arbitration by the British Government of all disputes between the Bhutan Government and the Chiefs of Kuch Behar and Sikkim; that they should cede to the British Government the whole of the *Duars*, together with certain hill posts protecting the passes into Bhutan; that they should deliver up two British guns which had been lost at Dewangiri, and return the agreement they had extorted from the British Envoy; and that, in consideration of the fulfilment of these terms, the British Government would pay the Bhutan Government, from the revenues of the *Duars*, an annual sum beginning with Rs. 25,000 and rising to Rs. 50,000. The Treaty extorted from the Envoy was given up and an apology was tendered for the insult offered to him; but as the guns which had been lost were in possession of the Tongsa Penlop, who had not signified his adherence to the terms, a separate agreement[1] was concluded, providing that no payment would be made to the Bhutan Government until the guns were actually restored. They were eventually surrendered on the 25th February 1866. The permanent arrangements effected were recorded in a Treaty concluded 11th November 1865; and by the Proclamation of the 4th July 1866 the *Duars* were declared to be annexed to the territories of Her Majesty the Queen. The Treaty is called by the Bhutanese the Ten Article Treaty of Rawa Pane or Pani.[2]

In accordance with the provisions of Article 5 of the Treaty of 1865, payment of the allowance to the Bhutan Government was temporarily withheld in 1868 in consequence of the Bhutanese having put a stop to intercourse between Bhutan and Buxa, and on account of their having disregarded the provisions of Article 4 by sending an officer of inferior rank to receive the annual payment.

In March 1880 a raid was committed by an official on a British village, Chunbati, near Buxa on the frontier, the object being the recovery of some persons escaped from slavery in Bhutan and settled in British territory. Six persons were carried off, and, ten of the raiders being satisfactorily identified, a demand was made for the restoration of the captives and the surrender of the raiders

[1] Aitchison LXII.
[2] Aitchison LXIII & LXIV.

in accordance with the Treaty. The Deb Raja delayed and made excuses. He was consequently told that the annual subsidy paid on condition of good behaviour would be withheld till he complied with our demands. While the matter was pending, two of the captives escaped and returned to Buxa, and eventually, on finding that the subsidy would not be otherwise paid, the remaining captives and eight out of the ten raiders were delivered at Buxa in July 1881, one raider having died and another having escaped on the road. The raiders were convicted, and the sentences passed were upheld by the High Court on appeal.

The Tibet Mission of 1903-04.

After 1881 the relations between the two Governments were not marked by any untoward event until the British Government deputed a Mission to Khamba Jong in 1903 to delimitate the frontier between Sikkim and Tibet. This caused some unrest among the Bhutanese, and vague rumours reached India of warlike preparations on their part, and of their intention of co-operating with the Tibetans in case of war. To clear up the situation and with a view to discussing the intentions of the Bhutanese, the Tongsa Penlop was invited by the Bengal Government to meet the Commissioner of the Rajshahi Division. As the invitation was not responded to, in order to bring pressure to bear on the Bhutanese, the payment of the annual subsidy was stopped, and to facilitate matters they were asked to communicate in future with Colonel Younghusband in the Chumbi valley. Eventually, owing to the ill-health of the Tongsa Penlop, the Thimbu Jongpen was deputed by the Bhutanese to confer with the British Commissioner. On arrival at Phari, about the middle of February 1904, he was able to convince Colonel Younghusband of the friendly and peaceful intentions of the Bhutanese, in consequence of which the withheld subsidy was paid.

Several high Bhutanese officials accompanied the British force to Gyantse and eventually to Lhasa. The Tongsa Penlop offered his services as mediator with the Tibetans but they were declined. He, however, accompanied the British Mission on to Lhasa and played an important part in the final negotiations between Colonel Younghusband and the Tibetans, materially assisting in bringing about the acceptance of the Treaty by the latter. To mark the appreciation of the British Government of the friendly attitude of the

Bhutanese, and of the efforts of the Tongsa Penlop to bring about a settlement, the King-Emperor was pleased to make the latter a Knight Commander of the Indian Empire. Mr. White was, in consequence, deputed to Punakha in March 1905 to present Sir Ugyen Wang Chuk with the insignia of the Order. Mr. White's Mission was accorded a most hospitable welcome, and has succeeded in establishing the most cordial relations with a race which at one time was most hostilely disposed towards the British Government.

---

# CHAPTER VIII.

## *MILITARY OPERATIONS.*

Operations in 1772.

THE first operations against the Bhutanese of which there is any account appear to have taken place in 1772. The Bhutanese had invaded Kuch Behar, and the ruling family of that principality solicited the aid of the East India Company. In consequence of this request a detachment of four companies of sepoys with two guns was despatched under Captain Jones for the purpose of driving back the invaders to their own frontier. This duty was so efficiently performed that the Bhutanese were not only driven beyond the frontier, but were followed into Bhutan by Captain Jones, who carried the three forts of Daling, Chichacotta, and Passakha (Buxa) and so pressed the Bhutanese that they were compelled to invoke the aid of the Tibetan Government.

Frontier affair in 1828.

The next occasion when British and Bhutanese arms clashed was in 1828, when, during the investigation of a case of aggression, the Jongpen of Doompa, who was in charge of the Buriguma *Duar*, attacked a frontier post, killing a native officer and some sepoys, and carrying off a number of men and women. The release of the captives and the surrender of the Jongpen was demanded, but the Bhutanese took no notice whatever of the representations. Finally the release of the captives was effected by a Jemadar and a party of Sebundies, who ascertained the place where they were confined, advanced upon it suddenly, and set the prisoners at liberty.

Operations in 1835.

In 1835, in consequence of numerous outrages committed on British subjects, a detachment of the Assam Light Infantry, under a native officer, was sent into Bijni to release some unfortunate captives. They gallantly stormed a stockade, rescued nine captives, and took the chief Bhutanese officer of the district prisoner.

# SKETCH MAP OF BHUTAN

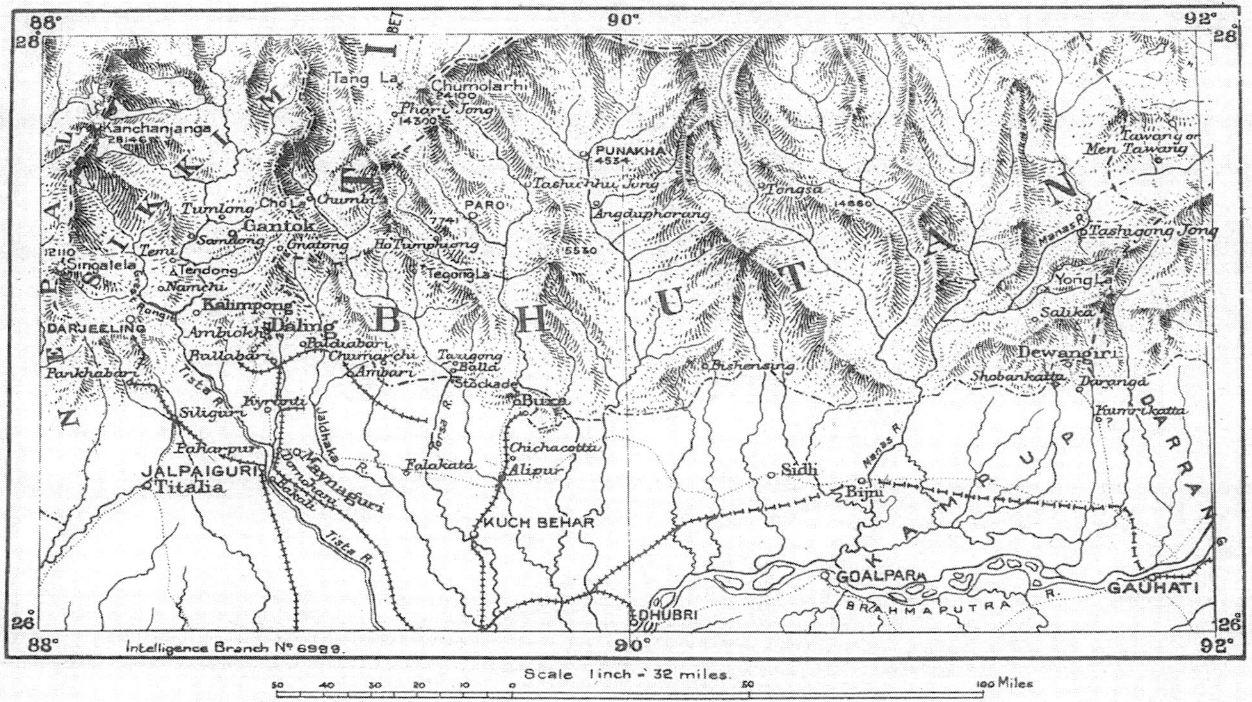


Scale 1 inch = 32 miles.

In February 1836, Captain Bogle advanced across the frontier with eighty Sebundies under the command of Lieutenants Matthews and Vetch to negotiate with the Dewangiri Raja about the surrender of some criminals. The Raja having come down from the hills, took up a strong position and built two stockades. He was ordered to retire, and on his failing to comply Captain Bogle proceeded to enforce his demand. The Bhutanese abandoned the first stockade on the approach of the British party and fell back upon the main body. Lieutenant Matthews at once charged them, and at the first volley the enemy broke and fled, leaving twenty-eight killed and about fifty wounded, with the loss of all their baggage.

Skirmish in 1836.

## Operations in 1864, 1865 and 1866.

In 1864, owing to the failure of Mr. Eden's Mission, and to the brutal treatment he had received, the Military authorities were informed on 24th August by the Government of India, that a force would be required to operate in Bhutan, and were further directed to decide upon a plan of operations, in the event of the Bhutanese Durbar failing to comply with the British demands for reparation. These demands were an ample apology for the insults offered to the Mission; the release of all captives; and the restoration of all property carried off by the Bhutanese during the last five years. The Bhutanese failed to comply with the conditions, and coercive measures were consequently decided upon. It was resolved not to make a regular invasion of the country, but to occupy, and, if expedient, annex, the Bengal *Duars*, a measure which would entail the advance of the British frontier for a varying depth of from twenty to thirty miles. To hold this line (of about 180 miles in length), and to prevent raids on the part of the Bhutanese, it was deemed essential to occupy all the dominant points, from Daling on the west to Dewangiri on the east.

The theatre of war may be described as an oblong, its four corners being represented by Daling, Dewangiri, Gauhati, and Jalpaiguri, the north and south sides each averaging about 200 miles in length and the east and west sides 50 miles each.

Sir Hugh Rose, the Commander-in-Chief, in a despatch dated 8th September 1864, stated that he did not approve of small detached columns, as the country was intersected by large rivers and swamps, which would render lateral communication difficult. Larger detached columns would, however, be suitable, as the Bhutanese were reported to be very unwarlike, and would probably not take due advantage of the isolation of the columns. He pointed out that the chief dangers to be guarded against were that the Bhutanese might induce the Tibetans and other tribes to join them, and that Sikkim, which, only two years before, had been subdued, might be a cause of trouble to us. He recommended that four columns should be formed, having for their objectives Dewangiri, Sidli, Buxa, and Daling.

Plan of operations.

3 Mountain Guns of the Eurasian Artillery Company.
1 squadron, 5th B. C.
43rd Assam Light Infantry.[1]
1 coy., Sibundy Sappers.
½ „ Bengal „
*In support at Gauhati.*
3 cos., 12th N. I.
Assam Local Artillery.

The Dewangiri column had assigned to it the country between the Manas river and Bor Nadi, which was known as the Kamrup District. The base was to be Gauhati, which was connected with Calcutta by water, as well as with many other stations on the Brahmaputra river. Their route was to Gumgaon (Daranga), a distance of fifty-eight miles, over a highly cultivated plain interspersed with bamboo jungle and large grassy uncultivated tracts. From here to Dewangiri was but ten miles, but the road chiefly lay up the stony bed of the Daranga river. The cavalry was to protect the Kamrup villages in the plain from raids by the Bhutanese. The remainder of the force were to threaten Tashigong, Eastern Tibet, and Punakha, by the main roads from Tongsa, thus diverting the Bhutanese from any general gathering for the protection of the Western *Duars,* and also protecting our right from any possible attack by the Akha and Michu tribes.

3 Mountain Guns of the Eurasian Artillery.
1 squadron, 5th Bengal Cavalry.
2 squadrons, 14th „ „
1 company, Sibundy Sappers.
½ „ Bengal S. and M.
Wing, 44th Assam Light Infantry.[2]
*In support at Goalpara.*
2 companies, 12th N. I.

The Sidli column, strength as per margin, was to operate in the Goalpara District, between the Sankos and Manas rivers, a country very favourable for the action of cavalry, but sparsely populated, and very little known.

[1] Now the 7th Gurkhas. [2] Now the 8th Gurkhas.

The Buxa Column was strongest of all, and was ordered to operate between the Jaldhaka and Sankos rivers, on the northern boundaries of Kuch Behar, through which state runs the main line of communications from India to Punakha, Tashichhu Jong (the summer capital of Bhutan), and Tibet. Its base was at the town of Kuch Behar, which was connected with Caragola Ghat on the Ganges by the Purnea and Dinajpur roads. Its object was to capture the strong fort of Chichacotta, making it into a depôt for sick and wounded and stores, and holding it with a wing of infantry, which would also keep up communication with Kuch Behar. The main body would then advance about twenty miles inland, and attack the strong and important fort of Passakha (Buxa).

½ Armstrong Mountain Train Battery.
Two 8-in. Mortars.
2nd Gurkhas.
11th Native Infantry.
1 squadron, 14th Bengal Cavalry.

The Daling Column was to operate between the Jaldhaka and Tista rivers, and had as its base Jalpaiguri, which was sixty miles distant from Kuch Behar, by a direct but bad road. There was a more circuitous and better road *viâ* Rangpur. It was in communication with Caragola Ghat *viâ* the Darjeeling road and also with Darjeeling by a good road through Pankhabari. The column was to occupy Daling and protect our flank from being turned *viâ* Sikkim and Tibet.

2 Armstrong Mountain Guns.
Two 8-inch Mortars.
1 coy., Sibundy Sappers.
Wing, 11th Native Infantry.
2 squadrons, 5th B. C.
*In support at Jalpaiguri.*
7 coys. H. M.'s 80th Foot.

The force was to be called "The Duar Field Force."

Arrangements for defending Darjeeling.

In the Commander-in-Chief's opinion, it was likely that the Bhutanese might attack Darjeeling as soon as the troops of the four columns had commenced their advance. He therefore recommended that the three companies of the 48th Foot at Darjeeling, which were about to be relieved by three companies of the 80th Foot, should be retained at that place for its defence together with the three relieving companies of the 80th. Two companies of the 17th Native Infantry were also afterwards ordered to Darjeeling. On 11th September 1864, the Government sanctioned the above measures.

Brigadier-General Mulcaster was appointed to command the Field Force, and Colonel Dunsford, with the rank of Brigadier-

General, to command the two left columns under General Mulcaster's directions. The Commander-in-Chief also recommended that two Civil officers should accompany the columns in order to gain a thorough acquaintance with the country. Accordingly Lieutenant-Colonel Haughton was appointed Chief Civil and Political Officer, Captain Lance and Mr. Donoghue were posted to the left columns, and Mr. Metcalf and Mr. Dribeng to the right.

A force of 726 infantry and 83 cavalry was organized as a police levy.

Proclamation.

On 22nd November 1864, a proclamation was issued, and distributed on the frontier. It shewed that outrages had been committed for years past by the Bhutanese on British subjects; that remonstrances on the part of the British had been disregarded, and the outrages continued; and that a pacific Mission had been insolently treated in open Durbar in 1863. For this insult the Governor General in Council had determined to withhold for ever the annual payments previously made to the Bhutan Government on account of the revenues of the Assam *Duars* and Ambari Falakata, which had long been in the occupation of the British. The Proclamation also shewed that, though the British wished to avoid an open rupture, no notice had been taken by the Bhutanese of a formal demand for the release of captives and the restitution of stolen property, and that the British were now compelled to annex the Bengal *Duars* of Bhutan, and the forts of Daling, Buxa, and Dewángiri. All inhabitants were warned to submit and to render assistance to the British, a guarantee of protection to life and property being given to those who did not resist our arms.

By the end of November 1864, all the preparations were completed, and the force ready to take the field. The original intention was that all the columns should advance simultaneously. This, however, was not carried out, the Dewangiri Column being delayed some days, and the Sidli Column some weeks, beyond the date that the columns on the left commenced operations.

The Daling Column.

On 28th November 1864, an advanced party of the Daling Column, consisting of a detachment of the Royal Artillery with two mortars, some detachments of Native Cavalry and Infantry under Major

Gough, V.C., and a few Bengal Native Police under Major Pughe, crossed the Tista river near Jalpaiguri, and marched to Bakali, near which was a small Bhutan outpost called Gopalgan, which was taken without resistance. On the 29th they advanced to Maynaguri, the stockade of which was found empty. The inhabitants readily submitted, and on the 30th Major Gough's party proceeded to Domohani, and found that the stockade there, a small one, had been deserted two nights before. By December 1st, a bridge-of-boats had been completed across the Tista river at Paharpur, six miles to the north of Jalpaiguri, and nearly opposite Domohani. General Dunsford's force marched across the river, and halted at Domohani for a day. On 3rd December the column advanced on Kyranti, and on the 4th reached the foot of the hills, encamping on the Chyle river, near the entrance of the pass leading to Daling. On the 5th the cavalry were sent back, and the remainder of the force marched up the ascent to Ambiokh, eleven miles distant, reaching it in four hours. This village was situated immediately below the fort of Daling. A message was then sent to the Jongpen, who replied that he would surrender the fort; but shortly after this the garrison were observed making hurried preparations for defence. Early on the morning of the 6th, the British force advanced, the guns and mortars shelling the fort from Ambiokh. A barricade was taken without difficulty, and from thence the attacking party advanced to the foot of the ascent, where they were exposed to volleys of stones and arrows and lost two men killed and several wounded, including two officers. Two $5\frac{1}{2}$-inch mortars were now brought up, and an unlucky explosion of a powder cask killed three officers and four men, whilst several others were wounded. An Armstrong gun was then ordered up from Ambiokh; after a few rounds a breach was effected, and the 18th Native Infantry took possession of the place, the Bhutanese evacuating it by the opposite side. Several buildings had been burnt, but though the place had been under a heavy fire for eight hours, only four bodies were found inside. Our casualties were three officers and seven men killed, and seven officers and fifty-six men wounded. On the 10th of December the fort of Dhumsong, which was about twenty miles from the Darjeeling frontier, surrendered without resistance, and was occupied by a detachment of fifty men of the 17th Native Infantry from Darjeeling. General Dunsford left a garrison at Daling, and, having completed his task in this part of the country now began to move his column down to the plains, for the purpose of proceeding along the foot of the hills to the Chumarchi pass, thirty miles to the east. On 22nd December the column reached Bullabari, twelve miles south of Daling. From here they turned eastward, and formed a camp at Tondu, midway between the Daling and Chumarchi passes. On December 29th a reconnoitring party of 150 men was sent on to examine the position of Chumarchi, and to occupy it if it was found undefended. On the party reaching a flat piece of ground about 600 yards below the crest of the hill, it was attacked by the Bhutanese, and before it could be withdrawn, twelve men were wounded. On December 31st General Dunsford came up with the main column, and made a reconnaissance of the position, and on 1st January 1865 opened the attack by shelling the fort. After a dozen rounds the position was rushed; the enemy immediately evacuated it, and flying over the hills, were intercepted by a party of 100 men under Captain Perkins. In the ensuing action the enemy lost thirteen killed, whilst our loss was two men killed and three wounded. One hundred men of the Bengal Police were left at Chumarchi, and the column returned on 2nd January 1865, to the camp at Tondu, whence General Dunsford proceeded eastwards with an escort of fifty men to inspect the posts at Balla and Buxa, which had been taken by the Buxa Column under Colonel Watson.

The Buxa Column.

This force had started from Kuch Behar simultaneously with the advance of the Left Column from Jalpaiguri. A reconnaissance had been sent forward from Kuch Behar on November 28th, through which it was ascertained that Chichacotta had been abandoned. The main column then advanced, and on the 7th December took possession of Buxa without opposition. From here they had returned to the plains and, marching westward, had occupied the Balla pass, thus completing the work assigned to them.

The operations of the two Right Columns now require to be noticed.

The Dewangiri Column.

On December 2nd the Dewangiri Column, commanded by Colonel Campbell, and accompanied by General Mulcaster, crossed the

Brahmaputra at Gauhati in a steamer and troop boat, and encamped on the north bank. On the 3rd it marched towards Kumrikatta, where it was proposed to establish a standing camp. On arrival at this place, on December 7th, fifty of the Bengal Police were sent on in advance, and on the 9th the column proceeded to the entrance to the Daranga pass. Early on the 10th it moved forward and entered the hills, marching up the bed of a torrent. About six miles up the pass the advanced guard was fired on from a stockade, and one man was wounded. It was ascertained that there were about fifty Bhutanese behind the stockade, which was open on both sides. As it was getting late and the baggage was still straggling in the rear, General Mulcaster now ordered the advanced guard to retire on the main body, and the whole force halted for the night. The column advanced the next morning (December 11th), but the stockade was deserted.

Just after starting General Mulcaster received a letter from Captain Macdonald, who had pushed on in advance with the Bengal Police, stating that he had captured Dewangiri. General Mulcaster accordingly pushed on with three companies to that place, where he found that the Raja and all his retinue had gone off early in the morning in the direction of Salika. The remainder of the column reached Dewangiri the next day, December 12th. Captain Macdonald only lost one man, and a few of the enemy were killed. On December 17th the column was broken up, six companies of the 43rd, and half No. 9 Company of Bengal Sappers and Miners, with two mountain howitzers and fifty 6-pounder rockets, being left as a garrison. The rest of the column[1] returned to Kumrikatta, where it was strengthened by a squadron of the 5th Bengal Cavalry. On the 26th it marched *viâ* Bijni to meet the Right Centre Column at Sidli, where a small garrison was left.

The day after General Mulcaster's arrival at Sidli, the 29th, the column marched for Bishensing, which was forty-two miles distant, over a very difficult and tedious route. Sometimes not more than three or four miles were made in a day, owing to the dense and tall jungle, through which paths had frequently to be cut.

[1] Strength: 2 companies of the 43rd Native Infantry and the Staff of the Eurasian Battery.

Bishensing was reached on 8th January, and a garrison of three companies of the 44th and fifty of the Bengal Police being left there, the remainder of the column returned to Sidli camp, except the two squadrons of the 5th Bengal Cavalry, which were sent to Jalpaiguri. There was no population in the country between Bishensing and Sidli, it being a vast teak and *sàl* forest.

The annexation being now thought to be complete, orders were given for the breaking up of the Duar Field Force early in February, the intention being to withdraw the regular troops and leave the occupation of the country to the Bengal Police. A few cavalry posts were, however, to be also established.

While everything thus seemed over, and the force was on the eve of breaking up, the Bhutanese were making preparations to attack the whole line of hill posts from Chumarchi to Dewangiri. Ample warnings of this were given at the latter place, but, for some unaccountable reason, no attention seems to have been paid to them. In addition to this, a letter was sent into camp by the Tongsa Penlop, but, as it was in Tibetan, no one at Dewangiri could read it, and it had to be sent on to Darjeeling, a distance of two hundred miles, for translation by Cheeboo Lama. It proved to be a caution to the Officer Commanding, to the effect that if he did not evacuate Dewangiri within a week of its receipt, compulsory measures would be adopted. At 5 A.M. on the morning of 30th January 1865, the Bhutanese managed to creep into the

Dewangiri attacked by the Bhutanese.

camp at Dewangiri, and commenced cutting the tent ropes. In a few moments the attack became general, but the troops succeeded in keeping the enemy in check until day dawned. As soon as their position could be made out, the 43rd Native Infantry and the Sappers charged them and drove them off, though they held their ground with considerable obstinacy for some time. The enemy also attacked the Jongpen's house, which was in charge of the Police, but here also they were driven off. This attack was conducted by the Tongsa Penlop in person. Our losses were Lieutenant Urquhart, R.E., and four men, killed, and Lieutenant Storey, 43rd Native Infantry, and thirty-one men wounded. The enemy's loss was estimated at about sixty men.

Though the Bhutanese had been repulsed they were by no means defeated, for they continued to hover about the camp and harass the garrison for the next three days. They succeeded also in cutting off the supply of water, which was conducted into the camp by a bamboo aqueduct from a spring 2,400 yards distant. On the 3rd February they threw up a stockade within 600 yards of the camp, and during the night succeeded in getting possession of the Daranga pass, thus cutting off communication by it with the plains. The troops were now getting short of water, as the only source of supply was a small and nearly dry spring.

It was deemed impracticable, with the force then available, to dislodge the enemy from the position they had taken up. Reinforcements had been asked for on January 30th, but General Mulcaster replied from Gauhati that he considered the force at Dewangiri ample for its defence. A supply of 25,000 rounds of ammunition was, however, despatched, escorted by thirty-six men of the 12th Native Infantry under Captain Cunliffe, but this party, finding the pass occupied, retired to Kumrikatta. On February 4th, as the camp was completely commanded by the stockade which had been thrown up, and water was running short, Colonel Campbell made up his mind to evacuate the place that night, and retreat to the plains by the Lebra pass. Two hundred and fifty men were told off to carry and escort the sick and wounded, 50 to carry the two 12-pr. howitzers, and 200 men to form the advance and rear-guards. At 1 A.M. on February 5th the place was silently evacuated, and the troops commenced their march, covered by the picquets, who kept up a fire to divert the enemy's attention. The main column unfortunately lost its way, and a panic ensued which caused the retreat to be one of extreme disorder, in the course of which some of the wounded were left behind, and the guns abandoned. The Eurasian gunners, about twenty in number, made an attempt to bring the guns on, but being unequal to doing so, threw them down a *khud* to prevent them falling into the enemy's hands. The Bhutanese however discovered them, and they were carried off to the seat of the Tongsa Penlop in the interior. The troops succeeded in getting clear of the hills, and reaching Kumrikatta camp. The total strength of the enemy, who, it was ascertained, were on this occasion assisted by Tibetans, amounted to about 1,500 fighting men.

British retreat from Dewangiri.

The attack on Dewangiri was but one of a series made about the same time along the whole line of hill posts to Chumarchi.

On January 25th Bishensing was attacked by several hundred men, but they were beaten off, our side only having two men wounded with arrows.

On February 3rd the Officer commanding Buxa proceeded on a reconnaissance with a small party, and captured a spy, who informed him that 1,200 men were on their way to attack Buxa and that they were expected to arrive there on the following day. Further on some Bhutanese were seen, but disappeared on being fired at. Previous to this 50 Gurkhas had arrived at Buxa, bringing the strength of the detachment up to 200 men. On the 6th Lieutenant Gregory with 150 Gurkhas proceeded to attack a stockade which the enemy had erected during the previous night. The party, however, found the enemy posted in an impregnable position in great force, and, being without guns, had to retire with a loss of two officers and thirteen men wounded. Most of the wounds were caused by bullets, which shewed that the Bhutanese were better armed than was anticipated. The enemy also shewed extraordinary rapidity and ingenuity in erecting stockades. On the 9th they were driven from one which they had commenced within five hundred yards of the post. By the 11th Buxa was reinforced and was then considered to be safe.

Buxa attacked by the Bhutanese.

Early on the morning of January 27th Tazigong, the stockaded post of the Balla pass, garrisoned by fifty men of the 11th Native Infantry, was attacked by the enemy. The Bhutanese advanced with great determination and endeavoured to force their way into the stockade, but the detachment behaved with great steadiness, and repulsed them, losing one sepoy killed and six wounded. As at Dewangiri, the Bhutanese, however, were not discouraged by their repulse, and proceeded to construct a stockade commanding the one occupied by the troops at Tazigong. On 4th February Colonel Watson, who had arrived with reinforcements, including two Armstrong guns and a mortar, determined to capture this stockade, but after engaging the enemy for a couple of hours, he found it impracticable to dislodge them, and retired with a loss of two officers

Balla attacked.

killed and several men of the 11th Native Infantry killed and wounded.

Chumarchi threatened.

At the same time Chumarchi was also threatened. The pass was held by 150 police, one of the sentries of which was attacked, and cut down at night. Here again the Bhutanese took up a strong position behind stone walls, whence the small force present was unequal to the task of expelling them. Reinforcements of 150 men of the 30th Punjabis and 2 mortars were therefore hurried to the front, the place was at once attacked, and the Bhutanese driven out. The position was, however, so situated as not to admit of being held by us, and the Bhutanese returned directly the troops retired to the plains. The police detachment, nevertheless, continued to hold their original position, and the Bhutanese confined themselves to their own entrenchments.

*Reinforcements.*
2 Batteries Artillery.
H. M.'s 55th Regiment.[1]
Hd.-Qrs., H. M.'s 80th Regiment.
19th Punjab Infantry.
29th " "
31st " "

On the news of these various attacks reaching Calcutta, immediate steps were taken for recovering our prestige, as well as for strengthening the posts remaining in our hands. Reinforcements were sent up, making an addition of 1,300 British Infantry, 2,000 Native Infantry, and 100 artillerymen, to the already large force in the *Duars*. Brigadier-General Tombs, C.B., V.C., relieved General Mulcaster in the command, whilst Brigadier-General Tytler, C.B., was nominated to succeed General Dunsford, who was compelled to resign on account of ill-health. The new troops were posted as follows:—One battery, the head-quarters, 55th Regiment, and the 29th Punjab Infantry were ordered to Gauhati to operate against Dewangiri; one battery, the left wing, 55th Regiment, the head-quarters, 80th Regiment, No. 2 Company, Bengal Sappers and Miners, and the 31st Punjab Infantry were detailed to join the brigade on the left, and the 19th Punjab Infantry the Centre Column at Kuch Behar. The whole of the 14th Bengal Cavalry was attached to the Right Column, whilst the 5th Bengal Cavalry was placed under the orders of Brigadier-General Tytler, C.B.,

[1] The left wing of this regiment was subsequently ordered to return to Dum Dum as its services were not required.

who commanded the Centre and Left Columns. Two 6-pounder guns and two 24-pounder howitzers with 300 rounds per gun were ordered to be sent for the defence of Daling Fort, 200 rounds per man were to be taken with the regiments, and 300 rounds per man were to be kept in the reserve depôt. The whole force was now divided into two independent commands, the Right Brigade under General Tombs, and the Left Brigade under General Tytler.

Meanwhile reports had been received that the Bhutanese, after their success at Dewangiri, were plundering the villages on the plains. Several small engagements now took place, but as the enemy always retired to the hills when hard pressed, little loss could be inflicted on them. Some prisoners were captured on the 15th February, and from their information it appeared that there were close on 2,000 of the enemy about Dewangiri, and that 1,000 men under the Tongsa Penlop had, seven days before, gone to Kuljarri, intending to make a raid into the Darrang District. The Right Centre Column had meanwhile been ordered to carefully and leisurely withdraw from Bishensing and Sidli and proceed to Gauhati, which they reached on March 10th. Three companies of the 44th Native Infantry were left at Datma for the protection of the Sidli and Bijni *Duars*. General Tombs, in a report to the Quartermaster-General, now recommended that the Bhutanese should be strictly blockaded in their hills, and that a force of 400 infantry and 50 mounted police should be established. He urged the necessity of having a patrol road made along the foot of the hills.

By the 29th March the following troops were collected at Camp Kumrikatta :—

No. 3 Battery, 25th Brigade, Royal Artillery.
Eurasian Battery of Artillery.
Head-quarters and right wing 55th Foot.
No. 7 Company, Bengal Sappers and Miners.
12th Regiment, Native Infantry.
29th „ „ „
43rd „ „ „
Head-quarters and 5 companies, 44th Native Infantry.
100 *Duar* Police.

Active preparations were made for the recapture of Dewangiri. In order to deceive the enemy as to his real intentions, General Tombs formed a small entrenched post about half a mile within the Shobankatta pass, and threw into it a garrison consisting of one company of Sappers and Miners, a detachment of the 12th Native Infantry, three companies of the 29th Native Infantry, two companies of the 43rd Native Infantry, and a troop of the 14th Bengal Cavalry, under the command of Major Langmore, whose orders were to patrol the pass daily, to make a feint at cutting a road, and to induce the enemy to believe that this route would be used for going to Dewangiri. These instructions were carried out, and the enemy were completely deceived; growing alarmed, they came in considerable force to this pass, and erected a number of stockades in it, while they left the other passes almost unguarded. On the night of the 31st March Major Langmore was recalled, but, in order to deceive the enemy, the tents were left standing, in charge of two companies of the 43rd Native Infantry. At 3 P.M. on April 1st a column, as per margin, advanced on Dewangiri under Colonel Richardson, with orders to proceed up the Daranga pass to a point distant about two miles from Dewangiri, where General Tombs would join them. The enemy was completely surprised and the column's advanced posts were established within half a mile of Dewangiri heights, without the loss of a single man. On the morning of 2nd April Colonel Hume with the main column joined General Tombs, and reported that the rear column with the reserve ammunition, supplies, etc., was also well up the pass.

Colonel Richardson's Column.

| | | |
|---|---|---|
| Eurasian Battery. | | |
| 1 company, | Bengal Sappers. | |
| 1 " | 55th Foot. | |
| 3 companies, | 12th Native Infantry. | |
| 3 " | 29th " | " |
| 1 company, | 43rd " | " |
| 4 companies, | 44th " | " |

On April 3rd General Tombs determined to attack. The pathway zigzagged up an exceedingly steep ascent with heavy jungle on both sides. At the spot where the advanced party was it became more level, and continued so for about 500 yards, until quite close to the plateau on which Dewangiri stands, the pathway leading to the Raja's house being cut on the side of the hill and commanded by numerous stockades and stone breastworks on the crest of it. At the east end of the plateau, facing and commanding the pathway, were, as far as could be seen, three stockades, the southerly, or nearest, being the strongest. The second stockade was lower down and smaller, and was in fact a blockhouse made of wood and stone, with a strong wooden roof. It was this face that General Tombs determined to attack, as it commanded the rest of the plateau. At 10-30 A.M. the troops were formed up for the attack, and fire was opened from two mortars and two howitzers, at a distance of about 620 yards, on the wooden blockhouse, a company of the 55th in skirmishing order being thrown forward to keep down the enemy's fire. At 11-30 A.M. the artillery had advanced to 400 yards; the company of the 55th had been reinforced by another, and the two were within 150 yards of the position, a party of them being in a stone enclosure, from which they had driven the enemy only 50 yards off. Behind this enclosure the storming party, consisting of three companies of the 29th, was formed up. The rest of the troops were held in reserve. The advance was now sounded, and the whole advanced party charged and stormed the position. Part of the enemy fled, but about 150 of them barricaded themselves in the large wooden blockhouse, determined to fight to the last. The only way in, except by the small door, which was strongly barricaded, and moreover was not discovered till all was over, was by climbing up the outer wall, which was fourteen feet high and between the top of which and the roof there was an opening of about two feet. Captain Trevor, Lieutenant Dundas, R.E., and Major Sankey gallantly led the way through this small opening, followed by three or four men of the 12th and 29th, and were almost immediately joined by other officers and soldiers. In half an hour the firing in the blockhouse ceased. About a hundred dead bodies were found piled up, and underneath them were about forty live men, who had crept there, feigning death. Many of these were fearfully wounded. Whilst this was going on parties were pushed on to the Raja's house and to the top of the Shobankatta pass, but the enemy fled so precipitately that but small loss was inflicted on them, as, owing to the intense heat and scarcity of water, the troops were too fatigued to pursue. The enemy lost at least 250 in killed and prisoners, independent of those who were wounded and got away. Amongst those killed was the Byagha Penlop, the chief next in importance to the Tongsa Penlop himself.

Dewangiri recaptured by the British.

The latter was present during the whole of the fight, but kept at a safe distance, and fled as soon as the shouts of the storming party were heard. General Tombs put down the enemy at 3,000 fighting men, while the British force numbered about 1,800 of all arms. Our loss was four officers and about thirty men wounded. The smallness of the casualty list being attributed to the deadly fire of the Enfield rifles, which the enemy had never felt before, and which seemed to completely paralyse them. Dewangiri being thus taken, it was decided to evacuate it, as the place was untenable during the rains. All the fortifications were accordingly destroyed, and the Raja's house levelled, and the force then returned to Kumrikatta, the last detachment arriving there on 6th April. Orders were given for the brigade to be broken up, but garrisons were left in important positions. On April 23rd General Tombs made over the command of the Right Brigade of the *Duar* Force to Colonel Richardson, C.B.

Operations by the Left Brigade.

It is now necessary to turn to the Left Brigade. General Tytler took over the command on 15th February 1865 from General Dunsford, and immediately commenced a thorough inspection of all the posts in his command, which included Darjeeling, Dhumsong, Daling, Ambari, Chumarchi, Buxa, and Pandu. The main difficulty in all these forts was an inadequate supply of water, which was very scarce in these hills. After his preparations were completed, General Tytler decided to attack the Balla pass, which the enemy were holding in force. On the night of March 13th Captains Perkins and deBourbell, R.E., and Lieutenant Cameron, R.A., explored a path leading to a ford at the west end of a spur on which the enemy's position stood. They advanced two and a half miles up the spur and returned without having been discovered. The Bhutanese evidently considered this flank of their positi on effectually guarded by the Torsa river. This reconnaissance determined the line of approach. On March 14th a turning column, consisting of two 6-pounder guns, two $5\frac{1}{2}$-inch mortars, forty sappers, and over seven hundred infantry, was assembled on the right bank of the Torsa, some three miles below the permanent camp, which was on the left bank. This column was concealed from the view of the enemy. It was ordered to leave its camp at dusk, and march to Santarabari, a village some three miles up the valley. To prevent the movement becoming known to the enemy, the village was seized by a small advanced party, and the inhabitants confined to their houses. The column quitted Santarabari at midnight, and reached the ford on the Torsa by daylight. By 6–30 A.M. the force had crossed, and commenced the ascent of the spur leading to the enemy's right. The remaining available troops, namely two 6-pounder guns, two 8-inch mortars, seventy cavalry, ten sappers and nearly 650 infantry, under Lieutenant-Colonel Watson, formed the column which was to attack the front of the enemy's position. Two small works which the enemy had constructed to cover the bridges over the Torsa, but which he had neglected to occupy at night, were successfully seized. By 5–30 A.M. the column had taken up its position, and an hour later both guns and mortars were in position. So silent were the enemy that it appeared possible that they had evacuated the works, and, to ascertain this, Captain MacGregor with a small party crept forward to reconnoitre. He was met by a brisk fire, and fell back, but not before he himself and four of his men were wounded. A slow fire from the mortars and guns was now kept up on the Tazigong

British attack on Balla stockade.

stockade, to keep the enemy's attention to his immediate front, which *ruse* succeeded admirably. At 11–15 A.M. a slight commotion, quickly followed by a dropping fire, was visible in the stockade situated on the saddle connecting the enemy's crowning work with the knoll which the turning column was directed to seize. Our troops were then seen rushing down the slope into and over the stockade on the saddle, and up towards the crowning stockade. General Tytler described it as the finest rush he had ever seen. On arriving at the fort, which was palisaded to a height of twenty feet, and backed by a 4-foot loopholed stone wall, the troops swarmed up the palisades sword in hand, and sabred the men who formed its garrison. The other positions were quickly abandoned by the enemy. A most successful turning movement had taken place, the troops engaged in it being upwards of sixteen hours on the march over very rough country. In spite of this the sepoys of the 18th and 19th, when they came in sight of the enemy's works, could not be restrained, and rushed the wall in a most gallant manner. The enemy's loss was forty-six, while three men were killed and one officer and nineteen men wounded on the side of the British. The force now moved towards Buxa, where the enemy had established themselves in stockades. On arrival at that place the *Soubah* commanding the position declared his willingness to retire if asked to do so. General Tytler at once sent a message to the effect that if he wished to prove his sincerity he must immediately evacuate his position and burn his stockades. At 2-30 P.M. the stockades were seen to be burning, and Buxa fell into our hands without a blow.

Chumarchi evacuated by the Bhutanese.

On the 24th General Tytler started for Chumarchi. The force detailed from Ambari for the reduction of this place was as follows :—two guns, one 8-inch and two $5\frac{1}{2}$-inch mortars, 150 police, and 420 infantry. A stockade some five miles from Chumarchi was evacuated by the enemy after a few rounds from the guns, and Chumarchi itself fell without opposition. This brought the operations for the season to an end. General Tombs now returned to Gwalior, whilst General Tytler was appointed to the command of all the troops in the eastern districts, and the troops in the *Duars*. The Government decided that the only two military posts to be maintained in the Bhutan hills were Daling and Buxa, whilst the plains were to be defended by the Police, supported by troops. At Buxa four guns, a Gurkha regiment, and three companies of the 30th Punjab Infantry were left, whilst at Daling were four guns, a wing of the 30th Punjab Infantry, and a company of Sebundy Sappers.

At the end of June 1865 the question was first mooted as to the possibility of an expedition into Bhutan itself, in the following cold weather, in the event of the Bhutanese not coming to terms with the British. The Government eventually determined that an advance should be made into the interior, and it was decided that the force should be divided into two columns, denominated the Right and Left Columns of the Bhutan Field Force. The Left Column was to advance from Buxa to Punakha, and the right from Dewangiri to Tongsa. Brigadier-General Tytler was nominated to the supreme command with the rank of Major-General, and Brigadier-General W. W. Turner, C.B., as second in command. The force was to be composed as follows :—two batteries of artillery, two companies of sappers, two wings of British Infantry, six regiments of Native Infantry, and 1,000 coolies formed into a corps of two wings, 500 men each. Active preparations were now carried on, but there was much sickness, chiefly scurvy, amongst the troops, which delayed an early advance on Punakha.

During the rains negotiations were carried on by the Deb and Dharma Rajas with a view to peace, but the Government did not on this account relax any of their preparations, as the Bhutanese were well known to be extremely treacherous. Orders were accordingly given on 4th October 1865 for an advance into Bhutan from Buxa and Dewangiri, and Colonel Richardson was ordered to seize the heights above the latter place. On 23rd October Dewangiri was re-occupied, not a Bhutanese being seen anywhere.

In messages received from Colonel Bruce on 4th, 6th, and 7th November the Government was informed that :—

(1) the terms of the treaty had been finally settled by the Bhutan Agents ;

(2) that they would execute a separate agreement to the effect that the Government of Bhutan was not entitled to any money payment, until the guns abandoned at Dewangiri had been restored ;

(3) that the treaty signed by Mr. Eden under compulsion would be given up, and a separate agreement would be signed ;

(4) that agents would be at once sent to the Tongsa Penlop for the guns. In the event of their not getting them, force would be used by the Bhutan Government to recover them ;

(5) the Bhutan agents, while withdrawing their claim to any money, appealed to the generosity of the Government, representing that a single payment would strengthen their hands in dealing with the Tongsa Penlop.

Hostilities were now suspended, but the Government ordered the road beyond Buxa to be proceeded with, and decided that the position already acquired should not be abandoned till it was known whether the Tongsa Penlop acquiesced in the treaty or not. On January 19th, 1866, General Tytler telegraphed to the Government that the Tongsa Penlop refused to give the guns up, and openly defied the British. In consequence of this, orders were given for an advance to be made against the Tongsa Penlop, and on February 4th Colonel Richardson proceeded from Dewangiri towards the Manas with three companies of the 26th Native Infantry, and one company of Sappers and Miners. On the 5th Colonel Richardson received a letter from the Lama Guru of Yongla saying that some of the Rajas meant to fight, and that they would probably destroy the bridge over the Manas at Salika. He at once determined to make a forced march to seize the bridge, and starting early on the 6th, had got to within a quarter of a mile of Salika when he was fired on by the Bhutanese. The position was rushed with a loss of two men wounded, and the column pushing on found the bridge untouched. Steps were now taken to store Salika with provisions, but on February 23rd the guns were delivered up to Colonel Richardson at the Manas bridge, and he returned to Dewangiri.

The force was now broken up, and peace restored.

---

### *BIBLIOGRAPHY.*

*Political Missions to Bootan.*—Doctor W. Giffiths, 1865.

*Report on the State of Bhutan and on the progress of the Political Missions to Bhutan,* 1863-64 and 1865.—The Hon'ble Ashley Eden.

*Report on Bhootan,* 1838, 1839.—Captain R. B. Pemberton.

*Political Mission to Bhootan,* 1865.

*An account of an Embassy to the Court of the Teshoo Lama in Tibet.*—Captain S. Turner, 1806.

# PART V.

# ASSAM.

# ASSAM.

## CHAPTER IX.

### *ASSAM PROPER.*

ASSAM Proper[1] includes the whole of the plains of the upper Brahmaputra valley. The only operations in this region in which British forces have been engaged were those of the First Burmese War in 1824, an account of which will be found in Volume V. Frequent allusion will, however, be found in these pages to the native kingdom of Assam, and it will be found convenient to understand something of the events which took place before the appearance of the British.

Ahom invasion.

The first event of certainty and importance was the invasion of the Shans in the thirteenth century. This people took the name of "Ahom,"[2] the Unequalled, and established a firm and settled government. But in the sleepy hollow of Assam they lost the qualities which had won them power and prestige, while, by adopting the language, customs, and religion of their Hindu subjects, they speedily sank into the position of a mere ruling caste. When their rule was weakened, rebellions broke out, and by the end of the eighteenth century the whole land was given over to confusion and misery.

Assam had been a part of the province of Bengal which was handed over to the English under the Moghul Emperor's *firman* of 12th August 1765. This deed had, however, never been acted upon as far as concerns Assam, and in 1819 the Governor General

[1] While generally alluded to as one country, Assam cannot be so considered historically, as it is made up of a number of different tribes and nations whose history must be separately considered. For this purpose the work has been divided into—

(1) Assam Proper.
(2) The Northern Hill Tribes—the Extra Bhutan Bhutias, Akas, Daphlas, Miris, and Abors.
(3) The North-Eastern Hill Tribes—the Mishmis, Kamtis, and Singphos.
(4) The Southern Hill Tribes—the Garos, Khasias, Jaintias, and Cacharis.
(5) The Nagas.
(6) Manipur.

[2] Assam is supposed to be the same word.

still spoke of this country as a foreign State. Nevertheless, in 1792 the Ahom Raja had appealed to the British for help; Lord Cornwallis admitted the obligation; and a detachment of sepoys under Captain Welsh, having entered Assam, speedily reduced the rebellious chiefs to order. It was then proposed that a brigade of British troops should be kept in the province at the Assamese expense, but before this project could be carried into effect Lord Cornwallis left India, and Captain Welsh was recalled by Sir John Shore, whose cautious policy was opposed to the enterprise. In consequence of this action, Assam was again given over to anarchy in 1794. Eventually the hands of the Government of India were forced by the intervention of the Burmese in the affairs of the country, which they had invaded and largely depopulated. Hostilities broke out with the Burmese in 1824, and they were in due course expelled from the valley, and also from the hill states of Jaintia, Cachar, and Manipur. The Government of India then assumed the suzerainty of Assam, leaving it at first under native administration; but in course of time, for one cause or another, various native rulers were superseded, and by 1842 the whole province was under British administration.

Captain Welsh's expedition.

First Burmese War.

The many years of misrule in Assam had reacted upon the surrounding hill tribes; they had become accustomed to regard the men of the plains as their lawful prey, and their continued depredations brought them into contact with the British Government. Accounts of the dealings of the latter with them will be found in the succeeding pages.

The Hill Tribes.

The British frontier has at no time coincided with that of the ancient Ahom kingdom. In many places it has not been judged worth while to assume control of the hill country which formerly belonged to the Ahoms, and the British administrative frontier includes less territory than the original treaty frontier. In other places, again, it has gone beyond it. Villages outside Assam administration have become enamoured of the security which British rule affords, and have applied to be taken into the province, and in this way the frontier has in places been stretched.

The limit of direct administration is known as the "Inner Line": a boundary maintained at the discretion of the Lieutenant-Governor, which British subjects of certain classes and external tribesmen are not allowed to cross without a pass. The inner line shown on the maps is not the British frontier: it is merely a line fixed by Government to guide the civil officers as to the extent of their jurisdiction.

The "Inner Line."

The favourable season for operations in Assam is between the 1st November, when the rains have ceased, and the 1st March, when the rivers begin to flood, and sudden storms render the navigation dangerous. The weather at this time of year is all that could be desired for campaigning, as it is neither so cold as to render a supply of warm clothing necessary, nor so warm as to incapacitate men from active exertion.

Season for operations.

---

*BIBLIOGRAPHY.*

*The North-East Frontier of Bengal.*—Mackenzie, 1884.

# CHAPTER X.

## *THE NORTHERN HILL TRIBES.*

FROM the eastern boundary of Independent Bhutan to the banks of the Sessiri, north of the Brahmaputra Valley, a series of tribes occupy the whole of the hill country between Assam and Tibet. These, with one exception, are akin to the Tibetans, and appear to be one people, though they are known to us under the different names of Bhutias, Daphlas, Miris, and Abors. The one exception mentioned above, are the Akas, who differ from their neighbours and have a language very similar to that of the Nagas. The country they inhabit is about 50 to 100 miles in depth, and 250 miles from west to east, but our knowledge of it is very slight. In many places, the inhabitants have difficulty in maintaining themselves in their mountainous and inhospitable regions: the neighbouring plains are a convenient outlet, and the plainsmen an easy prey.

In the days of a strong native rule in Assam, the hillmen appear to have been kept in good order, probably by drastic methods; and when the British Government took over that country, it found that its territory extended in many places to twenty or thirty miles into the hills. Previous, however, to the arrival of the British a period of weak rule had intervened, of which the hill tribes had made the most, and when we took up the reins of government these northern hillmen at first gave some little trouble.

Means of control over hill tribes.

The British hold over the hill tribes is a double one. The tribesmen desire access to the markets of the plains in order to trade; and many of them are in receipt of *posa*.[1] *Posa* is often inaccurately called blackmail: but enquiry will show that it was paid in the time of

[1] *Posa* originally meant a contribution for a common object—the blackmail subscribed in the plains to buy off marauding bands. The name is now applied to the subsidies paid to the hill tribes.

the Assamese kingdom to most of the hill tribes, and was not an uncertain exaction depending on the rapacity of the different hordes who might descend to levy it, but a definite revenue payment. As to the origin of it we are not concerned; suffice it to say that on arriving in Assam the British found it a recognized custom that the hillmen should have a share in the produce of the plains. At first they were allowed to descend and collect this revenue, but this was soon found to be inconvenient, and the *posa* rates were commuted by the British Government to annual payments conditional upon good behaviour. The power, vested in the local Governors, of cutting off access to the markets, and of stopping payment of *posa* is in most cases sufficient to keep hill tribes in order.

The term "Abor."

The term "Abor" as used in some of the older accounts of the tribes needs some explanation. It should be remembered that all the highland tribes north and east of Assam speak of those in the higher mountains as "Abors," that is to say, remote savages; and in many old maps and documents the reader is liable to be misled in consequence. We read of Daphla Abors, Miri Abors, Mishmi Abors and Naga Abors, and yet not one of these tribes call themselves by that name. To mark all the country north of Lakhimpur "Abor" conveys quite a false impression, and suggests the idea that these are a large and important race, instead of, as is really the case, a few weak tribes, scattered about in wretched little villages and quite incapable of defending themselves against a couple of hundred military police.

## The Extra Bhutan Bhutias.

The Extra Bhutan Bhutias are divided into three communities:—

1. The Sath Rajas,[1] of Kuriapara, or Monhpas, who call themselves subordinates of the Tawang Raja, a tributary of Tibet.
2. The Bhutias of the Bengia, a small and inoffensive tribe whose country is sixteen marches from our frontier. They also acknowledge their dependence on Tawang.

[1] Seven Rajas—a common title of the Bhutia Chiefs, not necessarily implying that they are actually seven in number.

3. The chiefs of Char Dwar, also known as the Sath Rajas, who occupy the valley land between the Daimara and Belsiri rivers, and acknowledge no external authority.

The only occasion when peace has been threatened by the Bhutias was in 1852, when one of the Sath Rajas of Kuriapara, known as the Geelong, took refuge in British territory, and was followed by a Tibetan Army who threatened to invade the plains unless he were immediately given up to them. Their ardour was cooled by the appearance on the frontier of 400 British light infantry and a couple of 6-pounders; and matters were satisfactorily arranged.

The Bhutias have given no trouble for many years.

## The Akas.

Between the Bhutias and the Daphlas dwell the Akas, who speak of themselves as Hrusso. As far as is known their western and eastern boundaries are the Dipota and Khari-Dikarai rivers. They are divided into two sections known to the Assamese as Hazarikhoas and Kapaschor,[1] which names so pleased the Hrusso that they have adopted them themselves. Both these tribes are believed to be limited in number; but to the north of them is an allied race known as the Mijis, about whom little is known.

Though small, this tribe has a great reputation for violence and audacity, and has more than once caused embarrassment to the Government of India. They themselves assert that they come from the plains, and belong to the original ruling stock, who were driven out by barbarian invaders from the east: they also claim noble origin, and certainly their bearing is in favour of this assertion. Their language is more nearly allied to that of the Nagas than any other, and they are lighter in colour than their neighbours. In person they are well made and strongly built, and have a very independent bearing.

The Hrusso country is, roughly speaking, the valley of the Bharoli river and its tributaries. This river valley is the only natural channel

[1] That is "Supported by, or eaters of a thousand" (hearths); and "cotton thief." The former named from their right, recognized by the Assam Government, to levy contributions from the *ryots* in the plains; the latter from the night attacks of the hillmen, who used to lie in the cotton fields waiting their opportunity. They levied contributions without the authority of the Assam Government.

of communication with the plains, but there is an easier and more roundabout route through the Bhutia country. The greater part of the tribe's territory is about 4,000 to 6,000 feet above sea level; it is in most places precipitous and densely wooded. A feature of it is the numerous plateaux and fertile valleys which it possesses and which enable the inhabitants to support themselves in bread-stuffs. They are the most successful and industrious of any of the northern hill tribes, and are quite independent of Assam for food supply.

The country.

The Hrusso are on fairly good terms with their neighbours, but hold little communication with any save the Mijis, with whom they are intimately connected. They have a few dealings with Tibet, and from Assam they obtain cloth, and iron for their weapons, which they manufacture themselves. These weapons are bows and arrows, the latter frequently poisoned,[1] and swords. Some writers speak of a light throwing spear, but none were noticed in 1883. They also possess a few muskets. Their positions are defended by *panjis*[2] and "booby traps."[3] The villages are unprotected and quite open, but skilfully built stockades[4] are placed in important positions, and would prove serious obstacles if in possession of men who had the heart to defend them stoutly. The tactics of the Hrusso consist rather in ambuscades, surprises and night attacks.[5] Small bodies of men will crouch quietly for hours in the jungle, hiding themselves with the aid of leaves and bushes which they plant in front of them, and wait for the arrival of a convoy, into which they will fire a volley of poisoned arrows; they then decamp down the hillside.

Arms and tactics.

1 The poison is aconite.

2 Bamboo stakes sharply pointed and hardened by fire, which are put into the ground where an enemy is likely to tread on them. They are likely to incapacitate an enemy not well shod.

3 A booby trap is a collection of rocks placed on a kind of scaffold of bamboos held in position by single canes which can be severed at a blow. It is usually placed so as to command a path ascending a hillside; as the path generally zigzags, the rocks, when liberated from the cage, strike it in several places before reaching the bottom.

4 They consist of double rows of bamboos fixed upright in the ground. The space between is filled with earth and stones to a height of four feet, and above that a *chevaux de frise* of pointed bamboos is fixed. These stockades are generally placed on a hill commanding a narrow approach, and so arranged that it is almost impossible to turn them.

5 During these they use a kind of primitive dark lantern to enable them to see their footing on the hillside. The torch is made of a piece of resinous pinewood, in front of which is held a piece of bamboo to which is fastened a leather flap. The torch is held close down to the feet with the leather flap in front of it.

The only way to cope effectually with this species of guerilla warfare is to adopt tactics similar to those of the enemy.

There is no settled government among the Akas, each village, and even each house, being independent. But from 1830 to 1870 a chief called Tagi Raja exercised almost absolute power over them, and was said to possess considerable influence among the Mijis as well, a little of which was doubtless inherited by his son Medhi. The Mijis treat the Hrusso as an inferior clan, their numbers being about 5,000 while those of the Hrusso are only one-fifth of the amount. [1]

Outline of History.

When the British first came in contact with the Akas they were under the influence of Tagi Raja. In 1829, however, this formidable freebooter was captured, and for four years was kept close in Gauhati jail. The Governor General's Agent then released him, expecting him to have learned better ways : whereupon Tagi recommenced his depredations. Amongst other enterprises, in 1835 he treacherously obtained entrance to the British outpost at Balipara, garrisoned by the 42nd Assam Light Infantry, and slaughtered sixteen persons, including the garrison of eight. For seven years after this, though vigorously hunted, he not only evaded capture, but continued to make raids on the plains. At length, weary of that life, he surrendered, and on taking an oath to keep the peace on the frontier, was pardoned and pensioned by the Assam Government.[2] This pension has since been continued to the Akas.

In 1875 the Kapaschor Akas threatened to give trouble, claiming an extensive tract of forest and other land on the Bharoli river, which was cut off by the demarcation of the boundary in 1874. Nothing further occurred at the time, and apparently the new boundary was quietly accepted ; but it is probable that this dispute, coupled with one or two very minor grievances, was the cause of the act of aggression which resulted in the expedition of 1883–84. This expedition did not result in the complete submission of the tribesmen, and was followed by a blockade of the frontier which was maintained until 1888, when the Aka Chiefs appeared before the Deputy Commissioner and tendered their submission.

[1] These numbers were estimated in 1884.
[2] *Vide* Aitchison LXX, CXIII, and CXIV.

Since that time the Akas have been well behaved and contented.

## The Aka Expedition of 1883.

The immediate causes which led to this expedition were as follows :—

In October 1883 Lakhidar, a Mauzadar, who had visited the village of Medhi, the son of Tagi Raja, the Kapaschor Aka Chief, in order to ask him to supply articles for the Calcutta Exhibition, and to send down a man and a woman to be modelled there, was forcibly detained ; and shortly afterwards Medhi's brother, Chandi, carried off a clerk and a forest ranger from Balipara. This second act showed that the first was not an isolated act due to enmity against the Mauzadar, as might otherwise have been supposed.[1] Demands for the return of the captives were ignored : on the contrary the Akas demanded grants of land and money payments as compensation for "insults."[2] The despatch of an expedition was consequently decided on by the Government of India, and its mobilization immediately proceeded.

There were two ascertained routes into the Aka country. One by Balukpung and up the Bharoli river ; and the other a short cut, leaving the Bharoli valley at Diju Mukh and rejoining it higher up. This latter route involved the crossing of the unfordable Bharoli river twice : but the Chief Commissioner was anxious to make a dash on Medhi's village and rescue the captives, and so the direct route was selected.

½ Kohat Mountain Battery.
½ company Sappers.
450 men, 43rd Assam Light Infantry.[3]
200 men, 12th Kelat-i-Ghilzai Regiment.[4]

*Flying Column.*

150 men, 43rd Assam Light Infantry.
50 men, Police.
454 coolies.

In December the force, composed of the marginally named troops, under the command of Brigadier-General S. Sale Hill, began to assemble at Diju Mukh, which had been selected as the base and was occupied on the 8th December by Lieutenant Cowley with a company of the 43rd Assam Light Infantry. Balarpung was held by 100 Frontier Police. The head-quarters of the force arrived on the 14th, and on the 17th a flying column

[1] The Mauzadar had assisted at the demarcation of the boundary in 1874.

[2] They were said to have understood that the British demanded the sale of a Raja and Rani for the Calcutta Museum.

[3] Now the 7th Gurkhas.

[4] Now the 12th Pioneers (The Kelat-i-Ghilzai Regiment).

under Major Beresford, left by the Diju route. The advance, though delayed by the roughness of the route and by cholera among the coolies, proceeded steadily. On the 19th the column reached the Bharoli river, the crossing of which was effected by the evening of the 22nd without opposition. The river there was about seventy to eighty yards wide and ten to fifteen feet deep, and had a current of four or five miles an hour. On the 23rd the Political Officer received intimation that the prisoners would be handed over immediately, and the column therefore remained halted. No Akas, however, appeared during the day to treat, and at midnight a sudden determined attack was made on the whole line of picquets. This attack lasted for an hour and a half: the night was very dark and foggy, and the jungle came right down to the bed of the dry *nala* in which the camp stood, circumstances very favourable to the methods of the Akas. The attack was eventually beaten off with a loss to the British of one killed and seven wounded. The Aka losses are unknown.

Akas attack flying column.

On the 24th and 25th a stockade was constructed covering the crossing of the Bharoli, and the column then advanced towards Medhi's village. The Tengapani was found to be held by the enemy in some strength, well posted behind stockades; and Major Beresford, not feeling himself strong enough to attempt the crossing, decided to wait for reinforcements.

The main body was now brought up, and on the arrival of the guns on the 6th January it was decided to attack the position, which consisted of one series of stockades about forty feet above the river, and a second 2,000 feet higher, crowning the steep ascent from the valley.

Attack on Tengapani position.

This position was attacked on the 8th January by sixty rifles, supported by a hundred more and by the guns. The enemy's fire died down after some twelve rounds had been fired by the guns, and on the attacking party advancing, the stockades were found to have been abandoned. This was fortunate, as the higher position was a formidable work situated at the head of a very steep rise to which there was but one approach.

The resistance of the Akas was now at an end. The British force remained in the neighbourhood until the 21st January 1884 in order to give the chiefs time to come in and make their submission, but this they would not do. They however sent in the captives, with the exception of the Mauzadar, who had died; and the expedition was then withdrawn.

## The Daphlas.

Between the Bharoli and the Sumderi river, north of Lakhimpur, dwell a collection of petty clans apparently quite independent of one another and incapable of combined action. To them we apply the term of Daphlas. Their own term for themselves is simply "Bangni" or "men." There is also a very similar tribe immediately north of the Daphla country, in the Kali valley, who are called Apa Tanangs or Ankas.

The country.

This range of country is about sixty miles from east to west, and forty from north to south, and consists of some very irregular hill systems running generally north-east and south-west, from 2,000 to 7,000 feet high. The northern boundary is the Lollupo range of some 10,000 feet. A great part of these hills has been cleared, particularly in the Ranga valley, where a good deal of land is under permanent rice cultivation. Elsewhere the original jungle is dense, and the hills steep. The Apa Tanang country is open and very fertile. Mr. McCabe, who visited it in 1897, describes it as a magnificent plateau, some ten miles in length, laid out in highly cultivated terraces. The Daphla country as a whole is much more accessible than the neighbouring hilly regions, and there are a number of passes into British territory.

The people.

The Daphlas are no doubt closely allied to their eastern neighbours, the Miris, although they differ from them in appearance. They are short, well-formed men of considerable development, with large, broad faces, square foreheads, high cheek bones, flat noses, and large mouths. They have a very independent bearing, but hold no communications with the Akas, whom they fear and dislike. What communication there is with Tibet we do not know, but the country is full of articles of Chinese manufacture.

The Daphlas are thought to number 10,000 and the Apa Tanangs 15,000, but these figures are mere estimations. Every village is independent, but in certain localities a number of villages acknowledge the leadership of a *gam* or chief.

Relations with British.

When the British first came into contact with the Daphlas they were giving a great deal of trouble to the plainsmen, and had a great reputation for warlike qualities. In fact they were thought to be the most formidable of our northern frontier tribes. This reputation has not survived closer acquaintance.

In 1835 the Daphlas made a determined raid into the plains and carried off some captives, who were rescued by a small British Military Expedition sent into the hills: after this outposts were kept along the frontier until 1852. At that time, however, the Daphlas seemed to settle down and they created no further disturbance until 1871, when some men of the Dikrang valley carried off a number of captives from British territory. A strong expedition was despatched into the hills, after a blockade had proved ineffective; the Daphlas showed no sign of fighting; and the captives were released and fines imposed.

The Daphlas have since that time been well behaved. But in 1896 a party of Apa Tanangs murdered one Poda Miri and his son within the Inner Line, and carried away three captives. An expedition of 300 men of the Lakhimpur military police was sent into their territory, and the release of the captives was effected without bloodshed. The Apa Tanangs have since been quiet.

## The Daphla Expedition of 1874.

The immediate cause which led to the Daphla expedition of 1874 was as follows:—In 1871 a severe outbreak of whooping-cough occurred among the Daphla inhabitants of Gohpore and Kullungpore Mauzas, and spread also among the hill tribes. The latter demanded compensation from the men of the plains among whom the disease had originated; and on its being refused, sent a party to the village of Antolla who killed five men and carried off thirty-five prisoners.

After some disagreement between the civil and military authorities as to the measures to be taken and the number of men required, a blockade was established on the frontier. On the seventy miles of frontier, mostly dense forest, sixteen posts were established, with the object of preventing the Daphlas from obtaining supplies of salt, iron, and opium from the plains; it was hoped in this way to bring them to reason and induce them to give up their captives. The whole force consisted of 600 men and was under the command of Major Arthur Cory of the 44th Assam Light Infantry. This officer was not given a free hand, the movement of troops and location of outposts being under the control of the Political Officer. Major Cory was also not allowed, as he wished, to attempt the rescue of the captives, although he on one occasion reconnoitred within a short distance of the villages where they were kept.[1]

This blockade produced no apparent effect on the Daphlas and in the autumn of 1874 an expedition was organized and sent to release the captives and punish the offenders. The force was ready to advance by the middle of November. The troops came by river to Dikrang Mukh and moved by road and river to Harmati.

| *Commanding*—Brigadier-General Stafford. | |
|---|---|
| British Officers .. .. | 30 |
| 42nd Assam Light Infantry[2] .. | 170 |
| 43rd " " "[2] .. | 110 |
| 44th Sylhet " "[2] .. | 212 |
| 16th " " " .. | 139 |
| Hazara Mountain Battery .. | 36 |
| Bengal Sappers .. .. | 64 |
| Total .. | 791 |
| Followers .. .. | 1,440 |

By the 8th December there were supplies at Harmati for 2,500 men for twenty-five days. The force then moved forward, only delayed by the necessity of making roads and getting up supplies, for the Daphlas made no sign of opposition. By the beginnng of January 1875 the force was in the middle of the offending villages and remained there several weeks. Small parties visited neighbouring villages and penetrated as far as Dilling, but no troops entered the Ranga valley. The captives were given up and fines imposed. It was found that the expedition had been organized on a ridiculously large scale. It must not be taken as a military example for it was projected and arranged by political authority and controlled by the civil power, and though its

1 Subsequent events fully proved the truth of Major Cory's assumptions; but a thoroughly false idea of the strength of the Daphla tribes had gone abroad: although the civil officer of Darrang estimated the whole fighting strength of the Daphla clans at 700 or 800 men, the quality of this force was thought so good, and the country so difficult, that 600 men had to remain inactive on the frontier while British subjects, who had been carried away captive, died of cruel treatment in Daphla villages in sight of British outposts.

2 Now the 6th, 7th, and 8th Gurkha Rifles.

results were politically satisfactory, the highest military authority did not view them with a like satisfaction, and the cost was very large.

## The Miris.

Between the eastern watershed of the Ranga valley and the Dirjemo river dwell the Miris, a quiet and inoffensive race who have never given any trouble to their neighbours. Their country consists of the lower catchment area of the Subansiri river, where they dwell on the low hills. The country of the Miris is more rugged than that of their western neighbours, the Daphlas, and the roads are of the most impassable description. To the north of them dwell the Lhokaptra, about whom nothing is known, while to the east dwell the Abors. The Miris carry on little cultivation and their villages are small and scattered. They have no settled government, no measures of defence, and no power of combination between different villages nor cohesion among clans. They are, in fact, poor, helpless, barbarous savages. They have just as much as they can do to keep themselves alive, and have little power either to help or to injure their neighbours. The British have always been on friendly terms with them, and the *posa* paid to them is perhaps more of a charity than that paid to any other frontier tribe.

It is believed that the Miris of the plains stand in some sort of servile relation to the Abors, to avoid which large numbers have settled in Assam as British subjects. Retaining their own language among themselves, they also speak Assamese, to which is due the name by which they are known in Assam, Miri or Mili, meaning go-between or interpreter, as they act as a channel of communication with the Abors of the hills.

## The Abors.

The people inhabiting the country about the Dihong river, whom we call collectively Abors, refer to themselves as Padam. They hold the territory between the range of hills forming the eastern boundary of the Miris, and the Sessiri river which divides them from the Mishmis. Of their northern boundary and neighbours we know nothing. The country varies much in character; that of the Pasi and Meyong communities on the right bank of the Dihong is comparatively low lying and consists of little broken ranges of hills; but near the left bank of the Dihong river, a wall of mountains rises up, and from there to the Dibong the region is very mountainous. The inhabitants of this country are called the Bor Abors. There are also several Abor communities living in the low country outside the mountains.

From the plains of the Brahmaputra valley the whole Abor territory rises up very steeply, like a wall, shutting out all view of the country beyond: and as the hillmen have always prevented strangers from visiting their territory, little or nothing is known about it. The 120 miles of the Dihong river immediately north of the British Frontier is still a goal for explorers. It can be seen from the south that the hills are partly cleared for cultivation in the neighbourhood of villages, but the higher ranges are uninhabited and wooded to their summits. Of roads there are none, and the only paths are difficult jungle tracks from village to village.

The people.

The Padam are the most formidable of the northern frontier tribes. They are physically superior to any of their neighbours, and have always been held in awe by them; and they were encouraged by the feeble conduct of the British troops in 1858 and 1859 to think the most of their own powers. Their numbers are considerable,[1] and they have a very definite tribal organization. All matters of importance are settled in open durbar by the vote of the majority. If the matter merely affects a particular village it is sufficient to discuss it in that village; but if of grave importance, it must be discussed by all the villages likely to be affected, and when once the majority have voted in favour of the motion the whole community will support individual members in their actions.

Arms and tactics.

The Abors are of Tibetan origin and have strongly marked Mongolian features. Their weapons are long straight *dahs* of Tibetan manufacture, spears, and arrows, the latter with iron heads, always poisoned.[2] It is on their *dahs* that they chiefly rely. Their villages are not defended in themselves, but have the principal

[1] It has been estimated that the Abors combined could turn out 10,000 to 15,000 fighting men.

[2] The aconite has little effect if the arrow is immediately removed and the wound washed.

approaches protected by stockades. These are very well placed, strongly built, and difficult to outflank. The defenders will stand well to them, and while troops in front are engaged, parties of Abors concealed in the jungle will deliver a flank attack, usually on the line of coolies. In the hills they rely greatly on "booby traps"[1] on which they expend great labour.

Outline of History.

When the British first entered Assam several officers visited outlying Abor settlements, but none were allowed to penetrate into the country. For some time no effort was made to obtain closer acquaintance with them, and they did not come into contact with the Government of Assam until 1848, when Major Vetch led a small expedition against the villagers of Doba, lying west of the Dihong, to demand the restoration of some Cachari gold-washers who had been carried off. The captives were restored; but the same night the British camp was attacked, and the assailants were only beaten off after hard fighting. To punish this treachery Major Vetch burnt a village.

Expedition, 1848.

In the succeeding years a number of small outrages on the part of the hillmen occurred, but the first serious affair took place in 1858, when the village of Sengajan, only six miles from Dibrugarh, was cut up by the Kebong village of the Meyongs, who wished to punish the inhabitants for denying them tribute. An expedition was sent against Kebong, but failed in its object, and only with difficulty got back to Dibrugarh. The next year a second expedition was sent up, but met with little better success. It burnt the village of Rumkang, and then returned without penetrating to Kebong. The Rumkang villagers came down in 1862 and in revenge raided a village near Dibrugarh, killing eleven villagers, and even crossed the Brahmaputra to the south bank. They had clearly not been impressed with any sense of the British power, and a force of 300 sepoys and two guns, under Lieutenant-Colonel Garston, was sent against them. This force went up the Dihong as far as the north of the Lallichapri and there commenced to parley.

Expedition, 1858.

Expedition, 1859.

Expedition 1862.

[1] See page 163.

with the raiders; the end of the conference being a treaty[1] by which the Abors were to receive a considerable yearly allowance, in consideration of their respecting the frontier.

This treatment displayed a remarkable degree of forbearance toward the Abors, to call it by no other name, and as soon as other chiefs got to hear of it they too come down to ask for *posa*, and were in turn given it.[2] It cannot, therefore, be wondered that the Padam began to believe that we were bribing them to remain good neighbours because we had felt ourselves too weak to compel them to remain so. The behaviour of the Padam was ever after sulky and insolent, and in 1880 it was understood that they intended to cross the Dihong in order to interfere with the trade road from the Mishmi country to Sadiya. To prevent such a movement British outposts were advanced to Nizamghat. Finally, in 1893, the Bor Abors broke into open hostility. An expedition was sent into the hills which occupied their principal villages after meeting with a good deal of resistance; and as they had not submitted when the column withdrew, a blockade was maintained against the whole country until 1900.

Expedition, 1894.

Since that time the Abors have been fairly well behaved.

## The Expedition of 1858.

The first operations calling for detailed notice occurred in 1858, in which year the Abors of Kebong and Rumkang raided an Assamese village near Tipi Tikri, within cannon shot of Dibrugarh, and killed about twelve villagers.

A punitive expedition composed of the marginally-named troops was decided on, and this little force arrived at Pasighat in March 1858. An immediate misunderstanding took place between Captain Bivar, Deputy Commissioner, Lakhimpur, and Captain Lowther, the Commanding Officer. The former wished to attack Kebong, some twenty miles up the river, while the latter did not wish to advance without clearing out the villages which would be left in his rear, and would most probably cut

*Naval Brigade.*
15 gunners.
*Local Artillery.*
15 privates.
Two 12-lb howitzers.
*Native Infantry.*
88 rifles.

[1] Aitchison, CXV. [2] Aitchison, CXV and CXVII.

him off. Eventually an advance was made by river to Pangighat, four miles from Kebong. A small party, under Captain Bivar, was left at this place, and the remainder of the force proceeded towards Kebong itself. On arrival within sight of the village the enemy opened fire and a bugler was killed, and, the path appearing difficult, Captain Lowther ordered a retreat to the river for the night, intending to attack the next day. In the night the Abors attacked the camp; the men became demoralized, and the force hurriedly retired to Passighat. It is worthy of note that the total British casualties only amounted to three sepoys and twenty-two coolies killed, wounded, and missing.

The whole of the neighbouring villages round, seeing the discomfiture of the expedition, now made common cause against it; and without attempting to inflict any punishment on the Abors, the force returned as fast as possible to the plains.

Three points call for remark in this expedition:—

1. There was an unfortunate amount of disagreement between the civil and military commanders. Both were subsequently blamed by the authorities. Captain Bivar had placed a great deal too much reliance on the information which he furnished to the military commandant and which proved faulty. Captain Lowther had failed to keep open any communication with his base during his advance.
2. The expedition advanced very near their objective—Kebong—without pressing home the attack; although the villagers were meantime preparing to surrender. The villagers afterwards asserted that they never intended to fight, but, an enterprising chief having, with his own hand, luckily hit the bugler with a sporting shot, and the British Commander having immediately ordered a retreat, they grew emboldened. One reason for the feebleness of the British Commander appears to have been want of faith in his guides.
3. The transport for the force was excessive. The force numbered only 140 all ranks, and the transport comprised 120 boats, 150 coolies, and 20 elephants.

### The Expedition of 1859.

Emboldened by the repulse of the expedition of 1858 the Abors of Kebong and other villages took up an advanced position, stockading themselves near Passi. It was evidently necessary to proceed against them, and an expedition was accordingly organized and followed the route of the former party as far as Passighat. They then turned west and attacked two stockaded positions, at Rumkang and Munku. The Abors clung obstinately to their stockades until driven from each at the point of the bayonet. The British losses were one killed and forty-four wounded, chiefly by poisoned arrows. After halting a few days the expedition abandoned the real objective, Kebong, and retreated leisurely to the plains.

*Commanding*—Colonel Hannay, 42nd Native Infantry.

| | Men. |
|---|---|
| Indian Naval Brigade | 60 |
| Native Artillery { 2 howitzers. 2 mortars. | |
| 42nd Assam Light Infantry .. .. | 300 |

This expedition was almost as unsatisfactory as the first; no real punishment had been inflicted on the offending community of Kebong, who were naturally again encouraged in their truculent attitude.

### The Expedition of 1894.

For thirty years the behaviour of the Abors had been growing more and more insolent and overbearing, when, in April 1893, the Bor Abors of Bomjur seized three Miri boats and carried them off. Miri envoys,[1] sent to demand an explanation, returned with this message :—

(1) That the Dumbuk and Silluk communities concurred in the seizing of the boats.

(2) That it had been done to punish the Miris for piloting *sahibs* up the Dibong.

(3) That as to any threat to stop their *posa*, they did not care if that were done or not ; but that if it were stopped, they would realize it themselves from British subjects as in former years.

Mr. Needham, Political Officer,[2] went up to Bomjur to discuss matters, but found the Abor envoys so insolent that he dismissed them, whereupon they openly defied him. Nine days afterwards three sepoys, on patrol close to the Bomjur blockhouse, were ambushed and killed; while in December a large party of Abors

[1] Miris have been commonly employed to carry messages to the Abors. See page 172.

[2] Further information on the expedition will be found in Mr. Needham's Report, 1894.—(*Official papers.*)

from Dumbuk set upon a patrol from Kherimpani, and succeeded in killing one sepoy.

An expedition was sanctioned on Christmas Day 1893, and the following instructions were issued to the Political Officer by the Chief Commissioner :—

Confine yourself to punishing villages you have good reason to believe concerned in the outrage, and any village that may offer resistance to the force, insisting on the restoration of murderers and sepoys' rifles. Do not go further inland than is absolutely necessary for the purpose, and give all villages clearly to understand that we have no desire to annex their territory, but only to punish offending villages. Old complaints about Miri slaves, and claims to territory which we have always disputed are on no account to be listened to.

The expeditionary force, strength as per margin, was ready at Sadiya on the 10th January 1894. At that time there were frontier posts at Bomjur, Kherimpani, Dikrang, Poba, Dibong, Sesseri, and Diphu, a total of 280 men; and the garrison at Sadiya, including the reserve for the expedition, was 308.

*Commanding*—Captain Maxwell.
*Political Officer*—Mr. J. W. Needham.[1]

| | | Rifles. |
|---|---|---|
| 44th Gurkha Rifles | .. | 100 |
| Lakhimpur Military Police | .. | 300 |
| Naga Hills Military Police | .. | 100 |
| Two 7-lb guns. | | |
| Followers .. | .. | 401 |

The first advance was made on Bomjur. The troops made a troublesome night march on the 14th January and attacked at dawn, but contrary to expectation no opposition was met with. A part of the village was destroyed and the remainder enclosed in a ring stockade. From the first the information given by the Miris proved quite unreliable.

A party of ten men was left at Bomjur and the force moved towards Dumbuk on the 20th. The enemy were found in strength holding a stockade about a mile distant from Dumbuk village, surrounded by dense jungle which impeded any turning movement. An attempt by the advanced guard to rush the stockade failed, and after some rounds of common shell had been fired with no visible effect, a general assault was made. The Abors fought well, standing to their defences and keeping up a discharge of stones and arrows,

Action at Dumbuk.

[1] Mr. Needham was in charge of all the direction and management of the expedition, except military details. He had been Political Officer at Sadiya for 11 years.

while the attackers were hacking at the *chevaux de frise* of *panjis* which prevented their reaching the stockade. The British lost three killed and twenty-seven wounded. By the time the work was carried it was too late to advance on the village and the party bivouacked on the position. Next morning Dumbuk was found deserted.

On the 25th a move was made to Mimasipu and Silluk. This advance was again opposed by the Abors, who defended a stockade on the road with some determination, and made a flank attack on the baggage. They did not, however, delay the advance long, and Silluk was entered that evening.

The three villages of Dumbuk, Mimasipu, and Silluk, the original objectives of the expedition, were destroyed. But it was now learnt that the village of Damroh had also taken part in the fighting, and an advance against it was consequently decided on. The force was ample for the purpose, but a difficulty was foreseen in the transport there being a great scarcity of coolies. Twenty days' rations were collected at Bordak, which was selected as the base, and which was reckoned to be four days' march from Damroh. The sick were sent back to Bomjur.

Mr. Needham, after consulting with some of the local *gams*, said that it was unnecessary to have a guard in charge of the camp at Bordak,[1] but, in order to cut down the column as far as possible, the spare men were left there. The force left Bordak on the 22nd February with four days' rations,[2] and reached Dukku without mishap on the 23rd. On the 24th a halt was made while provisions were brought in from the base by the Abor coolies. Next day the advance was continued, but, on account of the difficulty of the road, only six miles were covered, and, after the force had halted, a party reconnoitring a mile up the gorge was fired upon by the enemy. On the 26th the column only succeeded in moving two miles to Yamné, most of the day being spent in trying different roads; and the difficulties of transport were added

Advance on Damroh.

*Camp at Bordak.*
17 fighting men.
44 followers.

*Column.*
922 all ranks (including 400 rifles).

[1] Captain Maxwell concurred in this arrangement: but it must be remembered that all details as to the direction and management of the expedition had been placed in Mr. Needham's hands.

[2] More than this could not be taken owing to lack of transport.

to by a number of Abor porters absconding, leaving their loads in the last camp.

The British were now in a difficult position, as they had only two days' rations, including the loads left in the last camp, which had probably been destroyed by the enemy. It was decided to try to reach Damroh the next day with a flying column, which should burn the village and return the same day. This enterprise failed. The march was greatly delayed by the necessity for turning the Abors out of a great stone shoot they had arranged high up a hillside, and the column turned back at two o'clock without having reached their objective. A conciliatory message from the enemy arrived that day, and on the 28th the force halted to see if the Damroh *gams* would come in. Nothing was seen of them, however, and the next day, no rations having arrived from Bordak, the force was compelled to turn back.

Bordak was reached without difficulty, the villages of Silli and Dukku where the Abors endeavoured to oppose the retreat, being burnt on the way. Arrived there, the reason for the failure of supplies from the base was apparent. Bordak camp had been completely gutted. It afterwards transpired that the enemy had come into the camp in the guise of carriers, and that, while the loads were being distributed to them, they suddenly set upon the small garrison, out of which only one man succeeded in making his escape. It should be remembered that the men left behind at Bordak to form its garrison were all weakly, and were commanded by a native officer who had been too sick to accompany the column; furthermore they were expecting Abor coolies at the camp, to carry rations to the main force, and so were taken off their guard.

Mr. Needham wished to return immediately to the plains, but Captain Maxwell prevailed on him to stay to punish the villages of Padu and Membu, who must have been concerned in the destruction of the camp. Little difficulty was experienced; the enemy had a strong position covering Membu, and prepared to defend it, but their attention was held by the fire of guns in front, while the main body made a detour and disorganized the defence by appearing in rear. The two villages were destroyed, and the force then withdrew without further incident, reaching Sadiya on the 14th March.

The objects of the expedition had been fairly accomplished. The Abors have ten villages only, *viz.*, Bomjur, Dumbuk, Silluk, Mimasipu, Membu, Padea, Kumku, Sillu, Dukku, and Damroh. The primary object was to punish the first three for the murder of our sepoys. This was completely executed, all three villages being burned,[1] and quantities of crops being destroyed. Subsequently all the other villages were burnt with the exception of Dâmroh.

The British losses were—killed forty-nine; wounded, forty-five.[2]

1 A serious matter for the Abors, who employ in the building of their houses heavy planks, which must take a large amount of labour to make.

2 These figures include followers.

# CHAPTER XI.

*THE NORTH-EASTERN HILL TRIBES.*

## The Mishmis.

THE north-eastern corner of Assam is enclosed by a tract of mountainous country, of an extraordinarily precipitous and rugged nature, formed by the junction of the Himalayan range with the mountains of Upper Burma—the Daphabum termination of the Patkoi range. The rivers which unite to form the Brahmaputra break through these mountains by deep and precipitous gorges. The country is inhabited by four tribes of a common origin and language, known to us as the Mishmis. The boundaries of their territory are not accurately known, but west of it is the Abor country; northward is a snowy range cutting off the Tibetan district of Pomed; while to the east and south-east lies the Tibetan province of Zyul, which includes what is known as the Lama valley. Except on the Assam frontier the boundaries are quite undefined.

The whole of the country from the Sessiri river to the Daphabum is extremely precipitous; so much so that cultivation is very laborious and the inhabitants have some difficulty in maintaining themselves in food supplies. The mountains, which range up to 15,000 feet in height, and are divided by deep gorges, are covered with dense jungle; and a belt of forest, some twenty to thirty miles wide, extends into the Brahmaputra valley. There are no good communications, but only ill-defined paths up and down the mountain sides, which are in many places very dangerous to traverse. As to the climate we have no precise information, but it is probably similar to that of the other hill districts in Assam, which have a heavy rainfall from July to October, during which time the jungles are extremely malarious. Heavy snow falls on the hills in the winter.

The people.

The four Mishmi tribes inhabiting this region, and grouped by us under one heading, because of their common race and language, are the Midu, the Mithun, the Digarus, and the Mejus. Of these the Midu, called by the Assamese Chulikatta (or crop-haired, from their custom of wearing a fringe) inhabit the country north of Sadiya, from the Sessiri river[1] on the west to the Digaru river on the east; the Mithun, called by the Assamese Bebejiya (or outcast), inhabit the country north and east of the Chulikattas, about the valleys of the Ithun and Ithi rivers; the Tains, or Digarus, lie between the Digaru river and Brahma Kund; and the Mejus are found south-east of the Digarus, as far as the Daphabum.

These four tribes are in no way united, and exhibit some different characteristics. On the whole they are a weak race. They have in the past not only been subject to Assam, but have been subdued by such an insignificant people as the Hkamtis. The Chulikattas are the most numerous and the boldest tribe, while the Bebejiyas, occupying more remote country, have usually been thought to be the least civilized and the originators of outrages on the plains. The Digarus have always been friendly to the Sadiya Government. They are keen traders, and so highly appreciate the advantages of access to the markets in the plains that they have never given any trouble.

The Mishmis are a short, sturdy race, of fair complexion for Asiatics, and well knit figures, and are as active as monkeys. As a rule their features are of a softened Mongolian type, but are sometimes regular and almost Aryan. They all wear a kilt and short jacket, except the Digarus, who favour a kind of armless shirt. They carry a *dah*, a quiver of poisoned arrows,[2] bow, shield, and spear.

The chief evidence of prosperity among the Mishmis consists in the possession of hill-oxen (*mithun*) and numerous wives. Their sources of wealth are aconite, the valuable medicinal plant Mishmi *tita*, and the pods of musk deer.

Their numbers are unknown. Mr. Needham in 1899 described them all as "fearful cowards who would never dare attack a stockade by day or night." Certainly in 1899 the Bebejiyas did nothing to oppose the British advance, but that tribe always maintain that they are allies of the British *raj*. They are under the disadvantage

1 The Sessiri river is roughly the boundary between the Mishmis and the Abors: but the latter have villages beyond this line. The furthest east is Bomjur on the Dibong.

2 Their poison is aconite which grows in quantities in the hills.

of a complete want of organization, each village and even each house looking to its own interests.

The Chulikattas are the most formidable of the Mishmis. They are greatly detested by their neighbours, the Abors, and also by the Digaru Mishmis; and they are especially dreaded by the Sadiya population, in consequence of their prowling expeditions to kidnap women and children. They are full of deceit, and used to come down in innocent-looking parties of men and women to the plains, apparently groaning under the weight of merchandise imported for barter; they would proceed thus until they found an unprotected village; then, throwing aside their fictitious loads, they pounced upon the women and children and carried them off to the hills. They used to attack the other Mishmi tribes in this way, as well as Assamiese, but not the Abors, who were always on the alert.

Attitude towards the Government of India.

The majority of the Mishmis acknowledge their dependence on the Government of India, but the Mejus consider themselves also to a certain extent the allies of Tibet. This feeling dates from 1836, when the Tibetans gave them some help against the Digarus. Before the British took possession of Assam the Mishmis paid tribute to the Sadiya Khawa Gohains. They also appeared to have obeyed the orders of the Hkamtis and Singphos.[1]

Outline of History.

The internal history of the Mishmis consists entirely of inter-tribal wars; their external history of periodic raids into the plains, varied by an occasional blockade enforced by the British, or a military expedition sent against them in retaliation.

Various explorers have tried to penetrate the hills, but the difficulty in their way is that each village chief expects presents for a safe conduct. For this reason a traveller, to go far, must carry a great deal of money, in which case he will very probably be robbed.

The general object of explorers has been to visit the fertile Lama valley in Tibet. Many of them have been well received,

[1] As late as 1835 the Singpho Duffa Gam received assistance from the Mishmis in erecting his stockades.

but with two exceptions no one has reached that place.[1] The first was M. Krick, the French Missionary. He was not allowed to visit the capital, Roemah, but had a good view of the valley itself. This was in 1851. The same traveller, in company with M. Bourry, again entered the valley in 1854, on which occasion he and his companion were murdered by a Meju Chief, by name Kaisha, from motives of revenge and plunder. This murder was the occasion of Lieutenant Eden's successful minor expedition of 1855, and indirectly the cause of a bitter feeling amongst the Mejus against the British. Lieutenant Eden was helped by a chief named Lumling, and after the former's withdrawal, Kaisha's son obtained the help of the Chulikattas and exterminated the latter and his people, the Government of India refusing to send Lumling any aid.

The continual interference of the Abors with the trade route to Sadiya caused the British authorities at that place to advance their outposts to Nizamghat and Bomjur in 1880. This interference by the Abors had been a great obstacle to free intercourse between the Mishmis and Sadiya.

Raids on the plains on the part of the Mishmis were of continual occurrence, and in 1899, when the Bebejiyas had committed a very deliberate outrage on a Sadiya village, a force was despatched to penetrate their country. This expedition met with practically no opposition, and destroyed the villages concerned in the outrage. The Mishmis have since that time been perfectly well behaved.

### Lieutenant Eden's Expedition of 1855.

The murder by an independent party of Mejus of the two French Missionaries, M. Krick and M. Bourry, related above, took place to the east of the Mishmi frontier, to which the travellers had been escorted by the Digarus. The latter urged the British authorities to punish the murderers, and in February 1855 Lieutenant Frederick Grey Eden was sent by Lord Dalhousie to avenge the outrage. He took with him twenty picked men of the 1st Assam Light Infantry,[2] forty Hkamti volunteers, and a few hillmen as

[1] Mr. Needham reached the Lyal valley in 1885. It had previously also been reported on by the explorer A. K. in 1882, who entered it from Tibet.

[2] Now the 6th Gurkha Rifles.

carriers. After eight days' forced marching the party reached Kaisha's village on the Du river, surprised and captured it with the help of a friendly chief named Lumling, captured the chief and others, recovered the greater part of the stolen property, and released M. Krick's captured Singpho servant. The party then returned safely to the plains, and Kaisha was hanged at Dibrugarh.

### The Expedition of 1899.

On the 4th May 1899 six Bebejiya Mishmis, sent by Ahalon of the village of Abrangon, visited a small Hkamti village named Mitaigaon sixteen miles north-east of Sadiya, to buy salt. The Hkamtis were unable to provide the salt required, but gave them a *mithun* head. Having eaten this, the Mishmis went to the fire around which the Hkamtis were chatting, murdered two men and two women, and carried off two boys and a girl as captives, and also three guns.

The Government of India then decided to send an expedition into the Bebejiya country. Previous to its start, Mr. Needham, Political Officer at Sadiya, recovered one boy and one gun, and despatched a Chulikatta named Tora to Abrangon to demand the surrender of the remaining guns and captives and also of the murderers. Tora returned, bringing back the news that Ahalon, together with the remaining Bebejiya villages, intended to fight.

1 coy., Bengal Sappers and Miners.
2 coys., 10th Bengal Infantry.[1]
3 „ 42nd Gurkha Rifles.[2]
1 coy., 43rd „ „ [3]
2 coys., 44th „ „ [4]
2 mountain guns.
200 Military Police.

The expedition, strength as per margin, was assembled on 25th September 1899 under the command of Lieutenant-Colonel Molesworth, 44th Gurkha Rifles.

Its objects were laid down to be —

1. The punishment of the Bebejiyas for the recent outrage.
2. Recovery of the captives.
3. Exploration and survey of the country.
4. If subsequently thought desirable, the establishment of temporary posts to ensure complete pacification and recognition of British power.

[1] Now the 10th Jats.
[2] „ „ 6th Gurkha.
[3] Now the 7th Gurkha Rifles.
[4] „ „ 8th „ „

The force left Sadiya on the 1st December. The crossing of the Mahu pass, 8,900 feet, on the 29th was practically unopposed, a very fortunate thing, as much of the advance was over cliffs where the party had to pull themselves up by ropes, and a resolute defence of the stockades which had been prepared would have given much trouble. Colonel Molesworth was of opinion that the enemy had intended to oppose the advance, but, owing to the bad weather, had returned to their villages, and, on return to their defences, had found they were too late. The advanced guard entered Hunli on the 31st and found it deserted.

No opposition was met with, and the column reached Sadiya on the 8th February, having successfully carried out the objects of the expedition.

---

*BIBLIOGRAPHY.*

*The North-East Frontier of Bengal.*—Mackenzie, 1884.
*Report on the North-East Frontier of India.*—Michell.
*The Assam District Gazetteer of India, Vol. VIII*, 1905.
*Military Report on the Mishmi Country.*—Lieut. E. L. S. Ward, 1899.
*Statistical Account of Assam, Vol. I.*—Hunter.
*Bengal Records, XXIII.*
*Bengal Asiatic Society's Researches, XVII.*

---

## The Hkamtis.

Among the hill tribes drawn into the Brahmaputra valley by the attractions of the plains, on the decline of the Ahom power, were the Hkamtis.[1]

The Hkamtis, called Bor Hkamti[2] by the Assamese, are Shans, of the same race as the Ahoms, and live in the fertile valleys immediately to the east of Daphabum. They are a literary and cultivated people, and much more civilized than any of their neighbours, not excluding the Assamese. In religion they are Buddhists. Originally under Burmese rule, in their own home they are now independent, but about 2,000 of them are settled within the Assam frontier, and acknowledge the authority of the

[1] Shan for "Land of gold."
[2] Bor means, in Assamese, an independent savage.

British Government. Those outside the "inner line" pay no tribute; while the villagers about Sadiya and Saikwa are British *ryots*, paying revenue.

The Hkamtis first appeared in Assam towards the end of the eighteenth century, and settled on the Tengapani; but in 1794, probably in consequence of pressure from the then invading Singphos, they crossed the Brahmaputra, ousted the Khawa Gohain, or Assamese Governor of Sadiya, and, usurping his powers, reduced the Assamese *ryots* to virtual slavery.

On their arrival in the country, the British, finding the Sadiya tract entirely under Hkamti management, recognized the Chief as local officer of the Assam Government. He was to pay no revenue, but was to maintain a force of 200 men, who would be armed by the Company. In 1824 this force rendered material aid against the Singphos. In 1835 the old Hkamti Raja died, and the arrogant behaviour of the young chief, who openly disobeyed the orders of the Resident, compelled the Assam Government to remove and deport him.

The district was thenceforth in charge of a British Agent at Sadiya, who was empowered to collect revenue and administer justice, while the internal affairs were left to the chiefs.

At first the Hkamti chiefs seemed to be satisfied, and, on their rendering further good military service, the ex-Khawa Gohain was permitted to return and live among his people. They were not, however, really content, and the ex-Khawa Gohain fomented the hostile feeling. They had lost their profitable position of control over the Assamese; their slaves had been released; and they knew it was possible that they might be taxed.

Attack on Sadiya.

At length in 1839, a force of five hundred Hkamtis attacked the British post at Sadiya. Surprising it in the early hours of the morning, they fired the lines, killed Colonel White, the Political Officer, and then captured the stockade. The sepoys, however, behaved well and recovered the stockade in fifteen minutes, killing twenty-one of the enemy, and driving them off. The British losses were eight men, women, and children killed.

After this the hearts of the Hkamtis failed them, and, deserting their villages, they fled to the Mishmi hills. They subsequently submitted and were re-settled, mostly in new villages, and since that time they have been perfectly well behaved.

The Bor Hkamti country is little known. It was visited by Wilcox in 1828, by Woodthorpe and MacGregor in 1884, by Mr. J. Errol Grey in 1892, and by Prince Henry of Orleans in 1895.

---

*BIBLIOGRAPHY.*

*The North-East Frontier of Bengal.*—Mackenzie, 1884.

---

## The Singphos.

The Singphos, or Kachins as they are called in Burma, are a tribe inhabiting both sides of the Patkoi range, the mountain system which divides Upper Burma from Assam. Their boundaries are nowhere precisely defined. As neighbours they have: on the west the Naga tribes and Lakhimpur; on the north the Hkamtis; on the east the independent tribes of Upper Burma; and on the south Burma Proper. Their home is the Hukong valley, lying immediately to the south of the Patkoi range. There they are independent, and comparatively few Europeans have visited their country. Those Singphos who have left the Hukong valley and have settled in Assam acknowledge the authority of the Assam Government.

The Patkoi range is no formidable obstacle. From Bisa, in the Brahmaputra valley, to old Bisa, in the Hukong valley, is but seventy miles as the crow flies, and the passes are easy.

In the last century the upper portion of Assam, east of the Noa Dehing and south of the Brahmaputra, was considered the most fertile portion of the country. Suffering, as it did, from the incursions of the hill tribes at the breaking up of the old Assam kingdom, it subsequently became almost entirely overgrown with jungle, and is still to a great extent unreclaimed. Bisa, the centre of this country, stands ten miles from the mouth of the defile through which the Hukong valley road passes south-east. The Patkoi itself consists of a double system of mountains. The range nearest to Assam seldom exceeds 4,000 feet, and is succeeded by a depression, before the mountains again rise to the main range sometimes 5,000 and 6,000 feet in height. All these hills are heavily wooded, the southern slopes being even more densely so than the rest. The rains render all this hill country very malarious, and it is almost entirely deserted.

The Hukong valley is a broad plain some fifty miles in length by fifteen to forty-five wide. It is watered by the Chindwin river, a large stream whose width is never less than 150 to 200 yards, and by which large boats can enter the valley. The plain stands at a height of 1,000 feet, and is on all sides surrounded by hills which rise to 6,000 feet, the highest being to the north-east. The soil of this valley is very rich, but it is only sparsely cultivated. Save in the neighbourhood of villages the jungle is very dense, and the whole presents the appearance of a vast unbroken forest. Inter-village paths are quite overhung with vegetation, and during a march not a yard of the surrounding country can be seen.

The people.

The Singphos are certainly identical with the Kachins of Burma,[1] although they consider themselves distinct from, and superior to, the latter. They are a fine, athletic race, hardy and capable of sustaining great fatigue, and it is not uncommon to see them six feet high. They wear a jacket of coloured stuff, a plain checked cloth, and a white turban.

The Singphos have no caste prejudices but the men think it a degradation to do any kind of work. The whole of the domestic cares are performed by the women, even to cutting firewood. The agricultural labour is carried out by slaves. These slaves are obtained by raiding into neighbouring countries, and greatly outnumber the Singphos themselves. Their condition appears to be a happy one, in fact they are slaves in name only. They are permitted to marry, to acquire wealth, and to mix on an apparent equality with free men.[2]

When not actuated by feudal enmity, the Singphos are a singularly honest and moral race. Their only vices are drinking and opium-smoking. Neither men nor women are wanting in intelligence, but they are not a lively people.

[1] Singpho merely signifies in the Kachin language "a man."

[2] Mr. Needham, Assistant Political Officer, Sadiya, who visited the country in 1892, remarks that he heard not a single complaint from any slave during his journey. Mr. Errol Grey confirms this.

There is no common government; every village looking after its own interests. Sometimes groups of villages are united under a chief whom they call *Sawbwa*, but these chiefs have little real power. Local wars consist of surprises and house-burnings, ambuscades and cold-blooded murders. No prisoners are taken and no quarter asked. The villages are defended by strong and high stockades.

Arms and tactics.

All males between the ages of sixteen and forty are liable to serve in expeditions, and in 1835 it was thought that 9,000 or 10,000 men could be gathered together. The arms are *dahs*, spears, cross-bows, and matchlocks. These latter are kept in very good order, and powder is manufactured for them in the Hukong valley. For defensive armour there is a head piece of buffalo hide, and a shield of the same material.

The Singphos' mode of attack is peculiar. Covered with their defensive armour, a party will advance on all fours, in single file, towards the point to be gained, armed each man alternately with *dah* and spear. At intervals they stop to listen, and, if there is any sign of danger, they throw themselves on the ground, covering their bodies with their shields. When close upon the point of attack they rise up and rush in at the door of the stockade, or house, and, if not resisted, pass through it, cutting and stabbing every individual they find. Their object merely being to do as much mischief as possible in the first rush, as soon as this has been accomplished the party disperse. In these attacks severe wounds are inflicted, which give proof of dexterity in the use of their favourite weapon; but it should always be remembered that a night attack of Singphos is undertaken only when they are sure of doing injury to the enemy with impunity to themselves. The slightest resistance or signs of alertness on the part of the attacked changes the face of affairs entirely. This has been shown in the instances of attack upon our troops in Assam, where, although they have cut down sentries and a few unresisting individuals without arms, they have invariably beaten a hasty retreat directly any resistance was shown. It is, however, very dangerous for small parties of troops to be placed in any but the strongest stockades, for if overwhelming numbers get entrance in a night attack, the Singphos are so quick and expert at this sort of work, that a small party would be annihilated in an incredibly short space of time.

The first event in the history of the Singphos with which we are concerned is their appearance in Assam, where their incursions began during the troubles which followed the Moamariah rebellion at the end of the eighteenth century. They first drove the Hkamtis away from some of the lowlands near the Patkoi hills, and settled on the Tengapani and upper Bari Dehing. They were, however, not allowed to occupy this territory in peace, for in 1809 the Assamese drove them back, and they did not obtain any permanent footing in Assam until the Burmese invasion of 1818. During the disturbed times which followed that event they made the most of their opportunities, and carried off thousands of Assamese into slavery in the Hukong valley and Tengapani. The whole of Eastern Assam became well nigh depopulated, and the Assamese became so utterly broken that it was no uncommon thing for one Singpho to drive twenty Assamese bound before him.

Outline of History.

The British first came in contact with the Singphos in 1825 in the course of the Burmese war. This tribe had at that time been harrying the Hkamtis, and the latter had appealed to the British for protection. The Singphos then made advances to the local British officers and negotiations were entered into. It appears that the Singphos valued their lands in the Brahmaputra valley and had fears lest the British should expel them as they had expelled the Burmese. The difficulty in the way of a satisfactory settlement, however, lay in the slave question. The Government of India would not hear of slavery in any form within its dominions, and the tribes were unwilling to give way on this point. These negotiations, therefore, led to no result. The Singphos now threw in their lot with the Burmese, and advanced with them against the British, but were soon driven back by a force order Captain Neufville. The following year they entered into an agreement[1] by which those who had been subject to Assam acknowledged their dependence on the Government of India, and agreed to keep aloof from the Burmese and to provide facilities for British forces passing through their country. Under the terms of agreement 6,000 Assamese slaves were set free.

First contact with British.

[1] Aitchison, CXX.

In 1830 the Hukong valley men invaded Assam and were joined by their countrymen of Lattora and Tengapani. They numbered in all some 3,000 men, but on Captain Neufville approaching they withdrew without fighting.

In 1835 the Duffa Gam[1] came over the Patkoi to attack the Bisa Gam. He was driven out by Captain Charlton with 250 men, who took the Duffa Gam's stockade by assault. For the next few years there were many signs that the Singphos were in a most disturbed and discontented state, and in 1843 they broke out. A party of warriors came over from Hukong valley and being joined by some of the men on the north of the hills, attacked the British post at Bisa. The garrison, consisting of a jemadar and twenty men, foolishly surrendered when they had suffered some loss, upon which several were put to death and the others sold as slaves. The invaders then attacked the Koogoo and Ningru posts, but these were commanded by British officers and beat off their assailants. Shortly afterwards the British reversed the state of affairs and inflicted severe punishment on several villages.

The cause of the unrest among the Singphos was in great measure attributed to the loss of their dependants, the slaves, of whom the ordinary hillman in old days had possessed from forty to sixty. Under British influence these had melted away, and their former masters found themselves without means to cultivate their lands. The rising was the last effort of a rude and revengeful people to vindicate what they considered to be their rights. This fall in their prosperity was however a good deal due to internal dissensions, for, had it not been for continual internal strife, many Assamese were attached to Singpho life, and would have remained with their masters, who exercised a patriarchal care over them.

Since 1843 the Singphos have given no trouble, but they do not like the conditions of British rule, under which they must do their own work, and many have returned to the Hukong, where slavery still flourishes. Probably it is for this reason that they keep the valley jealously closed, knowing well that with European influence slavery must decline.

[1] The Singphos were at this time under the leadership of four important chiefs:—
The Lattora, Lattao, Bisa, and Duffa Gams.

The inhabitants of the valley seemed very well disposed to Mr. Needham who visited the country in 1892.

### Captain Neufville's Operations in 1825.

Early in 1825, 5,000 or 6,000 Singphos were ravaging in the Sadiya district and as far as Rangpur.[1] They were not at that time on good terms with the Burmese, for at the end of March a Burman force of five hundred men was defeated by them.

Captain Neufville, commanding the frontier force, proposed to move against the Singphos and considered that 200 men would be a sufficient force. He found, however, that the Noa Dehing valley was impassable and the Singphos alert. About this time negotiations were entered into by the enemy, but as already related, they came to nothing, and the Singphos then threw in their lot with the Burmese, who again advanced over the Patkoi in May. On the 7th of that month Captain Neufville advanced to attack 300 Burmese who had advanced along the Noa Dehing, and entrenched themselves twenty-five miles from its mouth. The British force, numbered two hundred, charged the Burmans with the bayonet and routed them with some loss.

On the 5th of June Captain Neufville advanced against Bisa with 180 men, leaving two gunboats and thirty sepoys to protect the passage of the Tengapani. He found the enemy, Burmese and Singphos, numbering about 200 foot and 50 horse, at Daffla, a place defended by a stockade of considerable strength, fourteen feet high. The enemy were driven out but escaped without loss.

Advancing on Bisa on the 11th, he found the Burmese drawn up in line, with their cavalry on the right. The enemy broke and fled precipitately upon the British force charging, without the latter firing a shot. They were pursued for some miles and fled in great confusion over the passes.

Three thousand slaves had now been released, but there remained as many more, whom the Singphos would not give up. Captain Neufville accordingly prepared to continue operations against that tribe and as it was thought that they numbered no more than 500 fighting men, it was arranged that the British force should hold

[1] The ancient capital of Assam, near Sibsagar.

the pass into Hukong, while the native auxiliaries, Hkamtis and Moamariahs, swept the country.

These operations reduced the Singphos to reason. Peace with the Burmese was concluded in February 1826, and in May of that year the Singphos also submitted.

# CHAPTER XII.

## *THE SOUTHERN HILL TRIBES.*

STARTING from the junction of the Manipur State and the Naga territory, where it adjoins the Patkoi range, a system of hills runs westward into the plains, and divides Assam from Sylhet. These hills have no distinctive name, but the precipitous cliffs in which they culminate in the south, the height of which varies from 3,000 to 6,000 feet, are called the Barail or Great Dyke.

These hills are occupied by four tribes, known as the Garos, the Khasis, the Jaintias, and the Cacharis, all of whom were driven there by more powerful neighbours who possessed themselves of the plains. The hills are now of no military importance, but have been the scene of a few minor operations in former days, for which reason a brief account of the tribes inhabiting them is here given. No doubt they have settled down more quickly than other hill tribes owing to their being surrounded by plains and the hills themselves being largely open plateaux. Had their territory been backed by mountain fastnesses they would probably not have proved so amenable.

The most remarkable feature of the Barail is the astonishing rainfall. The moisture laden current from the Bay of Bengal encounters these hills as the first obstacle, and deposits a rainfall which has been known to amount at Cherrapunji to over 800 inches in the year. The first ridge appears to exhaust the greater part of the moisture, for in the northern districts the fall is very moderate.

### The Garo Hills.

The western extremity of the Barail is occupied by the Garos, a section of the great Bodo race,[1] who were probably driven southwards from the plains of Kuch Behar. They were in early days in a state of intermittent conflict with the *zemindars* of the large estates lying at the foot of the hills. The exactions levied by the subordinates

[1] A race which originated between the upper waters of the Hoang-Ho and the Yangtse-Kiang.

of these landholders irritated the hillmen, and the belief that the spirits of their headmen required the souls of others to attend them in the next world acted as a further incitement to the despatch of raiding parties. At the end of the eighteenth century the Garos inhabiting the outer ranges had been brought to some extent under the authority of the *zemindars*, but the villages in the interior were entirely independent. Steps were taken by Government to release the tributary Garos from the control of the Bengali landlords, and it was hoped that by this means the practice of raiding would be stopped. It was difficult, however, to put down all oppression, and the hillmen continued to be turbulent. In 1848 an expedition was sent into the hills to punish the Dasamni Garos for having murdered one of their headmen with all his family because he attempted to collect the tribute due by them to Government. In 1852 seven Garo raids took place in which forty-four persons were killed. A blockade was established along the frontier, which produced some effect, but in 1856 the tribes broke out again and a succession of forays was made upon the plains. Between May 1857 and October 1859 nine raids were made into Goalpara and twenty heads taken. An expedition was despatched into the hills in 1861, the effects of which lasted for a few years; but, in 1866, a most murderous raid was committed on the Mymensingh district, and it was decided to establish a British officer in the hills. The success with which this experiment was attended was very striking; raids at once ceased, and since that date the Garo Hills have been quite undisturbed.

## The Khasi Hills.

The Khasi Hills form an irregular parallelogram about seventy miles from north to south and fifty from east to west. The neighbours of this territory are Jaintia, Sylhet, the Garo Hills, and Goalpara. The northern is a closely wooded tract rising for some twenty miles from the Assam valley; this is succeeded by an elevated undulating plateau between four and five thousand feet above the sea. It is on this plateau, at Shillong that the summer capital of Assam is now situated. The land then falls to the Sylhet plain—a steep face, some seven miles wide, densely wooded, malarious, and afflicted with a rainfall of some hundreds of inches in the year.

This country is inhabited by the Khyee, called by us Khasias, who, with the decay of the Ahom kingdom, had settled in the plains, but, on the advent of the British into Assam, were swept back into their own hills. For some time the British had no further dealings with them than the establishing of frontier posts, and their occasional exclusion from the markets of the plains; and until the year 1826 the hills were visited by no Europeans. About that time it became an object with Mr. Scott to establish communication by road between Assam and Sylhet. An opportunity presented itself in 1826, when the Raja of Nongklao expressed a wish to rent some lands in Assam; in return for the granting of this request Mr. Scott was able to obtain permission for a road to be made from Gauhati to Cherrapunji.

History.

For eighteen months after this agreement most cordial relations existed, and operations on the road were commenced. But in 1829 a survey party of about fifty men at Nongklao, under Lieutenants Bedingfield and Burlton, was suddenly attacked and cut up. Mr. Scott himself had a narrow escape, having just left for Cherrapunji. Troops were immediately called up from Sylhet and Assam to avenge this massacre, and a long and harassing war ensued. The Sylhet Light Infantry under Captain F. G. Lister defeated the Khasias at Mamlu on the 14th April 1829, retook Nongklao and stormed the strong position of Mogandi on the 21st May. The Khasias maintained a desultory conflict, in spite of their being hunted by Captain Lister from post to post, until the chief insurgent Tirat Singh gave himself up in 1833.

Expedition, 1829.

Since that time the maintenance of a British garrison at Cherrapunji, and afterwards at Shillong, has sufficed to maintain the Khasi States in perfect tranquillity.

The Khasi States are twenty-five in number. They are governed by chiefs in subsidiary alliance [1] with the Government of India, and control their own internal affairs

## Jaintia.

Jaintia embraces that part of the Barail which lies between the Khasi Hills and Cachar, and a part of the Sylhet plain extending

[1] Aitchison, LXXIII.

as far south as the Surma river. This State has never possessed any military importance.

The Government of India first came in contact with Jaintia in 1774, when a Major Henniker operated in the hills with a small force: there are no records of this movement nor of its cause. In 1824 when Cachar was taken under British protection, the Jaintia Raja entered into an agreement with the Government of India, by which he acknowledged allegiance to the Company. During the Burmese War in 1824 a detachment of 150 British troops was sent to reinforce the Raja of Jaintia, which move had the effect of dissuading the Burmese troops from entering that country.

In 1825 Mr. Scott marched through from Sylhet to Assam with an escort of three companies of the 23rd Native Infantry under Captain Horsburgh, in order to strengthen the Raja in his alliance. The Raja's allegiance, however, was very doubtful, and he subsequently, in 1832, caused four British subjects to be seized, carried off, and sacrificed to the goddess Kali. Unable to obtain the surrender of the murderers, the British Government, on the accession of the Raja Ram Singh, in 1832, took possession of the part of Jaintia lying in the plains: whereupon the Raja declared himself unwilling to retain possession of the hills. Upon this the hills also were declared a part of the British dominions, and in March 1835, Captain Lister, with two companies of the Sylhet Light Infantry, took possession of Jaintiapur. Since that time Jaintia has been peaceably administered as a British district.

## Cachar.

Cachar, the country of the Cachari tribe, lies north and south of the Barail, immediately to the west of the junction of that range with the Naga Hills. The northern half is hill country and the southern more or less lowland. It is sharply divided by the Barail, or Great Dyke, which attains a height of 6,000 feet in Cachar. North of the Barail the land has not been nearly so extensively cleared for cultivation as in the south, were the Barak valley is a broad and exceedingly fertile plain.

The Cacharis proper, who now number but a small proportion of the population, call themselves Dimasa. They are generally

1 Aitchison. LXXIV—CXII.

supposed to be a section of the Bodos, and migrated to their present territory about 1750. When the British first came in contact with them they were merely an unimportant tribe, living in a remote and jungly tract, and would have attracted no attention had they not been neighbours of the Manipuris and Nagas, and near to the path of the invading Burmese. The first connection with the British dates from 1762, when Mr. Verelst marched up from Chittagong with five companies of infantry to assist the Manipur Raja against the Burmese. This force reached Khaspur and remained there a year, but were prevented from further advance by the difficulties of the country.

First contact with British.

In 1809 Krishna Chandra, then Raja of Cachar, engaged in intrigues in Manipur, the consequence being that Cachar became the arena in which the Manipuri brothers Charjit, Marjit, and Gambhir Singh contended for supremacy and obtained possession of most of the Cachar valley. In 1819 the Burmese, then in Manipur, professed to regard Cachar as a dependency of that State and announced their intention of taking possession of it. This the Government of India would not allow; Gobind Chandra, of the Cachari royal family, was placed on the throne, on condition of his paying a tribute of 10,000 rupees annually.[1] This man was however assassinated in 1830, and as he left no heir, either natural or adopted, the country was annexed to the British crown in 1832, in compliance with the frequent and earnestly expressed wish of the people.

Annexation.

During the last years of Gobind Chandra one of his officers set up an independent kingdom in North Cachar; and on the Raja's death he claimed the throne. The Government of India would not listen to his claim to the whole kingdom, but settled him in a small tract of territory.[2] His family, however, proved quite unable to keep out the Nagas, and in 1854 the tract was taken over by the British and the family pensioned.

The history of Cachar since it came under British administration has been one of peaceful progress, the only events of importance being the Lushai raids of 1849–1871; and the Indian mutiny

[1] Aitchison, LXXI.
[2] Aitchison, LXXII.

of 1857, when some sepoys of the 34th Native Infantry from Chittagong made their way to Cachar, and were there dispersed by the Sylhet Light Infantry.[1]

## BIBLIOGRAPHY.

*The North-East Frontier of Bengal.*—Mackenzie, 1884.
*Treaties, Engagements, and Sanads.*—Aitchison.
*The Assam District Gazetteer.*—Allen, 1905.
*The Services of the Bengal Army.*—Cardew.

[1] Now the 8th Gurkhas.

# CHAPTER XIII.

## *THE NAGA HILLS.*

THE region inhabited by the tribes, both savage and semi-civilized, collectively known as the Nagas, is the long strip of more or less mountainous country, stretching from Jaipur to Cachar, which forms the natural south-eastern boundary of the Assam valley. Part of this country is under British administration, and forms the district of the Naga Hills, 3,647 square miles in area; part is inhabited by independent tribes. The hill ranges in this tract run mostly north-east and south-west. In the northerly parts they consist of small broken ranges, with narrow intervening valleys, for the most part covered with dense jungle, and uncultivated. Further south the hills are on a larger scale, and culminate at the junction of the Patkoi ranges and the Barail, when they attain a height of 10,000 feet. In the south the valleys are broad, and a good deal cultivated. In their natural state the hills are covered with dense evergreen forest, but in the country of the Angami Nagas, which used to be dominated by the Military Station of Kohima, most of the slopes up to a height of 5,000 feet have been cleared for cultivation at one time or another. Where this has been done, and the irrigation water-supply has since failed, they are covered for the most part with scrub, bamboo, and grass. The Angami Nagas have developed terrace cultivation to a high pitch, and little suitable land is unused. The principal crop is rice. Intimate acquaintance with the ground, and with every track used by the wild animals who haunt the forest, enables the almost naked Naga to move at will through a country much of which is a hopeless labyrinth even to our Gurkhas. The rivers of the country are mountain streams which do not attain any considerable dimensions before they reach the plains.

The climate is, on the whole, healthy. The rainy season, lasting from June to September, is, of course, steamy and unpleasant, but the rainfall is very moderate, averaging 63 inches annually.

The lower hills, however, which adjoin the plains, are malarious, and their inhabitants consequently few and weakly.

The only cart-road in the country is the road which runs from Dimapur in Assam to Manipur. The general direction of this road is from north to south. There is also a bridle-road which runs from Kohima north-eastwards, throughout the British Naga Hills, with some loops and offshoots. At the time of the expedition of 1880 the paths were even fewer than they are at present, and for the most part were found only practicable for coolies, while the cart-road was non-existent. Frequent allusion is made in official documents to a "political path." This was the track from Samaguting to Piphima, Nerhama, and Wokha. The only way of moving through the country is, as a rule, by footpaths of extreme difficulty, which not only climb steep slopes and descend into deep ravines, but are so closely shut in with dense jungle that troops are compelled to move along them in single file. One of the most striking features in the Naga Hills is the number of ravines, deep and densely wooded, which in the rains become the beds of torrents, and formidable obstacles. The Nagas make great use of these ravines as roads. They are naturally dangerous, being commanded by high banks.

The numbers of the independent Nagas are not known, but the country administered by the Government of India contains 102,000 people. They are of four great tribes; the Aos, Lhotas, Angamis, and Semas; and two quite minor ones—the Rengmas and Kacchas. These tribes speak different dialects, and vary greatly in fighting character; the Rengmas being very peaceable and well behaved, and the Angamis most warlike. Otherwise they do not differ greatly in physical and moral characteristics. Dr. Hunter thus described the Angamis:—

The people.

An athletic, and by no means bad looking race; brown complexion; flat noses, and high cheek bones; brave and warlike, but also treacherous and vindictive. Many Nagas have regular features and Grecian noses, and do not in any way recall a Mongolian or Dravidian stock. Though complete savages, they are tolerably truthful towards one another and remarkably chaste. Their dress consists of a dark blue or black kilt, ornamented with rows of *cowrie* shells, and a thick cloth of home manufacture thrown loosely over the shoulders. The arms of the Angamis are the spear and shield; the former seven feet in length with a long and broad head, thrown usually at twenty-five yards range. They also carry at all times the *dah*, a heavy knife, narrow-bladed at the hilt, but widening toward the point, and used for many purposes. They have also a certain number of fire-arms.

The internal relations of the independent Nagas with one another resemble greatly those of the Pathan tribes on the North-West Frontier, and their tribal system appears to have advanced to about the same stage. No clan has any recognized chief, but each is divided into numerous sub-divisions, who may, indeed, combine for some great purpose, but are for the most part at deadly feud. The heads of villages are recognized as superiors and natural leaders, but have little real authority. Villages often contain several distinct sections of perhaps quite different clans, and some of these are generally at war with the others. The neutrals in this case are absolutely indifferent to the good or bad fortune of their neighbours.

The chief object and ambition of the Angamis and other backward clans used to be the collection of human heads, and no man was of any account till he had taken at least one. Any head was good, so long as it was that of a hostile clan; the skulls of women and children were prized equally with those of any male foe. The death of any individual had to be avenged by that of one of the murderer's section; and although years might elapse before an opportunity for satisfaction occurred, the debt was never forgotten, but handed down from father to son, murder being followed by murder, and vengeance by retaliation, through many successive generations.

Villages are built on the summits of hills, and are strongly fortified with stockades, deep ditches, and massive stone walls; and the hillsides are thickly studded with *panjis*. The approaches are tortuous, narrow ways, only wide enough to admit the passage of one man at a time. The sites of villages are, however, sometimes ill chosen, being commanded by adjacent heights, and opposition would therefore be useless against modern fire-arms.

The numbers of able-bodied men, all of whom are probably fighters, may be taken at one-fifth of the population. In 1880 the Angamis could produce 8,000 warriors.

The early history of the Naga Hills is not well known; nor would its inclusion in this work be of any interest. The country up to the Patkoi came nominally under British rule with the rest of the Muhammadan possessions in Assam in 1765, but no British officials came into contact with the Nagas until 1832. In that year Captains Jenkins and Pemberton made their way from Manipur to Assam, with the idea of opening communications through the Angami Naga country, then unknown. They had a large escort of Manipur troops and had to fight the whole way. In the same year, and with the same object, Lieutenant Gordon and Raja Gambhir Singh of Manipur penetrated to Kohima.

Outline of History.

The East India Company paid no special attention to the Nagas until 1835, when the Angamis raided some villages in North Cachar. From that time the raids became frequent, and the Company, unwilling to institute a permanent hill district, endeavoured to control the hillmen by occasional expeditions and promenades. Between 1839 and 1847 seven expeditions entered the Naga Hills: the Naga men learned that their fastnesses were not impregnable, and were occasionally profuse in expressions of submission; but their raids continued.

In 1847 it was thought that a Resident in the hills would keep the Angamis in order, and a native, one Bogchand, was sent to Samaguting. The Angamis killed him, not liking his high-handed ways; and a punitive expedition from Assam having failed, a strong force[1] entered the hills in 1849 and inflicted severe punishment on the recalcitrant tribesmen.

British Representative in the hills.

Having settled with the Angamis for the murder of Bogchand, the Government decided that the future policy should be one of absolute non-intervention. Accordingly, by 1857, the troops were withdrawn. This was of course the opportunity of the Nagas, and they celebrated the occasion by making twenty-two raids into British territory within the year. The raids continued constantly in the succeeding years; the frontier officials being actually instructed not to interfere, anxious as they were on occasions to respond

Non-intervention Policy.

1 334 men and 4 guns.

to appeals for intervention in the constant fighting which went on in the hills. The Assam frontier was contracted, first to Dimapur, then behind the great Namba Forest to Borpathar.

Thus in the case of the Angamis the policy of non-intervention absolutely failed. The tribes in the north were, however, more easily dealt with; they had developed a liking for trade, and by the closing to them of the markets in the plains the frontier officials were always able to bring them to reason. At last, in 1862, in consequence of the continued raids, the Commissioner was constrained to report:—

> It is not creditable to our Government that such atrocities should recur annually and with unvarying certainty, and that we should be powerless alike to protect our subjects or to punish the aggressors. It is quite certain that our relations with the Nagas could not possibly be on a worse footing than they are now. The non-interference policy is excellent in theory, but Government will probably be inclined to think it must be abandoned.

The Lieutenant-Governor wrote at that time in a letter to the Government of India:—

> The treaties with Burma and Manipur recognize the Patkoi and Barail ranges of hills running in a continuous line from the sources of the Dehing, in the extreme east of Assam, to those of the Dansiri, in north Cachar, as the boundary between those countries and British India. There is no intermediate independent country; and, while the wild tribes who inhabit the southern slopes of those ranges are subject to Burma and Manipur, those who inhabit the northern slopes are subject to the British Government. These latter, including the Angami Nagas, are independent only in the sense that the British Government has refrained from reducing them to practical subjection, and has left them, except at occasional intervals, entirely to themselves; and it is clearly open to the British Government in point of right, as it is incumbent on it in good policy, to exercise its sovereign power by giving them the benefit of a settled administration.

British Resident in the hills.

In accordance with this opinion, in 1866 a Deputy Commissioner, Lieutenant Gregory, was sent to Samaguting. The effect was immediate; the Angamis made two raids subsequent to Lieutenant Gregory's arrival, but that officer was able to mete out to them prompt punishment. All raiding into Cachar and the plains ceased forthwith, and with rare exceptions has never been resumed. The primary object for which the Naga Hills District had been established had thus been achieved: namely the protection of the peaceful inhabitants of British territory. But no progress was made in the work of civilizing the Nagas themselves, the inter-tribal feuds continuing to rage with unabated ferocity.

The Chief Commissioner was anxious to extend the influence of peace, and about 1874 there were signs that some of the Angamis appreciated the merits of immunity from attack. At this time survey operations on the Assam border were extended into the Naga Hills. These surveys appear to have had a very disturbing effect on the Naga mind, and one party was treacherously attacked; Lieutenant Holcombe and eighty men were killed, and Captain Badgely and fifty others wounded; and but for the courage and skill of Captain Badgely, and the discipline of his men, the whole would have been destroyed. A punitive expedition under Colonel Nuttall, C.B., 44th Sylhet Light Infantry, was immediately organized, and was completely successful, destroying all the villages implicated in the outrage, and recovering nearly all the arms and plunder taken from the survey party. The expedition was composed of detachments of the 42nd and 44th Native Infantry and some frontier police from the Naga Hills, the total force numbering 308 men of all ranks.

1875 Punitive Expedition.

For some months after this expedition the Nagas maintained a comparatively peaceful attitude, but in the following year they again displayed their hostility by an attack on another survey party, in which Captain Butler, the Deputy Commissioner, was killed in an ambush. There were no other casualties, and the escort next day destroyed the villages implicated. After this the conduct of the Nagas continued peaceable in 1876, but in 1877 they raided into North Cachar. This raid was punished by the expedition of Captain Brydon, related below.

1877 Expedition.

The head-quarters of the district was then advanced to Kohima. Mr. Damant who was now Deputy Commissioner, took a favourable view of the situation; but, as a matter of fact, trouble was brewing. Kohima was in the middle of the group of the turbulent villages of Konoma, Jotsoma, and Mozima, of which two had probably gained confidence from their lenient treatment in 1877. They now found that the existence of the garrison at Kohima not only put an end to their head-hunting pursuits, but entailed the payment of tribute, and their resentment broke out in October 1879. Mr. Damant then visited Konoma with an escort of eighty-seven men, and, on approaching the village, was shot dead. His escort, which was unprepared for attack, was dispersed, and, only fifty men returned to Kohima, nineteen of them being wounded. The Nagas of Konoma had now irretrievably committed themselves, and in a few days the whole Angami country was in a blaze of insurrection. On the 16th October Kohima was attacked. The place was not well fitted for defence; its garrison consisted of only 158 men, while the enemy amounted by their own account to 6,000; the water-supply was cut off, and the rations were scanty; but the place succeeded in holding out, and reinforcements reached them on the 26th October.

In five years three British officers had been murdered by hill-men, and it was evidently time that the Nagas should be taught a lesson. A punitive expedition was accordingly sent into the hills.

1880 Expedition.

The 44th which had reached Goalundo on its way to take part in the Afghan War was recalled; Konoma was taken, and the district assessed to revenue. The Nagas, however, did not immediately settle down, and minor expeditions were sent against them in 1883, 1885, 1888, 1889, 1892, and 1905. From these expeditions the Deputy Commissioner came to the conclusion that a good effect was exercised on the Naga mind by the burning of his home. "It is an undoubted fact," he says, "that the burning of a village leads almost immediately to the establishment of good relations with the inhabitants. Strangely enough, after they have been burnt out, the people seem to consider that they have become the children of the *Maharani*."

Since the last expedition much has been done to open up the country, and the Naga communities are now apparently settled down as revenue-paying subjects of the British Government.

## The Expedition of 1875.

In consequence of the treacherous attack and massacre of Lieutenant Holcombe's Survey party at Ninu on the 2nd February 1875, at the end of the same month a punitive expedition was despatched into the hills. It consisted of detachments of the 42nd and 44th Native Infantry, numbering 308 in all, and was commanded by Colonel J. M. Nuttall. Leaving Dibrugarh on the 27th February, the expedition advanced by Bor Matan, across the Tesing and Desang rivers, through a thickly-populated country, to the large village of Ninu, which was taken after a smart skirmish on the 19th March. A week was spent in scouring the country with detachments and in the destruction of villages which had taken part in the massacre of February. On the 26th the column was re-united at Ninu, when, the persons most directly implicated in the massacre having been captured or given up, the troops returned to Dibrugarh, arriving there on the 11th April.

### The Expedition of 1877.

| | |
|---|---|
| 42nd Assam Light Infantry .. | 210 |
| Police .. .. .. | 50 |
| | 260 |

*Political Officer*—Mr. Carnegy, Deputy Commissioner.

In November 1877, in consequence of the Angami raid into North Cachar, a force under Captain Brydon was despatched from Gauhati against the important village of Mozima. A party of fifty men of the 43rd Assam Light Infantry co-operated from Golaghat. On the 5th December the troops reached Samaguting; on the 6th Piphima; on the 7th Pachima; and on the morning of the 8th they moved on Mozima, only a few miles distant. The column having been fired on by the inhabitants, the village was attacked, carried by assault, and burnt to the ground. The burning was unintentional. The men of Mozima, joined apparently by warriors from Konoma and Jotsoma, then took to the jungle and the hills, and continued hostilities. Captain Brydon's little detachment, owing to its weakness, could do no more, and was now virtually placed on the defensive. This radical fault in the expedition, the smallness of its numbers, had been noticed by the Commander-in-Chief at the commencement of the operation; but as the political authorities were misinformed with regard to the attitude of the Nagas, and did not anticipate much resistance, it was allowed to proceed. In Naga warfare the enemy are always greatly favoured by the extreme difficulty of the country; and the Angamis well understand the importance to themselves of harassing and interrupting the communications of an invader. On this occasion they took full advantage of Captain Brydon's forced inactivity, cut him off from his base, and repeatedly threatened Samaguting, which was, however, secured by a sufficient garrison. Captain Brydon, in view of his somewhat precarious position, wisely declined to hazard an attack on Konoma as desired by the political officers, and constructed a stockade at Mozima, which could be held by 100 rifles, while with the remainder of his force he cleared the road to Samaguting. In the meantime Brigadier-General Nation, commanding the Eastern Frontier district, hastily despatched from Shillong, on his own responsibility, a reinforcement of 100 men of the 43rd Assam Light Infantry under Lieutenant MacGregor, 44th Sylhet Light Infantry. This action received the full approval of the Commander-in-Chief, who further authorized him to take any steps he might deem necessary for bringing the expedition to a successful termination. On the 9th January Lieutenant MacGregor with nineteen of the 43rd Native Infantry and twenty of the 44th Native Infantry, accompanied by Captain Williamson, Assistant Political Officer, reached Mozima. Shortly

Angamis treat for peace.

afterwards the Angamis, seeing reinforcements beginning to arrive, and being threatened in rear by a force from Manipur, commenced to treat for peace. Up to this time their desultory attacks had been incessant; the picquets were fired at every night, and attempts had been made to poison the water. They were now probably getting somewhat tired of hostilities, which, if unsatisfactory for us, were certainly not profitable to them: a great quantity of their grain had been captured or destroyed; and the men of Konoma and Jotsoma possibly reflected that, with the strengthening of the expedition, the same fate might overtake their own villages as had already befallen Mozima. Konoma was the first to submit, and the example was speedily followed by the rest.

Owing to the inopportune death of Mr. Carnegy, the Political Officer, who had ventured outside the camp at night and had been accidentally shot by a sentry, the negotiations with the hostile clans were conducted by Captain Williamson, who, unaware of the true circumstances of the case, let off Konoma and Jotsoma scot-free, and imposed very easy conditions on Mozima. On the 18th January, the terms imposed upon Mozima were complied with, and, peace being thus formally concluded, the expeditionary force fell back on Samaguting.

## The Expedition of 1880.

The death of Mr. Damant on the 13th October 1879 and the subsequent attack on Kohima have already been briefly referred to on page 206.

Kohima besieged.

Fortunately the garrison of Kohima had had thirty-six hours for preparation, and had used them well. The post consisted of two large unfinished stockades; the gateway had no doors; the palisading was weak and rotten; and no earthworks had been thrown up; so that there was virtually no protection against the enemy's fire, while all around, except on the north side, ample cover for the besiegers was afforded by jungle and uneven ground.[1] The greatest danger of all, however, lay in the number of thatched buildings with which the stockades were literally crammed: one spark of fire might destroy the whole place and drive the defenders from the palisades.

The strength of the garrison being quite unequal to holding both stockades, the military, or eastern, stockade was selected, and the night of the 14th was passed in energetic endeavours to put it into a state of defence. Earthworks were thrown up, the gateway was barricaded, and the western stockade was, as far as possible, destroyed; all stores, ammunition, and easily removable property being first taken over to the other.

| | |
|---|---|
| 43rd Assam Light Infantry .. .. | 78 |
| Frontier Police .. .. | 40 |

The garrison was under the command of Captain Reid, 43rd Assam Light Infantry, the other British officer being Mr. Cawley of the Police, one of Mr. Damant's assistants. There were two ladies in the post, Mrs. Damant and Mrs. Cawley. The

[1] The unprepared condition of Kohima to resist attack excites comment. It was a newly established post in the heart of most difficult and dangerous country; but so far from having been well situated, well fortified, and well supplied, the reverse appears to have been the case. Moreover, a number of women, children, and non-combatants were allowed to reside there. It seems to have been regarded as a civil station, instead of what it actually was—an advanced military post. There also seems to have been some disagreement between the civil and military authorities, not only long before the siege, notably in regard to clearing around the post, with which Mr. Damant interfered; but also during the defence. These questions were afterwards the subject of an enquiry.

Mr. Damant was perhaps unduly confident as to the pacific attitude of the Angamis.

soldiers had rations for a month, but the police and non-combatants, women and children, a total of four hundred and thirteen souls, had but three maunds of rice, and absolutely nothing else. The long aqueduct furnishing the main water-supply was so constructed that a kick or a stroke of a hoe would render it useless, while the two springs near the stockade could only be approached as long as the garrison was strong enough to drive away the besiegers from their vicinity. The proposed roads of communication had never been completed, and the Nagas quickly destroyed and cut off the garrison from all communication with the plains.

Directly news was received at Kohima of the attack on Mr. Damant's party, letters and telegrams were despatched by runners to Samaguting, but they were all intercepted and destroyed. A party who volunteered to convey the intelligence to Wokha just got through in time; half an hour later they would have been cut up, as the Konoma men occupied Nerhama shortly after they had passed.

The eastern stockade having been made to some extent defensible, the garrison awaited the expected attack with tolerable confidence. On the morning of the 16th October the first parties of the enemy made their appearance, and, favoured by the ground, began firing into the stockade. They were, however, driven off by a small sortie. The aqueduct had been rendered useless by the enemy, and advantage was taken of the respite to send out a party for water. In the course of the day some Nagas of the Chitonoma clan [1] succeeded in throwing up a *sangar* about 550 yards north-west of the stockade, though the work was considerably delayed by marksmen of the 43rd. Repeated efforts were made on the 16th and 17th to fire the houses in the stockade, but fortunately without success. The enemy were otherwise quiet.

At noon on the 19th Mr. Hinde arrived from Wokha with a welcome reinforcement. Mr. Cawley's message, despatched on the evening of the 14th had reached Mr. Hinde on the evening of the 16th, and he had started the next morning with all available men, and had succeeded in accomplishing his difficult journey in safety. The Nagas were aware of his approach, and had made preparations to resist it; but by the

*Mr. Hinde's reinforcements.*

| | |
|---|---|
| 43rd Assam Light Infantry .. .. | 43 |
| Police .. .. .. | 22 |

[1] The Chitonoma clan is a sub-division of the Kohima people.

exercise of great skill and caution, by avoiding the villages, and by marching at night, he escaped all the dangers which threatened him, and finally, with some assistance from the friendly clans of Kohima, he marched into the stockade without the loss of a man. On the 21st a message was got through to Samaguting. At daybreak on the 23rd, the collected Nagas attacked in earnest, and the din of their war cries around the stockade showed how large were the numbers engaged in the assault. It has since been said by the Nagas themselves that 6,000 men, comprising contingents from almost every Angami village, were present; of these, 500 had fire-arms. The little garrison had now been at their stations since the evening of the 14th; they had lived on quarter rations with a short supply of filthy water, and had been exposed to the weather night and day. The Wokha reinforcement, having come by forced marches without baggage or even greatcoats, were the worst off. Many men were also suffering from sickness or from wounds, but all who could hold a rifle stood up to the defences.

The enemy kept up a heavy and well-directed fire, but the danger from their bullets was as nothing compared to that arising from their incessant attempts to fire the houses inside the stockade. Masses of burning rags attached to heavy missiles obtained from the ruins of the western stockade fell constantly on the thatched roofs, but were as quickly swept off with long bamboos. It was only by the exercise of the greatest activity and vigilance that the garrison averted a conflagration which would have destroyed the stockade and all within it. While numbers of the enemy were thus endeavouring to fire the houses, the remainder continued to advance under cover of logs and rocks, which they rolled before them. Their fire never slackened, and their picked shots were posted to mark down any man who might expose himself for an instant.

During the night of the 23rd, after the moon had set, the garrison succeeded in unroofing some of the houses, and burning the thatch; but this was not effected without the loss of two men, as the enemy continued to fire whenever they could get a chance. Earthworks and barricades were also constructed to oppose those which the enemy were rapidly throwing up on all sides. In these works the garrison made use of meatsafes, chests of drawers, tables, and anything they could lay their hands on. Meanwhile the enemy, on their side, had not been idle, and daylight disclosed strong lines of entrenchments within forty yards of the palisading. The fire of the enemy from behind these almost quelled that of the garrison, and rendered a large portion of the defences almost untenable. The sick and wounded were now laid out in the open behind some rising ground which protected them from bullets, and the women and children sought refuge in the same place. The European ladies and children were stowed in the ovenshed, the only shot proof building in the stockade. At this time only forty-five of the 43rd Assam Light Infantry were really fit for duty, the police were somewhat demoralized, and altogether the position of the garrison appeared well-nigh hopeless. To their great relief, however, the attack slackened about midday, and vague rumours began to fly about regarding the advance of a force from Manipur.

Kohima hard pressed.

The Nagas now showed a disposition to treat, and negotiations were opened the next day. On the 26th, Lieutenant-Colonel Johnstone, Political Agent, Manipur, arrived with 2,000 Manipuri levies, some Cachar police, and thirty-four rifles of the 34th Native Infantry, the Nagas disappearing on his approach. He had got together and brought this force through a hundred miles of difficult country in eight days from the time he received news of the outbreak.

Relief of Kohima.

Having relieved Kohima Colonel Johnstone was anxious to push on at once and punish the Angamis of the village of Konoma, who were then in a submissive frame of mind; but this he was not allowed to do.

Immediate action was, however, advisable, as the present season was favourable for operations, and the crops of the Nagas, on which they greatly depend, were still uncut. Brigadier-General Nation, commanding in Assam, was accordingly given a free hand and at once proceeded to organize a column with all the troops available at the moment, which included :—

Punitive expedition.

| | |
|---|---|
| The 42nd Assam Light Infantry ; | The 44th Sylhet Light Infantry ; |
| The 43rd „ „ „ | Two mountain guns ; |

Total—1,135 all ranks ;

in addition to the Manipuri troops, and 200 Military Police,

General Nation assembled his head-quarters at Piphima on the 14th November. His chief anxiety, with the small force at his command, was to arrange for the security of his communications, for he anticipated that with the fall of Konoma the Nagas would infest the road as far as Borpathur, the whole course of which was surrounded by dense forest country most suitable to their operations. This road was held by posts of Frontier Police strengthened by detachments of the 43rd Assam Light Infantry; but the insecurity of the country was such that it was unsafe for the *dâk* or any officer to leave camp for a few miles without an escort of fifteen to twenty men. The Chief Commissioner decided on the following policy towards the Nagas :—

> Konoma to be absolutely destroyed and rebuilding prohibited. Headmen implicated in Damant's murder to be captured and executed. All other villages concerned in the rising to be subjugated, and complete disarmament of fire-arms enforced. Terms of submission should include payment of substantial revenue in grain and nominal revenue in money, together with contribution of labour. Dismantling of village walls and defences left to discretion of Colonel Johnstone.

An advance from Piphima was made on the 14th November, Colonel Nuthall, C.B., being sent with 200 men of the 44th Assam Light Infantry to surprise Sachima, about twelve miles distant. The village was reached at 9 A.M. on the 15th, and found to be deserted, but no sooner had it been occupied than the enemy attacked. Dispositions for its defence were hastily made by Colonel Nuthall, but so determined were the enemy that it was not until the arrival of the main body the following day that they were finally driven off. Meantime Major Evans and a detachment of the 43rd Native Infantry had attacked Sephima, a village ten miles north-east of Piphima. Having arrived within a mile of it, he halted till dawn on the 16th, when the village was rushed and destroyed.

The main body remained at Sachima, which was a beautiful camping-ground with an important strategical position, within easy striking distance of Konoma, until the 22nd November, when, two guns having arrived from Dimapur,[1] an advance was made on Konoma.

[1] Two 7-pr. mountain guns. They were carried by coolies, worked by a detachment of the 44th Native Infantry and commanded by Lieutenant Mansel, Royal Artillery.

Konoma stood on the crest of a hogbacked hill which rises abruptly from the plain to a height of about 1,200 feet. The hill itself is the termination of a spur falling in rear to a saddle, and then rising again abruptly to join the peaks of Japvo. In front and on both sides there is tolerably level ground, which has been carefully terraced for rice cultivation. On either side the ridge is so steep and wooded as to preclude the possibility of attack from the flanks. The village extends some way down the western slope. Its position necessitated an attack from one or other of its narrow extremities. The north end faced the advancing troops and General Nation decided to attack it, as the enemy had other posts higher up the hill on the south side which would have brought a flanking fire to bear on troops attacking from that direction. Detachments of the 43rd and the 44th Light Infantry were at the same time sent round to take up positions on the spur to the south, so as to intercept the flight of the enemy.

Attack on Konoma.

| | | |
|---|---|---|
| 43rd Assam Light Infantry | .. | 133 rifles. |
| 44th Sylhet „ „ | .. | 359 „ |
| Frontier Police .. | .. | 26 „ |
| 2 guns. | | |

It soon became apparent that the strength of the defences was much greater than had been supposed. Immense labour had been expended on them, and it is said that no less than 400 houses, out of the 600 in Konoma, had been destroyed, to clear the ground and perfect the entrenchments. These consisted principally of a series of terraces, their scarps revetted with stone and topped by walls or stockades, perfectly bullet-proof and admirably loop-holed. Each terrace formed a separate fortification defensible from either side. The whole place was a mass of redoubts, and retrenchments within retrenchments, so that an entrance gained at any point only gave possession of a small area; and as the hill rose towards the centre, the inner entrenchments successively commanded those below them. Outside, the ground visible from the walls had been carefully cleared of jungle and covered with obstacles in the shape of *panjis* and bamboo entanglement, similar obstacles being also set in front of the inner defences. The only two defects in the whole elaborate system were, a deficiency of flanking fire, and the fact that each terrace, being adapted for all-round defence, would, when taken, afford some shelter to the assailants.

About 10 A.M. covered by a well-directed fire from the guns, a part of the 44th advanced to the attack. The enemy very deliberately reserved their fire and caused the assailants some loss, huddled as they were in the only available approach; but the Gurkhas gallantly pressed on, and, rushing the first line of defence, possessed themselves of the north end of the village. They were now faced by the inner line, a stone-faced scarp surmounted by a loopholed stockade, the whole about twelve feet high. Two assaults on this stockade failed. They were led with the greatest bravery by Lieutenant R. K. Ridgeway, the Adjutant of the 44th, who was severely wounded, and was granted the Victoria Cross for his gallant conduct. The attacking party were too few, and their isolated efforts were everywhere met with overwhelming showers of stones and missiles of every description. Night was now coming on, and it was decided to hold the ground already won, and attack again in the morning; when day dawned, however, it was found that the Nagas had abandoned the position.

Assault of Konoma.

The stoutness of the defence created surprise. True, it was believed that several thousand men were behind the walls and stockades of Konoma, and that half of them were equipped with fire-arms, including many Sniders and Enfields; but such preparations and such stubborn resistance were a new feature in Naga warfare. It was afterwards known that during the day the enemy made two attempts to break away in rear, but were each time driven back by a heavy fire from the detachments on the south. These detachments having through some mistake been withdrawn at nightfall, the Nagas were able to make their escape to the precipitous cliffs on the top of the Chaka spurs (about 9,000 feet) of the Japvo mountain.

The British casualties in this action were forty-four killed and wounded, including two British officers killed. The Naga losses were, according to their own accounts, about double that number.

Konoma, the first objective of the expedition, had been taken; nevertheless the situation was far from satisfactory. The enemy, still undismayed, held the Chaka entrenchments, a position of even greater

Second Phase.

strength, and one which, after recent experiences, it would have been madness to attack with the 450 men still remaining; the fighting men of other Angami villages were openly in arms; and, lastly, in rear was a line of communications nearly a hundred miles in length, through a most difficult country, about thirty miles of which was exposed to the attacks of the hostile Nagas. In the face of these difficulties the main body retired to Sachima pending the arrival of reinforcements; a detachment remaining at Konoma.

Operations were now confined to protecting the communications and reorganizing the transport. The enemy continually harassed *dâks* and messengers, and it was clear that their confidence had not been shaken.

By the middle of January General Nation had a force sufficient in itself to attack the Chaka position, but found himself unable to move with any degree of vigour, being entirely dependent for transport on coolies locally obtained from friendly Nagas. As has been frequently experienced, the military question had become entirely one of transport. Measures were taken to reorganize this department on a proper basis, but owing to loss of time in correspondence, and other delays, the operations were completed before any improvements had been effected.

During February and March there was a series of skirmishes connected with endeavours to prevent supplies being brought in to the enemy's stronghold, and to capture and occupy Paplongmai. The Nagas meanwhile maintained a guerilla warfare, constantly firing at sentries, convoys, and water parties, but making no sustained attack, save on the Nichiguard outpost, on which in one week they made three night attacks, without, however, causing serious damage. Altogether in these petty onslaughts they inflicted throughout the expedition a loss of nearly fifty killed and wounded.

One party of Nagas executed a most daring raid, which, as it disclosed our weakness in an unexpected quarter, requires to be specially mentioned. Late in January a party of fifty-five men of Konoma, with only seven fire-arms among them, started from Paplongmai, marched down the bed of the Barak through Manipur territory, and, crossing by a disused road into British territory, surprised the Baladhan tea-garden at night, slew the manager, Mr. Blyth, and sixteen coolies, plundered what they could, and burned everything in the place. They then marched back, unmolested, by the same route. The distance in a straight line cannot be less than eighty miles, which, even for Nagas, is a good four days' march; following the tortuous course of the Barak it must have been nearly 120 miles.

Submission of Nagas.

By the middle of March further reinforcements[1] were coming up, and it was possible to enforce a stricter blockade of the enemy's position at Chaka, and to make reconnaissances against it, with a view, if necessary, of taking it by assault; happily this was not necessary, the Nagas showing a disposition to treat, and finally submitting on the 27th March. Those villages which had taken part against us were punished by fines in grain, cash, and unpaid labour. The Nagas also had to surrender fire-arms, and the villages which had taken up arms against the expedition were destroyed. Konoma, in addition, had its land confiscated and its inhabitants dispersed. Some modification of these terms was afterwards made.

Transport difficulties.

As usual in hill campaigns the greatest difficulties arose from the transport. The force was based on the Brahmaputra, and as far as the hills good roads were available; within them the communications were of the worst possible description. At the commencement of the campaign, perhaps owing to the attention of Government being occupied with the affairs in Afghanistan, the expedition had to organize its own transport arrangements. By the time a properly organized system was started the operations had been concluded.

The bad conditions under which the transport animals had to work were in some degree aggravated by unwise treatment. The condition of the Government elephants was poor from the beginning. The grain ration issued to them was only six or eight seers a day, whereas planters in the district give their elephants twenty seers when in hard work. The first fifty elephants arrived at the end of their six weeks' march from Dacca in a starving condition; they had been under no European supervision, and were in no state to face the difficulties of the hill roads. The mortality was consequently considerable and the cost of the elephant train from November 1879 to

[1] The 18th Native Infantry.

June 1880 amounted to Rs. 4,03,091. With regard to the transport ponies, these unfortunate animals were, at the beginning of the campaign, actually issued a ration of only one seer of grain a day, although they were said to be getting "no fodder," there being no grass-cutters, and all the large store of compressed forage being accumulated at Golaghat. Small reason for surprise that these luckless animals were soon reported to be "getting emaciated."

The fact of the matter was that previous lessons, all of which went to show that hastily organized transport will invariably break down, were disregarded. The result was that not only were the troops put to the greatest discomfort, but operations were also very seriously delayed. Nor did this policy result in economy. The mortality among the Government elephants amounted to 60 per cent.; among the hired elephants to 30 per cent. This was nothing new, for the same thing had been experienced in the Bhutan war. Much time and money would have been saved if the three Assam battalions, which were constantly employed on minor wars and expeditions about that time, had been always equipped to take the field at short notice.

### *BIBLIOGRAPHY.*

*The North-East Frontier of Bengal.*—Mackenzie, 1884.

*Report of the Naga Hills Expedition.*—Captain P. J. Maitland, 1880

# CHAPTER XIV.

## *MANIPUR.*

MANIPUR is a protected State lying between Burma on the east, the Naga Hills on the north, Cachar on the west, and the Lushai Hills on the south. It was known to the Shans as Kasé; to the Burmese as Ka-thé; to the Ahoms as Mekheli; and to the Cacharis as Magli. The old Assamese name is Moglau.

The State covers an area of 8,456 square miles, and consists of a small, but most fertile valley, isolated from the neighbouring kingdoms by an encircling zone of mountainous country. The general trend of the hills is north and south, and the greatest altitude is attained in the extreme north where the Mao Thana is overhung by the peak of Japvo nearly 10,000 feet above the sea. The hills run, as a rule, in irregular serrated ridges, rising here and there into peaks; but west of the valley they assume a more open and rolling character. Between Cachar and Manipur they are covered with dense evergreen forests and bamboo jungle, but round the valley itself there is comparatively little tree growth, and the sides of the hills are, for the most part, covered with grass.

The Manipur valley is about twenty miles in width by thirty in length; it stands at an elevation of some 2,600 feet, and possesses a temperate climate and moderate rainfall.[1] The principal features are rice-fields, swamps, small muddy rivers, bamboo clumps, and barren low hills. The general drainage runs southward into the Chindwin and Barak rivers. The rivers of the country have no navigable importance, sinking as they do to insignificant streams a few inches deep in the dry weather; but in the rains they are liable to floods, and sometimes delay traffic for days.

[1] Seventy inches.

The only town worthy of the name is Manipur or Imphal, which consists of a collection of villages surrounding the Raja's enclosure or *Pât*. The villages consist of numerous small houses built of reeds plastered with mud, and with thatched roofs, each house standing in its own enclosure of about half an acre.

There are three roads connecting Imphal with the outside world: the cart-road over the Naga Hills to the Assam-Bengal Railway at Dimapur (134 miles); the bridle-path to Cachar; and the bridle-path to the Chindwin valley.

The people.

The population is estimated at 285,000.[1] The Manipuri is tall, well-built, and muscular, his complexion fair and his features often regular. In some the Mongolian strain is very marked, in others the finely-chiselled nose and well-set eyes suggest a completely different origin. From certain points of view there is much that is attractive about the race: they are clean and neat, dress themselves well, and live in excellent houses; men and women alike are clever artizans; the women shrewd and quick. All this is fair enough; but there is another side to their character, for even the honour that proverbially prevails amongst thieves seems to be absolutely unknown to them. Their history is a painful record of feuds in which blood relationship was rather a danger than a security. The patriarchal instinct is non-existent, and *chacun pour soi* is the motto of all. Loyalty seems to be unknown: when a man is in power his fellows cringe before him; deprive him of his office and they will spurn him. Calm and even tempered, they are generally cowards, though now and then displaying reckless courage. Their nature seems to have little capacity for affection, and altogether it is dangerous to trust them in any way. As a people they are religious, and the attendance of a Brahman at all occasions of any importance is regarded by them as a necessity. They abstain from liquor and intoxicating drugs, and will not touch animal food of any kind. Seventy-five per cent. of the population are employed in agriculture.

The origin of the Manipuris is a matter of uncertainty, but by tradition they are an amalgamation of several hill tribes: the

1 Manipuris, 181,000 men.
Nagas, 59,000 „
Kukis, 40,000 „

Koomals of the east; the Moirangs of the south; and the Meitheis and Looangs of the north-west.

The Army.

Their army had its origin in the old Manipur Levy, a body of 500 men raised by Raja Gambhir Singh in 1824, at the invitation of the Government of India. This body was armed and paid by the Company, and served under its directions. It was afterwards increased to 1,000 and again to 2,000, and two British officers were attached to drill and discipline it. In 1835 the one remaining British officer was withdrawn, and subsequently the efficiency of these troops deteriorated. The greater part were infantry; there were eight old 3-pr. brass field guns, and the pony cavalry were once famous. In 1889 the infantry, regular and irregular, numbered 6,200; the cavalry *nil*. The irregular troops were Kukis, naturally better soldiers and more courageous than the Manipuris. The men were of good physique, capable of bearing great fatigue, willing, and obedient; but the officers were very incompetent. About half the infantry were armed with smooth-bore muskets.

Outline of History.

The kingdom of Manipur first emerges from obscurity as a neighbour and ally of the Shan kingdom of Pong. It first achieved importance under Gharib Nawaz, who occupied the throne for forty years, during which time he was constantly engaged in warfare with the Burmese, with considerable success. In 1754 Gharib Nawaz was killed by one of his sons; and this was the beginning of a dreary tale of invasion and of internal wars of the most savage and revolting type.

First contact with British.

The Burmese invaded the valley in 1762, and, the Raja having sought the aid of the Company, a treaty of alliance was negotiated by Mr. Verelst on 14th September of that year. The small force which Mr. Verelst commanded could not, however, overcome the difficulties of climate, disease, and transport, and got no further than Khaspur, near Badarpur in Cachar, whence they were eventually recalled. Jai Singh was anxious to have British troops in Manipur, and willing to maintain them, but the idea was not at that time entertained by the Company; and it was not until 1824, when the Burmese, during the course of the First Burmese War, came in contact with the British in Assam, that the Manipuris were armed by the British. Thus supported, the Manipuris not only cleared their own territory, but invaded Burma, and occupied the Kubo valley.[1]

Burmese turned out of Manipur.

At the conclusion of the war, in 1826, the Company recognized the Raja of Manipur. It is said that at that time the adult male population of Manipur did not exceed 3,000 men; the country having undergone years of incessant oppression and anarchy.

After the final defeat of the Burmese and the appointment of a British Resident in Manipur in 1835, the State was secured from outside interference. It was not, however, destined to enjoy quiet, for many efforts were made on the part of various members of the Manipur ruling family to gain possession of the chief power in the State. The Lushais and Kukis were also a very disturbing element on the frontier, troubling the country with continual raids.

In 1879 the Manipur State rendered signal service to the British Government in the Naga war; it being the force furnished by that State and led by the Political Agent, Colonel Johnstone, which prevented a great catastrophe at Kohima.[2] In recognition the Raja received a decoration and a considerable quantity of arms and ammunition. In 1885 the State again gave great assistance to the British arms in the Kubo valley.

Manipur assists the Government of India.

The last revolution, the moving spirit in which was Tekendrajit, the *Senapati* or Chief Military Officer in the State, and the younger brother of the Raja, Sur Chandra Singh, took place in 1890.

Revolution of 1890.

At this time, Sur Chandra Singh having voluntarily abdicated, and taken refuge in Cachar, the Government of India recognized his second brother, the Jubraj, as Regent, and decided to intervene with a sufficient show of strength to make it understood that they intended to be masters of the situation. The presence of the *Senapati* was thought to be inimical to future peace, and it was decided to deport him. The Chief Commissioner of Assam, with an escort of 400 men of the 42nd and 44th Gurkha Rifles[3] under command of Lieutenant-Colonel Skene, proceeded to Manipur for

[1] This they held until requested to give it up in exchange for a subsidy by the Company, *vide* Aitchison CXIII.

[2] See page 212.

[3] Now the 6th and 8th Gurkha Rifles.

this purpose, and arrived at the capital on the 22nd March 1890 where there were also 100 men of the 43rd Gurkhas.[1] He was received with every mark of respect, and announced that a durbar would be held in the Residency on the same day. As the *Senapati* did not attend, on the plea of ill-health, the durbar was postponed until next morning, when he again failed to appear. The Regent was then informed that he would not be recognized unless he could produce the *Senapati*; and shortly afterward an ultimatum was sent to the palace, to the effect that if the missing man were not at once forthcoming he would be arrested by force.

Early on the 24th British troops surrounded the *Senapati's* house. A serious engagement ensued, the Manipuris opening fire at 6 A.M. and mortally wounding Lieutenant Brackenbury. When the house was captured the *Senapati* was not in it. Firing continued all day, but at 8 P.M., Mr. Quinton, the Chief Commissioner, arranged an armistice and sent to invite the Manipuris to discuss terms. A message was received at the Residency inviting the Chief Commissioner to meet the *Senapati* outside the fort, and Mr. Quinton, accompanied by four other officers, went out to meet him. They were never seen again by Europeans. It subsequently transpired that they were invited into the fort, that Mr. Grimwood was attacked and mortally wounded by a man in the crowd, and that subsequently all were bound and beheaded by the orders of the *Senapati*.

Lieutenant-Colonel M. D. Skene.
Mr. F. St. Grimwood, C.S.
Mr. H. W. Cossins, C.S.
Lieutenant W. H. Simpson.

Meantime, in the Residency anxiety grew apace. About midnight a voice called from the fort in Manipuri—"The Chief Commissioner will not return," and shortly afterwards fire was again opened on the Residency. It was then decided by the officer who had assumed command, in the absence of Colonel Skene, to retire to Cachar.

No time was lost in giving effect to this decision. The retreat was hampered with constant attacks, and the small force was somewhat scattered. Fortunately, on the 26th, near Laimatak, they fell in with Captain Cowley, who had been ordered up in support with 200 men of the 43rd Gurkhas from Cachar.

[1] Now the 7th Gurkha Rifles.

Preparations were immediately made for a punitive expedition. An advance was made in April, and by the end of May all the Manipuris concerned in the murders had been captured. Some were executed, other deported: and the Manipur State was declared forfeit to the British Crown. It was, however, regranted to Chura Chand, a minor of five years of age, member of a junior branch of the ruling family.

Expedition, 1890.

No events of importance have since occurred in Manipur, with the exception of some Kuki raids, the last of which took place in 1893.

### The Expedition of 1891.

On March 27th, 1891, news was received at Tamu of the disaster in Manipur. Lieutenant C. J. W. Grant, 2nd Burma Infantry, commanding the detachment at Tamu, immediately volunteered to rescue the supposed prisoners, and having received permission to advance, left early on the 28th. He had with him thirty men of the 43rd Gurkha Rifles, and fifty of the 12th Madras Infantry.

The advance to Thobal was made under continued desultory opposition; and on arrival at that place a force of Manipuris, estimated at 800 to 1,000, and covering a front of one and a half miles, were found occupying a position defending the passage of the river. The little British force was met by a heavy fire, but, advancing by rushes, they drove the enemy from their defences on the far bank, and, quickly crossing the river, took up a defensive position in the village. The enemy now gathered in some numbers, Lieutenant Grant estimated them at 2,000, and for ten days continued to attack the little force with some determination. Lieutenant Grant endeavoured to secure the release of prisoners as a condition of his retiring, and one prisoner (Mr. Williams, a civilian) was produced; but all accounts agreed that there were no other European prisoners in the town of Manipur. On the 9th orders to withdraw were received from Captain Presgrave, who was advancing in support with seventy-five men, and the force moved back unmolested towards Tamu followed up closely by the enemy.

Lieutenant Grant was awarded the Victoria Cross for his gallantry in this fighting, and his force received proportionate rewards for their good service.

*Cachar Column.*

*Commanding*—Colonel R. H. F. Rennick.

| | | | |
|---|---|---|---|
| No. 8 Mountain Battery | .. | 2 | guns. |
| 18th Bengal Infantry | .. | 364 | rifles. |
| 42nd Gurkha Rifles | .. | 99 | „ |
| 43rd „ „ .. | .. | 275 | „ |
| 44th „ „ .. | .. | 112 | „ |
| 1-2nd „ Regiment | .. | 708 | „ |
| Calcutta Volunteers, Pioneers | .. | 48 | „ |
| Surma Valley Military Police | .. | 202 | „ |
| Total | .. | 1,870 | „ |

*Kohima Column.*

*Commanding*—Major-General H. Collett, C.B

| | | | |
|---|---|---|---|
| No. 8 Mountain Battery | .. | 3 | guns. |
| 13th Bengal Infantry | .. | 100 | rifles. |
| 42nd Gurkha Rifles | .. | 200 | , |
| 43rd „ „ .. | .. | 400 | „ |
| 44th „ „ .. | .. | 300 | „ |
| Assam Military Police | .. | 200 | „ |
| Total | .. | 1,200 | „ |

*Tamu Column.*

*Commanding*—Brig.-General T. Graham, C.B.

| | | |
|---|---|---|
| No. 2 Mountain Battery | .. | 4 guns. |
| 4th Battalion, King's Royal Rifles | | 1,800 |
| 2-4th Gurkha Regiment | .. | |
| 12th (Burma) Madras Infantry | .. | |
| 32nd ( „ ) „ „ | .. | |

*Lines of communication.*

5th Madras Infantry.

The main punitive expedition was organized in three columns, as shewn in the margin, based on Cachar, Kohima, and Tamu. They were ready to move on the 15th, 20th, and 23rd of April 1891, respectively. Cachar is nine marches, or 126 miles, from Manipur, over very difficult country: Kohima eight marches, or 105 miles, over an easy route; Tamu five marches, or sixty-eight miles. The latter route is an easy one, but Tamu itself is remote, and, at that season of the year, when the waters of the Chindwin river are low, difficult of access.

It was first intended that the main advance should be from Kohima, as it was anticipated that the Cachar Column would be delayed by the difficulties of the route and of transport. Two preliminary movements were ordered. The first was under the command of Captain Macintyre, who advanced with 200 police and burned Mao Thana, after a sharp skirmish with the enemy, on the 31st March: a prompt action which was considered very creditable to Captain Macintyre by the Commander-in-Chief, and which had the effect of clearing most of the road from Kohima to Manipur The other minor operation was carried out by Colonel Browne, who was ordered on the 1st of April to take 300 rifles of the 18th Bengal Infantry half-way to Manipur from Cachar, to aid fugitives and keep open the road.

The departure of the columns was so arranged that they might be expected to reach Manipur simultaneously on the 27th

April. The Tamu Column was the only one which encountered serious opposition. It left Tamu on the 23rd April and advanced to Palel without opposition. On the arrival of head-quarters there on the 25th information was received from a reconnoitring party that there was a large number of the enemy in an entrenchment six miles north of Palel, at Bapam. This entrenchment was attacked by the marginally-noted force under the command of Captain Rundall, 2-4th Gurkhas. It was an oval work, some fifty yards long by forty broad, and consisted of a parapet and ditch, defended by a *chevaux de frise*, and by a deep *nala* full of water. There were also deep shelter trenches in the work. Captain Rundall opened on the enemy with shell and rifle fire, and ordered an advance when the enemy seemed to him sufficiently discouraged. The Manipuris, however, re-appeared from their trenches and continued to offer a stubborn resistance even after the attacking party had gained possession of a part of the work. But they could not withstand the desperate hand-to-hand fighting of the British; and breaking from the works in a north-easterly direction they were pursued by the mounted infantry, and completely routed. The British casualties in this action amounted to two killed and thirteen wounded.

Action at Bapam.

| | | |
|---|---|---|
| 2-4th Gurkhas | .. | 250 |
| 12th Burmas | .. | 50 |
| Mounted Infantry | .. | 43 |
| 4 guns. | | |

The Tamu Column reached Manipur on the 27th without further incident, and the other two columns arrived on the same day. That from Kohima had met with no resistance; while Colonel Rennick had brushed aside the efforts of the enemy to impede his progress without incurring any casualties. As usual in hill campaigns the chief difficulties met with by all the columns were those of transport and climate: difficulties only realized by those who have served in mountainous and malarious jungle country. The Cachar Column had to cope with cholera amongst other troubles.

In this campaign the usual difficulties were accentuated by the remoteness of the bases, and the necessity for immediate action; but the spirit and behaviour of the men were excellent throughout, and earned the high appreciation of the Commander-in-Chief.

With the arrival at Manipur the military operations were brought to an end, and by the middle of May most of the troops had returned to their own stations.

The Regent and his brothers were fugitives, and the search for them was carried out principally by military police.

---

*BIBLIOGRAPHY.*

*The North-East Frontier of Bengal.*—A. Mackenzie, 1884.
*The Manipur Expedition*, 1891.—Official account.
*The Assam District Gazetteer*, 1906.
*Treaties, Engagements, and Sanads.*—Aitchison.

# PART VI.

# THE LUSHAIS.

# THE LUSHAIS.

## CHAPTER XV.

### *THE COUNTRY AND PEOPLE.*

THE Lushai Hills lie on the eastern frontier of India, and cover an area of about 6,900 square miles, which is, roughly speaking, the size of Wales. On the north they are bounded by Sylhet, Cachar, and the native State of Manipur; on the east by the Chin Hills District; on the west by the native State of Tippera, and the Chittagong Hill Tracts; and on the south by the Arakan district of Burma.

Country.

The whole tract consists of a mass of hills averaging from 3,000 to 4,000 feet in height, running fairly regularly north and south. Their slopes are steep and are cut up by many deep and almost precipitous ravines. Throughout the whole region there is no level ground extending beyond a few hundred yards, and even short stretches are rare. The western and southern portion of the hills are densely wooded, chiefly by bamboo and evergreen trees: towards the east and north, where the rainfall is not so heavy, the country is more open, and the oak and pine take the place of the thick jungle prevailing elsewhere. The rivers are mountain streams, and with one exception are only navigable for a few miles into the hills. The exception is the Dhallesar river, which is navigable by boats all the year round as far as Changsil, and for the greater part of the year nearly as far as Aijal.

The best season for operations is from November to March. During this period of four months the hills are at their best. The weather is dry, cold, and bracing; the camping-grounds healthy, and the roads and paths easy for men and animals. Towards the end of March, owing to the constant jungle fires, the air becomes filled with smoke and dust particles, producing dense haze, and obstructing all signalling by heliograph. Moreover, the prolonged drought reduces the water-supply in many places to a seriously inconvenient extent. Soon after March the heat and rains begin to set in. During the rainy season, the climate is far from healthy, especially in the valleys and lower ranges. The roads and paths are slippery and troublesome, and small landslips are common. Both men and animals are constantly bitten by leeches, even on the Government roads, and a variety of venomous flies, mosquitoes, and sandflies make life in camp almost intolerable. Fever and dysentery are the prevailing complaints during the rains. From November to February, in the early mornings, dense, almost motionless, masses of cloud-like vapour lie in the valleys, which give the hilltops the appearance of islands in a sea of cotton wool. Thin fogs often remain till mid-day, but do not appear to have an unhealthy effect, for the months during which they prevail are the healthiest in the year.

There are now a fair number of Government roads adapted for infantry with mule or bullock transport. Where there are no Government roads narrow Lushai paths connect the different villages, but these frequently run for long distances along the bed of some stream, and for this reason are entirely unsuitable for anything but infantry with coolie transport. All the Government roads in the interior connect either Aijal or Lungleh, with the different Military Police outposts. The principal road of all is that between Aijal and Lungleh, which not only connects the North with the South Lushai Hills, but secures through communication between Cachar in the north and Chittagong in the south.

The people.

The population of the Lushai Hills is, with the exception of a few immigrants, all of one race. It is of Mongolian origin. There have been various clans and families,[1] but minor differences have become gradually merged under the preponderating influence of a few clans, and at the present time nearly every village is ruled by a chief of one of the five royal Lushai families. The customs of the different clans vary in several particulars, but there is a general

[1] Old reports teem with a bewildering number of names of tribes. This classification was to a great extent transitory or imaginary.

resemblance among them all. The extent of variation amongst them is by no means constant. The Ralte, Paithe, Thado, and Lakher are easily distinguishable, and a brief acquaintance with them makes it apparent that they are not real Lushais. The same may be said of the clans known as Hmar and Poi. The remaining clans are so much alike that one might live a long time in the hills without being aware of any difference whatever.

The race is distinctly a short one, the men ranging from about five feet two inches to five feet four inches in height, while the women seldom reach the height of five feet. Both men and women are stoutly built, and have very muscular and well-developed legs. Their most noticeable characteristic is their fondness for tobacco and beer. Excessive indulgence, and a damp and depressing climate, have combined to produce a sullen and morose race.

It used to be the general opinion that the Lushais were great head-hunters.[1] Better information seems to show, however, that the primary object of their raids was to obtain loot and slaves. Undoubtedly a man who had killed another in a raid was looked up to; and to prove their prowess the raiders would usually take the heads of those slain, to exhibit in their villages, but the actual killing and taking the head was more an incident in the raid than the cause of it.

The language spoken by the bulk of the population throughout the hills is known as the Dulien dialect, the word Dulien being merely another name for Lushai. The few Raltes, Hmars, Paithes, etc., in the country, who are all kindred tribes, usually classed under the general name of Kukis, have each dialects of their own which are unintelligible to Lushais. On analysis, however, these other dialects show many points of resemblance with the Dulien tongue, and go far to prove the connection that undoubtedly exists between the Lushais and other Kuki tribes.

Rice is the staple food of the inhabitants, and except when there is a bad harvest there is, as a rule, more than sufficient to

1 The name Lushai, according to Colonel Lewin, one of the greatest and earliest authorities in the hills, was derived from *lu* a head, and *sha* to cut. This was, of course, a mistake, as the name of the clan is Lushei not Lushai, and moreover the word *sha*, "to cut," is never used in the sense of cutting off a man's head. The word is probably compounded of *lu*, a head, and the adjective *shei*, meaning long, in allusion to the way in which the Lushais bind their hair in knots at the back.

supply the wants of the inhabitants. The surplus supply is, however, not large, and never sufficient for export purposes.

Each village is ruled by a chief who, in his own village, is supreme. His house is the poorhouse of the village, and all who have no means of support are received there and get food in return for their labour. Formerly a person who had committed some serious crime could enter the chief's house and thus escape vengeance.

Villages and houses.

Villages are generally built on the top of a ridge or spur, and in former days the choice of a site was much influenced by its defensive capabilities. When we first occupied the hills, every village was strongly defended, two and even three rows of stockades being found in some cases. The gateways were commanded by timber blockhouses, and at all suitable points on the roads blockhouses were built. The approaches to all these works were well planted with *panjis.*

Arms and tactics.

From a military point of view, the Lushai Hills is simply a mountainous district inhabited by more or less savage tribes with a propensity for raiding and committing depredations on the neighbouring plains, if not kept under proper control by an armed force sufficiently strong, not only to mete out punishment when required, but also to establish and maintain free communication throughout the district. Men sixty and seventy years of age can remember the time when guns were hardly known, and fighting was carried on with spears or bows and arrows. Now-a-days the weapons of the people are flintlock muskets, spears, and *dahs.* The Lushais' idea of warfare is essentially a system of surprises and ambushes. In their estimation the greatest triumph that can be achieved is to surprise a village at dawn, dash in before the men have time to make any resistance, capture as many women and children as possible, and, loading them up with their own property, get away before their relations can organize a rescue party. Ambushing armed parties is regularly practised; but our experience has been that the ambusher was always so anxious to get off with a whole skin, that his fire was apt to be ineffective. A raiding party, even after a march of several days, will retire without firing a shot if the enemy are found to be on the alert.

The despatch of punitive expeditions from the plains is a matter of considerable difficulty and expense for the following reasons :—

1. The very limited amount of supplies obtainable in the country makes it necessary for troops to carry their own rations.
2. The nature of the roads and smallness of the camping-grounds impedes the movements of any large body of troops.
3. An enormous amount of transport is required in proportion to the fighting strength of the troops : and the difficulty of maintaining that transport in an efficient state is very great.
4. Climatic difficulties necessitate all operations on a big scale being commenced and completed during the cold weather.

Outline of History.

From the earliest period of which we have any knowledge, the Lushai Hills have been inhabited by a collection of tribes known to the Bengalis as Kukis. They were constantly a terror to their neighbours outside their own hills, as well as being frequently engaged in internal warfare. The chief of Chittagong appealed to Warren Hastings for help against them in 1777 and until recent years they have made repeated excursions beyond their own frontier. During the weak rule of the last Rajas of Cachar, the Cachar valley was almost depopulated by these hillmen, and at the same time the district began to be invaded by refugee bodies of Kukis, driven out of their own country by more powerful clans.

The Lushai hillmen attracted serious attention in 1844 when Lalehokla, a chief of the Palhan Kukis, raided a village of Sylhet and carried off twenty heads and six captives. The Indian Government called on the Raja of Tippera to assist in punishing Lalehokla ; but as the steps he took to accomplish that object were considered altogether inadequate and unsatisfactory, it was decided to send a party of the Sylhet Light Infantry under Captain Blackwood to avenge the outrage. The expedition was entirely successful. Assisted by a Kuki Chief, our troops surrounded Lalehokla's village, destroyed the grain in the neighbourhood, and speedily reduced the chief to submission. He was then transported, his life having been pardoned on condition of his surrendering himself. The transaction was unfortunately looked upon as breach

Captain Blackwood's Expedition, 1844.

of faith by the Lushais, who interpreted the promise of pardoning his life as a free pardon; and in consequence of this, great difficulty was experienced in future expeditions in inducing the chiefs to come personally to tender their submission.

In 1849 simultaneous raids were made in Sylhet, Tippera, and Cachar by a chief called Mulah; and Colonel Lister, Political Agent in the Khasi Hills, was sent with a force of 6 native officers and 229 men to exact retribution. He succeeded in destroying Mulah's village,[1] and released about 400 captives, but, beyond proving to the Lushais that we could penetrate their jungles, little effect was produced on the tribe at large. After returning from this expedition, Colonel Lister gave it as his opinion that to effect a permanent impression on the Lushais, an expedition of at least 3,000 men would be required, and that a road would have to be constructed running into the heart of the country. He also advocated the formation of a Kuki levy to act as scouts and collect information. The Government of India approved of these recommendations and a Kuki levy was actually raised. The special object of the latter was, however, speedily nullified by the attempt to turn these savages into regular disciplined troops. Their special qualifications as scouts and trackers were never exercised, and when the time came for them to be employed, they proved utterly useless for the work for which they were originally intended. The effect of Colonel Lister's expedition was nevertheless considerable and for twelve years no further raids occurred.

Colonel Lister's Expedition, 1849.

In 1850 the Chiefs Vonolel[2] (father of Lalbura), Vutara, and Lalphunga offered to pay tribute to Government in order to secure immunity from the attacks of the Pois, but it was not then considered advisable to do more than maintain friendly relations with the tribes, and so secure the safety of our border.

Nothing further of any importance occurred till January 1862, when three villages near Adampur were burnt and plundered. There was some talk of sending an expedition, but the Government of India thought it inadvisable to adopt forcible measures, as it was

[1] Ngura, village on Shentlang, twenty miles north of Aijal.

[2] The Lushai name for Vonolel is Van-hnuai-liana.

feared that they would result in bringing down the Lushais on the many tea-planters who had now settled close to the border. Accordingly Captain Stewart, the Deputy Commissioner, began to negotiate with Sukpilal[1] for the delivery of the captives in his possession. About the same time he also concluded a treaty with Vonpilal, son of Mulah, who agreed, in consideration of a small money payment, to commit no raids himself, and to refuse all countenance to other chiefs in any like attempt. The negotiations with Sukpilal came to nothing; that chief failed to give up the captives demanded, and an expedition was therefore organized to compel their release. Before it could start, however, the rainy season set in, and the operations were eventually abandoned.

Soon after this Sukpilal resumed negotiations by sending in annual presents, and after considerable trouble four captives were also released. One of the difficulties alleged with regard to the returning of the captives was that they had contentedly settled down and married Lushais. This statement, though doubted at the time, was probably true, as it was proved on subsequent expeditions that Lushai captives did not always hail with joy their release from captivity.

General Nuthall's Expedition, 1868.

Towards the close of 1868 some villages in Manipur and Hill Tippera were attacked. This was followed by a raid upon the tea-gardens of Loharbund and Monier Khal in January 1869. The attacks on the tea-gardens were attributed to Sukpilal and Vonpilal, and a large punitive expedition, composed of military and police, was set on foot. The season was, however, too late for effective measures, and the operations were a failure. The result of this expedition considerably diminished our prestige with the Lushais, and the policy of conciliation and concession, which was tried immediately after it, only served to confirm the tribes in the notion that the British were powerless to injure them.

Between December 1869 and March 1870 Mr. Edgar, Deputy Commissioner of Cachar, and Major Macdonald, visited Sukpilal at his village, and between them fixed a new boundary, which after-events soon proved to be an altogether futile piece of labour. Even

[1] The ancestor of many of the most important chiefs of the present time. He died in 1880, when he was ruler over the whole of the Western Lushais.

before Mr. Edgar's return to Cachar a series of raids had begun which exceeded in magnitude and ferocity all that had gone before.

Raids in 1871.

The first raid occurred in the Chittagong Hill Tracts, and was supposed to have been committed by a body of Shendus, 200 strong. Poyakukie in Hill Tippera was burnt on the 21st January 1871, and Alexandrapur, a tea-garden in Cachar, was looted on the 23rd. Mr. Winchester, a planter, was killed, and his daughter, aged six, was carried off as a captive. About the same time the village of Ainakhal was burnt, twenty-five persons being killed and thirty-seven taken captive. On the 26th January the Lushais attacked the garden of Monier Khal. Fortunately the manager had received warning of the raid, and had removed his coolies. He himself, with two other Europeans and a guard of thirty-seven soldiers and police, remained in the stockade, where he was reinforced, by Mr. Daly of the Police, with forty men. The Lushais sustained the attack for seventeen hours, but were finally driven off with a loss of fifty-seven, the loss on the British side being seven killed and as many wounded. On the 28th a party of eight sepoys were overpowered, and all but one killed, not, however, before they had accounted for twenty-five Lushais. On the 23rd February seven coolies were killed and wounded on Jhalnachera tea estate.

Similar outrages continued to occur in Sylhet, Tippera, and Manipur until well on in March. The identity of the tribes concerned in these several outrages was not clearly established for some time, but subsequent information leaves no doubt of the complicity of the Eastern Lushai chiefs, Lalbura, Lenkham, Bungteya, and Poiboi; of the Sylu chief Savunga, and his sons Lalagnura and Laljika; and of the Howlang chiefs Sanvunga, Benkora, and Saipuiya.

The 1871 Expedition.

In consequence of these raids the expedition of 1871-72 was despatched.[1] It was completely successful, and peace was re-established on the following terms:—

(i) That Government agents should have free access to Lalbura's villages.

(ii) That the guns taken at Monier Khal and Nandigram should be surrendered.

[1] See page 244.

(iii) That a fine of two elephant tusks, one set of war gongs, one necklace, ten goats, ten pigs, fifty fowls, and twenty maunds of rice should be paid.

These were lenient terms, but their effect was that for nearly twenty years the Eastern Lushais gave no serious trouble.

Attack on a party of police in 1883.

In November 1883 a party of police were attacked near Demagiri by some Malliam Pois, acting as scouts for a large body of Eastern Lushais. A follower was shot, and two of the police were drowned by the capsizing of a boat. After this the country remained quiet until the early part of 1888, when a small survey party, commanded by Lieutenant Stewart of the Leinster Regiment, was surprised and massacred by a head-hunting party of Shendus, who had ventured across the frontier. The outrage was entirely unprovoked, and it afterwards transpired that the motive of the attack was not any grievance against the British Government, but the fulfilment of an obligation which Howsata, one of the chiefs of the Shendus, was under, to obtain the heads of two foreigners for his father-in-law Jahuta. By accident the raiding party came across Stewart's camp, and, finding it absolutely unguarded, except for a sepoy sentry over the arms, they considered the opportunity to attain their object too good to be lost. Their first volley from the jungle killed the sentry and the two British privates, who were Lieutenant Stewart's assistants, and wounded the other sepoys of the Military Police. Two sepoys, with Lieutenant Stewart himself, were the only ones able to get at their ammunition when the attack began. They defended themselves with great gallantry, killing several of the enemy, but at length Lieutenant Stewart was shot through the chest, and the two sepoys, having exhausted their ammunition, then retired through the jungle, and eventually effected their escape.

The season being too far advanced, the idea of sending a punitive expedition had to be postponed until the following cold weather. When the time came, however, its despatch was again postponed on account of the unsettled state of the Chindwin district, which, in the opinion of Government, rendered it inexpedient to take any further action against the Eastern Lushais for the time being. Instead of the expedition, 250 men of the 9th Bengal Infantry were sent to strengthen the police outposts with a view to preventing further raids, but these half-measures did not have the expected result. In December 1888 an attack of unusual ferocity was made on a village within British territory, and only four miles from our outpost at Demagiri. Twenty-one villagers were killed, and fifteen carried off captive. The event was soon followed by a series of raids on a larger scale in the Upper Chengri valley early in January 1889, during which a hundred persons were killed, and ninety-one carried into captivity.

Renewed raids.

While these raids were in progress a punitive expedition had been organized and was already on its way to Demagiri, which was chosen as the base of operations. This expedition successfully accomplished the punishment of the villages responsible for the murder of Lieutenant Stewart, and established a fortified post at Lungleh within the enemy's country, connected by road and telegraph with Demagiri.

Colonel Tregear's Expedition, 1888-89.

A much larger expedition was organized in the following year. Its general object was: To punish certain tribes that had raided and committed depredations in British territory; to subjugate tribes as yet neutral, but now brought by force of circumstances within the sphere of British dominion; to explore and open out as much as possible of the, as yet, only partly known country between Burma and Chittagong; and, if the necessity arose, to establish semi-permanent posts in the regions visited, so as to ensure complete pacification and recognition of British power. As the operations were to be directed as much against raiding tribes of Chins on the Burma frontier, as against raiders in the Lushai Hills, and as the movements from east to west, and *vice versâ*, were intimately connected, it was determined to treat the whole as one combined operation styled the Chin-Lushai Expedition, to distinguish it from other operations which had taken place in the past. This expedition succeeded in releasing a number of captives and destroyed the chief offending village.

Chin-Lushai Expedition, 1889-90.

Previous to these operations, the policy of the Government since 1872 had been to maintain a line of outposts connected by patrol paths; and, while cultivating, as much as possible, friendly intercourse with the chiefs, to abstain from interference in their internal affairs. It was now decided to endeavour to put down raids once for all by proving the British power to occupy their country, and by establishing military posts in their midst. Two such outposts, with a garrison of military police, were established at Aijal and Changsil.

For a time the Lushais appeared to have accepted the situation, and attended a durbar held by Captain Browne, the first Political Officer appointed to the Northern Lushai Hills, at which they swore an oath of friendship. On the 10th September 1890, however, they, without any warning, suddenly rose in a body, made a combined attack on Aijal and Changsil, and killed Captain Browne, a sepoy, and a number of coolies. Repeated attacks on the stockades were successfully resisted by the garrisons of these two posts until the arrival of reinforcements from Cachar on the 26th September. The relieving party included 200 Military Police, the officer in command of which, Captain Swinton, had been killed while advancing up the narrow channel of the Dhallesar river to Changsil. The garrison of Changsil was further augmented by the arrival of 200 men of the 40th Bengal Infantry on the 30th September; and on the arrival of Mr. McCabe, the new Political Officer, punitive operations were immediately commenced, and severe punishment meted out to all the villages in the neighbourhood.

Attack on Aijal and Changsil, 1890.

Punitive measures, 1890.

The summer and winter of 1890 passed uneventfully among the tribes on the Chittagong frontier; but in January 1891, although the Lushais had shown no signs of further hostility it was considered advisable to move a body of troops into the hills to visit as many villages as possible, and to establish British authority. The force, consisting of 400 men of the 43rd Gurkha Rifles under Colonel Evans, and 20 Military Police, visited Lalbura's and Poiboi's villages and returned to Changsil without encountering any opposition.

Meanwhile Mr. Murray, Assistant Political Officer, South Lushai Hills, proceeded on tour with an escort of fifty rifles, Chittagong Police. He found the Chief Jacopa recalcitrant, and attacked his village; but being assailed by very superior numbers he eventually retired to the Kaladan post. A punitive expedition was sent off on the 20th, consisting of 100 men of the 2-2nd Gurkhas and 45 rifles, Chittagong Police, under command of Captain Hutchinson. It burned Jacopa's village, destroyed his grain, and returned to the Kaladan post on the 3rd March. No further operations took place on the Chittagong side during the cold weather.

Raid, 1892.

In 1892 the Western Lushais were in a state of submission; but Lalbura, a chief of one of the eastern tribes, resisted the British authority. In February he attacked the Political Officer, who was visiting his village, and in April raided the tea estate of Booruncheria, killing forty-two and carrying off thirteen prisoners. There being reason to expect more trouble, the forces in the North Lushai Hills were reinforced by 300 men of the 18th Bengal Infantry under Colonel Rennick, and those of the South Lushai Hills by 300 of the 3rd Bengal Infantry. The local troops were at this time 540 Frontier Police in the seven posts of Lungleh, Demagiri, Lungsin, Fort Tregear, Lalthuama, Rangamaṭia, and Burkhul.

Punitive operations, 1892.

On the Assam side, retributive measures were commenced by the police on the 10th of April 1892. This party consisted of 225 men of the Assam Frontier Police, and 75 men of the 18th Bengal Infantry, all under the command of Captain Loch, Commandant of the Surma Valley Frontier Police Battalion. The force left Aijal on the 10th of April 1892 for Poiboi's village, which, after some resistance, was captured and destroyed. The force then destroyed all the grain in the neighbourhood, and hunted the Lushais out of all their temporary camps, thus depriving them of shelter at an inclement season of the year. A somewhat smaller force of 250 men captured Bungteya's village, and pursued the same tactics as those mentioned above. A good many of the minor chiefs now made their submission, but Lalbura resolved to make a stand at Maitè. This place was captured on the 25th of May 1892, and again the same tactics were pursued. As the men had suffered much from the climate, and Lalbura was now a fugitive with a small following, Captain Loch's force returned to Aijal, which was reached on the 8th of June 1892. All the principal chiefs, except Lalbura, and most of the people implicated in the late rising had surrendered at various times during the above operations, and agreed to furnish free labour.

Although the power of the hostile Lushais was broken by these operations, it was found advisable to despatch another expedition in December 1892, in order to protect friendly villages, our convoys, and communications, and to impress on the native tribes once for all a sense of British superiority. This force, acting in concert with a column from Aijal, completely effected its object; and without meeting any resistance established the authority of Government throughout the whole tract of country where it had been resisted.

At the beginning of 1893 the Lushais might be considered as having been divided into four main groups,—the Western Lushais, the Eastern Lushais, the Howlongs, and the Kairuma group. Of these the last named, which consisted of seven villages, were by far the strongest combination in the hills. The first three groups had settled down quietly, but the Kairumas remained sullen, and disregarded the orders of the Political Officer. Consequently, late in 1893 three small columns were sent against them from Aijal, Lungleh, and Falam respectively. Their movements coincided exactly in accordance with the pre-arranged plans, and severe punishment was inflicted on the recalcitrant villages.

Operations, 1893.

This was the last of the long series of military expeditions; and since that time the record of the Lushai Hills has been one of peaceful and steady progress. The internal management of the country is left to the chiefs, subject only to a general supervision by the Superintendent, who administers justice.

## CHAPTER XVI.

*MILITARY OPERATIONS.*

### The Expedition of 1871-72.

THE first expedition against the Lushais which calls for detailed mention was that of 1871. It consisted of two columns, starting from Cachar and Chittagong, respectively, and each column included half a mountain battery, a company of Sappers and Miners, and 1,500 Native Infantry. In addition, a separate contingent was supplied by the Raja of Manipur. Transport was reduced to a minimum; no tents were allowed, the numbers of followers were cut down as far as possible, and only six seers of baggage were allowed to each sepoy.

Operations of the Cachar Column.

The objective of the left or Cachar Column, under command of General Bourchier, was the village of Lalbura, son of Vonolel, who had been mainly concerned in the raids of Monier Khal. Tipai Mukh, on the Barak river, was selected as a secondary base of operations. Up to this point water communication was to a certain extent available, and the route of the force was, roughly speaking, along the course of the Barak valley.

The column reached Tipai Mukh on the 9th December and at once began to build store-houses, hospitals, and stockades, preparatory to its advance into the enemy's country. On the 13th the advance began, and except some threatening demonstrations, no opposition was experienced till the 23rd December. On the latter date, the troops, while ascending the hill on which the Kholel villages lay, were received by a volley from a number of Lushais in ambush. The village was at once taken with a rush, and was then destroyed. On the following days several hostile villages in the neighbourhood were similarly dealt with. On the 26th December the force evacuated Kholel, and returned to camp in the valley below. A few days later, the enemy made complete submission. On the 30th and 31st, peace offerings were accepted, and the year closed in comparative quiet.

Early in January the force continued its advance, and towards the end of the month began to close upon Poiboi, one of the most powerful chiefs in that quarter. On the 25th the General was warned by Poiboi's ministry that he would be attacked if he went on. No regard was, of course, paid to this, and the troops were accordingly attacked on all sides, while traversing a particularly bad piece of ground. The men, however, behaved with great coolness, and the Lushais were driven off with considerable loss. This attack proved that Poiboi and Lalbura had joined their forces to oppose our advance. Parties were sent out to burn Poiboi's villages, and the artillery came into action for the first time, striking wonder and terror into the minds of the Lushais, and causing them to abandon their stockades in a panic. Poiboi now desired to come to terms with the General, but the latter replied that he would only treat in Chelam, the chief village of the tribe. The column accordingly proceeded to occupy this village, which was found deserted by Poiboi and his followers. Nothing could persuade this chief to come in personally and tender his submission, nor was he ever captured.

Preparations were now made for the final stage of the operations, the capture of Lalbura's village, for which service 400 men and two guns were detailed. On the 12th February, the troops started, and after five days' marching arrived in view of the valley of Cham Phai, Lalbura's head-quarters. On the 17th, the village itself was reached, and being found deserted was at once burnt to the ground. It appeared that the Soktes, old enemies of the Lushais, had taken advantage of the panic caused by the advance of the British column to make a fierce attack on Lalbura. The latter had succeeded in beating them off with loss, but their attack had created a diversion and prevented Lalbura from occupying a stockade prepared across the route of the column, from which he intended to oppose our advance.

On the 20th February, the conditions were complied with, and next day the force, having accomplished its task, set out on its return to Cachar. While these events were occurring, the right, or Chittagong Column, under command of Brigadier-General Brownlow, was accomplishing its task with equal success. The object of this force was primarily to reach and punish the Syloo Chief Savunga, who had been concerned in the raids on West Cachar, and in the murder of Mr. Winchester. General Brownlow arrived in Chittagong on the 28th October, and at once began operations by establishing a depôt at Kasalong, up to which point troops, stores, and provisions could easily be conveyed by means of the Karnafuli river. Above Kasalong the river was found broken at intervals by rapids, but by dint of considerable labour these difficulties were overcome, and a boat service was established as far as Demagiri, which was converted into an advanced depôt.

Chittagong Column.

About ten miles from Demagiri the force left the Karnafuli valley and commenced their regular hillwork, marching north by east to attack Vanunah, the first great Syloo chief on the Belkai range. On the 14th December this man's village was taken and burnt by a party of 160 men, 2nd Gurkhas. Head-quarters was established there and parties were despatched against the neighbouring village, which were all destroyed together with immense quantities of grain, without any loss on the side of the British.

Head-quarters occupied the village of Savunga on the 11th January 1872, and Rutton Poia, our ally, was despatched to treat with the Howlongs. The force in the meantime bivouacked and awaited his return. A week later Rutton Poia was successful in inducing the Howlongs to surrender Mary Winchester, the child who had been captured in the raid on Alexandrapur in 1871. She had been well treated, and was found none the worse for her captivity. Negotiations were carried on with the Howlongs for some considerable time, and finally, on the 18th of February, the chiefs Sangbunga, Lalbura, and Yatama, who represented the whole of the northern portion of the tribes came in. An oath of friendship was taken with these chiefs, and on their returning all the captives, peace was proclaimed and presents exchanged.

Rutton Poia sent to treat with Howlongs.

On the 27th the Lushais made their submission, and peace was granted them on the same terms as to the Howlongs.

On the 28th the force began its return to Demagiri, and by the 3rd of April the last of the troops had arrived in Calcutta. The results of this our months' campaign may be briefly summed up as being—

Return of Expedition, and its results.

1. The complete subjection of two powerful tribes inhabiting upwards of sixty villages, of which twenty that resisted were attacked and destroyed.
2. The personal submission of fifteen chiefs, and their solemn engagement on behalf of themselves and their tributaries for future good behaviour.
3. The recovery of Mary Winchester, and the liberation of upwards of 100 British subjects who had from time to time been made captives.
4. The survey officers attached to the expedition were able to triangulate 3,000 square miles of country, more than half of which was surveyed in detail.

Our casualties throughout the campaign were only forty-seven among fighting men, and 118 among followers. The deaths among the latter were nearly all due to an outbreak of cholera.

Casualties.

## The Expedition of 1888-89.

The next expedition which demands special notice was that of 1888-89. It consisted of about 1,150 men, and was placed under the command of Colonel Tregear, who was directed to punish the raiders and to establish a post in the vicinity of Vandula's village. The first thing to be done after collecting the force at Demagiri was to complete the construction of the road to Lungleh, which had been decided on as absolutely necessary. Advanced parties were sent ahead to select camps and to cover the working parties on the road, and on the 2nd March 1889 the work was completed. A small party under Captain Shakespear was then sent towards the Kaladan river to reconnoitre the approaches to the Shendu territory. This party returned on the 10th of March and reported that the road as far as the Kaladan was fit for mules, and that Howsata's village was only one day's march beyond, on a fairly good road. They

2 guns, No. 2 Mn. Battery.
200 men, Madras Pioneers.
250 ,, 2nd Ben. Infantry
400 ,, 2-2nd Gurkhas.
250 ,, 9th Ben. Infantry.

also reported that the Shendus evidently did not expect to be attacked. On receipt of this information Colonel Tregear at once wired for permission to despatch a flying column against Howsata, and sanction having been obtained, a force under command of Colonel Tregear himself left Lungleh on the morning of the 15th. On the 20th of March Howsata's village was reached. On the approach of the column the enemy abandoned the village and escaped into the jungle, after first setting fire to their houses. The troops completed the destruction of the village, and recovered Lieutenant Stewart's gun, thus showing that they had punished the right people. They then returned to Jahuta's village, which was also destroyed; after which they began their homeward journey and reached Fort Lungleh on the 25th without any further sight of the enemy.

| | | |
|---|---|---|
| Bombay M. B. | .. | 1 gun. |
| Sappers and Miners | .. | 26 |
| Native Infantry | .. | 209 |
| Frontier Police | .. | 40 |

The expeditionary force was now rapidly withdrawn. The fortifying of Lungleh was completed on the 15th of April, and it was then handed over to the Military Police, who furnished a garrison of two companies with one British Officer.

## The Chin-Lushai Expedition, 1889-90.

The Chin-Lushai Expedition was composed of columns operating from Burma and Chittagong, the former acting against the Chins and the latter against the Lushais. The operations of the Burma Columns lie outside the scope of this chapter, and it will suffice to say that communication was eventually established at Tao with the Chittagong force.

The duties of the Chittagong Column was to move from Lungleh to Haka, making the road as it advanced. The troops for this column, which was placed under the command of Colonel Tregear, arrived at Chittagong between the 10th November and 10th December 1889, and were sent up as quickly as possible to Demagiri which was again selected as the base. Some delay, however, occurred, owing to the great sickness among the transport

No. 2 Company, Bengal Sappers and Miners.
3rd Bengal Infantry.
Detachment, 9th Bengal Infantry.
2-2nd Gurkhas.
Wing, 2-4th Gurkhas.
28th Bombay Pioneers.
Detachment, Chittagong Frontier Police.
Total about 3,400 men.

coolies. The road to Haka was at once started, and by the end of December a good mule road had been traced as far as Teriati.

On the 28th January the marginally-named column started northwards to punish the Lushais concerned in the raid on the Chengri valley and upon Pakunna Rani's village, who had escaped punishment last season. The column, moving partly with cooly transport and partly on 900 rafts down the Klong or Dhallesar river, effected a junction with a force of police from Cachar, under Mr. Daly, at Lienpunga's village. They then punished all the villages concerned in the raids on Chittagong, built Fort Aijal, and marched out of the hills through the Cachar district, the last detachments arriving at Calcutta on the 6th April 1890.

*Commanding*—Colonel Skinner.
80 men, Ben. S. and M.
250 " 3rd Ben. I.
300 " 2-2nd Gurkhas.
102 " 28th Bo. I.
50 Frontier Police.

Meanwhile the main column, which had been compelled to send nearly all its cooly transport with the northern party, had made steady progress with the construction of the road to Haka, and had sent a party forward who succeeded in meeting the Burma troops at Tao on the 26th February.

Roads were constructed from Fort Tregear to Fort Lungleh, and from Lungleh to Tao gap, and the native track from Tao gap to Haka was made passable for mules. A site for a permanent post was selected on the Darjow range, which was completed on the 4th of May, and called Fort Tregear. The wing of the 2-4th Gurkhas was then pushed across to Haka, and the remainder of the troops returned to Chittagong, the last being despatched to Calcutta on the 19th May.

Permanent posts were left at Fort Lungleh and Fort Tregear, with posts along the line of communication with Demagiri.

---

*BIBLIOGRAPHY.*

*North-East Frontier of Bengal.*—Alexander Mackenzie, 1884.
*Report on the Lushai Expedition of* 1888-89.—Captain Chamber.